The Concise Marrow of Christian Theology

Classic Reformed Theology

Volume 1. William Ames, *A Sketch of the Christian's Catechism,* translated by Todd M. Rester, and introduced by Joel R. Beeke and Todd M. Rester

Volume 2. Caspar Olevianus, *An Exposition of the Apostles' Creed,* translated by Lyle D. Bierma, and introduced by R. Scott Clark

Volume 3. Johannes Cocceius, *The Doctrine of the Covenant and Testament of God*, translated by Casey Carmichael, and introduced by Willem J. van Asselt

Volume 4. Johann Heinrich Heidegger, *The Concise Marrow of Christian Theology*, translated by Casey Carmichael, and introduced by Ryan Glomsrud

The Concise Marrow of Christian Theology

Johann Heinrich Heidegger

Translated by Casey Carmichael
Introduced by Ryan Glomsrud

REFORMATION HERITAGE BOOKS
Grand Rapids, Michigan

The Concise Marrow of Christian Theology

Reformation Heritage Books
2965 Leonard St., NE
Grand Rapids, MI 49525
616-977-0889
orders@heritagebooks.org
www.heritagebooks.org

Printed in the United States of America
19 20 21 22 23 24/10 9 8 7 6 5 4 3 2 1

Library of Congress Cataloging-in-Publication Data

Names: Heidegger, Johann Heinrich, 1633-1698, author. | Carmichael, Casey, translator. | Glomsrud, Ryan, 1978- writer of introduction.
Title: The concise marrow of Christian theology / Johann Heinrich Heidegger ; translated by Casey Carmichael ; introduced by Ryan Glomsrud.
Other titles: Medulla medullae theologiae Christianae. English
Description: Grand Rapids, Michigan : Reformation Heritage Books, 2019. | Series: Classic reformed theology; vol 4 | Includes bibliographical references and index. | Summary: "An introductory text on systematic theology from the seventeenth century"— Provided by publisher.
Identifiers: LCCN 2019031077 (print) | LCCN 2019031078 (ebook) | ISBN 9781601786005 (hardcover) | ISBN 9781601786012 (epub)
Subjects: LCSH: Theology, Doctrinal—Early works to 1800. | Reformed Church—Doctrines.
Classification: LCC BT75.3 .H4513 2019 (print) | LCC BT75.3 (ebook) | DDC 230/.42—dc23
LC record available at https://lccn.loc.gov/2019031077
LC ebook record available at https://lccn.loc.gov/2019031078

For additional Reformed literature, request a free book list from Reformation Heritage Books at the above regular or e-mail address.

This volume is
gratefully dedicated to

Rev. Dr. W. Robert Godfrey

for his service as president of
Westminster Seminary California (1993–2017),
where he ensured that many ministers were
instructed in the foundations of theology,
which was the very aim of J. H. Heidegger in writing
The Concise Marrow of Theology.

Contents

Series Preface ix
Biographical and Historical Introduction xi

The Concise Marrow of Christian Theology

Dedicatory Epistle 3
Preface to the Reader 7
I. On Theology in General 9
II. On Holy Scripture 13
III. On the Existence and Divinity of God 21
IV. On the True Triune God 29
V. On the Decrees of God 35
VI. On the Creation of the World 41
VII. On the Providence of God 49
VIII. On Angels 55
IX. On the Covenant of Works 61
X. On the Sin of Man 67
XI. On the Covenant of Grace 75
XII. On the Economy of the Covenant of Grace under the Patriarchs 83
XIII. On the Economy of the Covenant of Grace under the Law of Moses 89
XIV. On the Decalogue 95
XV. On the Ritual Law of Moses 107
XVI. On the Judicial Law of Moses 113
XVII. On the Person of Jesus Christ 117
XVIII. On the State of Jesus Christ 123
XIX. On the Office of Jesus Christ 129
XX. On the Economy of the Covenant of Grace under the Gospel 139
XXI. On the Grace of Calling 145

XXII. On the Grace of Justification . . . 153
XXIII. On the Grace of Sanctification . . . 161
XXIV. On the Constancy of the Covenant of Grace . . . 171
XXV. On External Worship, Especially about the Sacraments of the New Testament . . . 177
XXVI. On the Church . . . 185
XXVII. On the Government of the Church . . . 191
XXVIII. On Glorification . . . 201

Scripture Index . . . 213
Subject Index . . . 231

Series Preface

There are at least three reasons why classic Reformed theology ought to be studied and thus why this series of critical English translations should exist. First, Reformed orthodoxy forms the intellectual background of modern theology which can only be understood properly in light of its reaction to and rejection of Protestant orthodoxy. Second, Reformed orthodoxy obviously merits attention by those who identify with the Reformed confession; it is their heritage and thus shapes their theology, piety, and practice whether or not they realize it. Third, despite the disdain, disregard, and distortion which Reformed orthodoxy suffered during the Enlightenments in Europe, Britain, and North America, contemporary scholarship has shown that, whatever one's view of the theology, piety, and practice of orthodoxy, on purely historical grounds it must be regarded as a vital intellectual and spiritual movement and thus a fascinating and important subject for continued study.

We call this series "Classic Reformed Theology" because, by definition, a period is classical when it defines an approach to a discipline. During the period of Protestant orthodoxy, Reformed theology reached its highest degree of definition and precision. It was then that the most important Reformed confessions were formed, and the Reformed churches took the form they have today. For these reasons, it is more than surprising to realize that much of the most important literature from this period has been almost entirely ignored since mid-eighteenth century. As difficult as it may be for those in other fields to understand, the list of scholars who have extensive, firsthand knowledge of some of the most important primary texts in the study of Reformed orthodoxy (e.g., the major works of Olevianus, Polanus, Voetius, Cocceius, Heidegger, and van Mastricht, to name but a few) can be counted easily. Further, few of the texts from this period, even some of the most important texts, have been published in modern critical editions. Thus, until recently, even those with the ability and will to read the texts from the classical period of Reformed orthodoxy could do so only with difficulty since some of these texts are difficult to locate outside of a few libraries in Europe and Great Britain. Technological developments in recent years, however, are beginning to make these works more widely available to the academic community. Coinciding with the development of technology has been a growing interest in classic Reformed theology.

Finally, a word about the plan for this series. First, the series seeks to produce and provide critical English translations of some of the more important but generally neglected texts of the orthodox period. The series does not intend to be exhaustive, nor will it be repetitive of critical translations already available. Most of the texts appearing in this series will be translated for the first time. It is the sincere hope of the editor and the board that at least one volume shall appear annually.

Biographical and Historical Introduction

Johann Heinrich Heidegger and The Concise Marrow of Christian Theology

Ryan Glomsrud

> All things besides God are subject to the providence of God…the giving of life, birth, the whole course of life and its end. For God has determined the limit of life, since there is "a period for man on earth."
>
> —J. H. Heidegger

The inscrutable providence of God was manifest in the life and times of Johann Heinrich Heidegger (1633–1698), who achieved the height of his career when he became professor of theology at Zürich in the wake of tragedy. On June 5, 1667, the renowned church historian and scholar of oriental languages, Johann Heinrich Hottinger (1620–1667), died in an accident while crossing the Limmat River. While embarking on a journey with his family, the boat in which Hottinger and his family were sailing was capsized in the fast-moving currents, and the professor and his children were drowned. By all accounts, "the calamity shook the city of Zürich, and all Europe mourned."[1] Man's days are "mercenary" Heidegger later wrote, quoting Job 7:1: "and 'his days and number of months are determined.'"[2] Within a few months of the accident, Heidegger was invited to assume Hottinger's vacant academic chair, and he taught and served the church in Zürich until his own death in 1698 at the age of sixty-five.

Despite the fact that Heidegger's textbooks of theology were among the most prominent in Europe at the beginning of the eighteenth century, very little has been written about him. This introduction will review the most important biographical details before placing the Zürich professor in his academic and ecclesiastical

1. James I. Good, *History of the Swiss Reformed Church since the Reformation* (Philadelphia: Publication and Sunday School Board of the Reformed Church in the United States, 1913), 143.

2. Heidegger, *Concise Marrow*, VII, VII.

context. In conclusion, we will provide a basic orientation to *The Concise Marrow of Christian Theology* (1697), so ably translated by Casey Carmichael.

A Mercenary Life

Heidegger was born in the small town of Bäretswil, canton of Zürich, about ten kilometers from the southern shores of the Zürichsee. At the time of his birth, in 1633, the village was still reeling from the plague that had ravaged the population in 1629.[3] Much of Europe was also suffering from political and military conflict as a result of the Thirty Years' War (as we now call it), that great struggle of German princes and their allies against the Holy Roman Empire.[4] In fact, the period from 1638 to 1648—the years of Heidegger's youth and education, which he pursued in Zürich, Marburg, and Heidelberg—was a time of renewed tension. It was a less violent time than previous decades, but there was no shortage of difficulties.[5] The University of Heidelberg, for example, that jewel of the Reformed educational system, had its doors shuttered by imperial forces in 1622, although not before a Vatican secretary sent from the pope plundered the library and carried off to Rome more than three thousand of the most valuable books.[6] The school was then reopened in 1629 with a Jesuit faculty until it was recovered by Protestant forces some time later. A similar tragedy befell the University at Marburg, captured in the mid-1620s. Hostilities did not cease until the leading parties were able to negotiate a settlement at the Peace of Westphalia in 1648.[7]

It must have seemed like a new day in Europe for the young Swiss student as he traveled north after the war. The Reformed faith was restored to the Palatinate (in fact, Hottinger helped rebuild the reputation of Heidelberg's university before moving to Zürich), and while a student Heidegger formed some of his strongest connections to German-speaking and Bohemian theologians of the Reformed tradition. For a time, he took up residence with "one of the most prominent theologians of his day in the Reformed Church of Germany," Ludovicus Crocius (1586–1655).[8] He also became friends with J. L. Fabricius (1632–1697) and later wrote a biography of the theologian and teacher, whose

3. See *Historia vitae Johannis Henrici Heideggeri, theologi Helvetio-Tigurini, cui non pauca historiam ecclesiae temporis ejusdem, nec non literas concernentia inseruntur* (Zürich: David Gessner, 1698).

4. See the very accessible Peter H. Wilson, *The Thirty Years War: Europe's Tragedy* (Cambridge, Mass.: Harvard Belknap Press, 2011).

5. Richard A. Muller, *Prolegomena to Theology*, vol. 1 in *Post-Reformation Reformed Dogmatics* (Grand Rapids: Baker, 1987), 47.

6. James I. Good, *History of the Reformed Church of Germany, 1620–1890* (Reading, Pa.: Daniel Miller Publisher, 1894), 41–42.

7. According to Good, 852 books were eventually returned to Heidelberg in 1815 from France, where Napoleon had taken them after his victory over Rome. Good, *History of the Reformed Church of Germany*, 43.

8. Good, *History of the Swiss Reformed Church*, 144.

work he also edited.[9] Neither Crocius nor Fabricius are well known today, but they were both teachers responsible for helping to train a generation of pastors and scholars and were, in their time, influential pedagogues—Crocius as rector of an important gymnasium in Bremen and Fabricius as rector of the very influential Danzig Academic Gymnasium.[10]

After completing his studies, focusing especially on philology and study of the sacred Scriptures, Heidegger married and traveled. From 1660 he came to know Johannes Cocceius (1603–1669), his slightly older contemporary who was likewise a philologist and professor of Hebrew, first at Franeker (1636–1649) and then at Leiden (from 1650).[11] Because of the challenges that German universities had faced during the Thirty Years' War, these Dutch schools at Leiden (established in 1575) and Franeker (established 1585) became almost disproportionately influential in the seventeenth century, with Leiden as perhaps the most famous and important in the world.[12]

Not only was there a new balance of power in Europe, but a generational shift occurred in the history of theology that is important to recognize. During the decade from roughly 1630 to 1640, a number of the most important theologians, professors, and authors died, including Johannes Wollebius (1589–1629), the longtime professor of Old Testament from Basel; two champions from the era of the Synod of Dort, the great William Ames (1576–1633) of Franeker and Franciscus Gomarus (1563–1641) of Leiden and later Groningen; and a host of important but lesser-known theologians, such as Johann Heinrich Alsted (1588–1638) of Herborn; Antonius Walaeus (1573–1639) of Leiden; Johann Heinrich Alting (1583–1644), who had taught at Heidelberg until its closure in 1622 and then resumed teaching duties in Groningen; and finally Marcus Wendelin (1584–1652), rector of another influential gymnasium in Zerbst. The theological world that Heidegger inhabited was international in scope and was overseen by these early orthodox theologians. Heidegger himself became a leader in the formation of the next generation of Protestant orthodoxy.

---

9. See *Joh. Ludovici Fabricicii Opera omnia: Quibus praemittitur Historia vitae et obitus ejusdem*, ed. Joh. Henrico Heideggero (Zürich: Davidis Gessner, 1698).

10. A generation and more of Polish-Lithuanian theologians, including Bartholomaeus Keckermann (1572–1608), received valuable training in Danzig; see Dariusz M. Bryćko, "The Danzig Academic Gymnasium in Seventeenth-Century Poland," in *Church and School in Early Modern Protestantism: Studies in Honor of Richard A. Muller on the Maturation of a Theological Tradition*, ed. Jordan J. Ballor, David S. Sytsma, and Jason Zuidema (Leiden: Brill, 2013), 339.

11. Willem J. van Asselt, *The Federal Theology of Johannes Cocceius (1603–1669)*, trans. Raymond A. Blacketer (Leiden: Brill, 2001).

12. See Anthony Grafton, *Worlds Made by Words: Scholarship and Community in the Modern West* (Cambridge, Mass.: Harvard University Press, 2009); and Anthony Grafton, *Joseph Scaliger: A Study in the History of Classical Scholarship*, vol. 2, *Historical Chronology* (Oxford: Oxford University Press, 1993). See also Howard Hotson, *Commonplace Learning: Ramism and Its German Ramifications, 1543–1630* (Oxford: Oxford University Press, 2007), 276.

The Academy

Richard Muller has defined Protestant orthodoxy as a period of Christian history that "extends for nearly two centuries past the Reformation—a phase of intellectual development of Protestantism that stands some three times the length of the Reformation."[13] It grew organically out of the Renaissance and Reformation itself, and its theologians, pastors, and teachers were responsible for overseeing the strengthening of confessional boundaries for the church and providing rigorous theological education in a variety of contexts.[14] As a preliminary note, it is crucial to understand this academic-ecclesiastical context for appreciating the nature and genre of Heidegger's work presented in translation here.

Muller provides a helpful chronology, dividing the tradition into early, high, and late orthodox periods.[15] Early orthodoxy (1565 to 1640) was an age defined by the successors of the first generation of Reformers as they built on the biblical and confessional foundations (laid by Luther, Calvin, and the rest), worked through theological challenges that came up in the church (including the Arminian controversy and its resolution at the Synod of Dort in 1618), and even consolidated the tradition during the difficulties of the Thirty Years' War. In the Swiss cities, the later Zürich Reformers Heinrich Bullinger (1504–1575) and Peter Martyr Vermigli (1499–1562) were eventually succeeded by lesser-known figures such as Johann Wilhelm Stucki (1542–1607) and Kaspar Waser (1565–1625). Basel's early orthodox figures are more familiar, including Amandus Polanus von Polansdorf (1561–1610) and Johannes Wollebius.[16] Geneva's theologians of this period are also widely known, if rarely read, including Calvin's most important successor, Theodore Beza (1519–1605); Lambert Daneau (c. 1535–c. 1590); Antoine de la Faye (1540–1615); Antoine de Chandieu (1534–1591); Giovanni Diodati (1576–1649); and Théodore Tronchin (1582–1657).[17]

With Heidegger we have the rising generation of high orthodox churchmen (1640 to 1725) who dealt with a number of controversies both within and outside of the church. Many of these challenges arose out of the new philosophical movements that were gaining popularity in Europe. It was the so-called Age of

13. Richard A. Muller, *After Calvin: Studies in the Development of a Theological Tradition* (Oxford: Oxford University Press, 2003), 4.

14. Muller, *After Calvin*, 5. See also Carl R. Trueman and R. Scott Clark, eds., *Protestant Scholasticism: Essays in Reassessment* (Carlisle, UK: Paternoster Press, 1999); Willem J. van Asselt and Eef Dekker, eds., *Reformation and Scholasticism: An Ecumenical Enterprise* (Grand Rapids: Baker Academic, 2001); and Willem J. van Asselt, *Introduction to Reformed Scholasticism* (Grand Rapids: Reformation Heritage Books, 2011).

15. See Richard A. Muller, *Post-Reformation Reformed Dogmatics*, vol. 1, *Prolegomena to Theology*, 2nd ed. (Grand Rapids: Baker Academic, 2003), 1–100.

16. See Wollebius in English translation in John W. Beardslee, ed. and trans., *Reformed Dogmatics* (Grand Rapids: Baker, 1977).

17. See Scott M. Manetsch, *Calvin's Company of Pastors: Pastoral Care and the Emerging Reformed Church, 1536–1609* (Oxford: Oxford University Press, 2013).

Reason, falling roughly into two phases from 1640 to 1685 (roughly the period of Heidegger's productivity) and then the full-flowering of the Enlightenment from 1685 to 1725. In the first phase, philosophers such as René Descartes (1596–1650), Benedict de Spinoza (1632–1677), and Thomas Hobbes (1588–1679) challenged received wisdom, each in his own way, and set the tone of discussion for intellectual disciplines. In theology, the usefulness of Descartes's philosophy in particular was a topic of intense and not always peaceful debate.[18] By the end of Heidegger's life, the intellectual landscape in Europe had changed, and this brought a number of challenges for the church and theological academy, not the least of which was the status and role of the Bible for theology. The late orthodox period (1725–1770) endured the decline of the orthodox consensus as scientific revolutions and the late eighteenth-century crisis of metaphysics inaugurated a new, disruptive period in modern European thought.[19]

It was very much a transitional age, then, when Heidegger achieved prominence as a theologian. In older scholarship, unfortunately, there have been a number of false narratives about Reformed orthodoxy, or Protestant scholasticism, as it is sometimes called. It used to be argued that Reformed orthodoxy represented a devolution from the simple, biblical piety of the Reformation.[20] Negative descriptions of ivory scholastic towers were not uncommon, and generations of students dismissed Protestant orthodoxy without study or consideration.[21] But the Reformation was always at least in part an educational movement from the very beginning. As Muller explains, "Once Protestantism had been established as an institutional church with its own confessional orthodoxy, the situation changed and the task of teaching theology in academies and universities encouraged the development of a new appropriately scholastic approach to theology."[22] The Reformed orthodox churchmen were both pastors and scholars, then, and the two vocations were not in conflict. If anything, their pastoral sensibility facilitated their interest in teaching and pedagogy. At present, the older models of scholarship have become increasingly irrelevant, and there is currently a thriving field of study of Protestant orthodoxy. These things are worth emphasizing by way of introduction, because first impressions of Heidegger's text, with its terse, stripped-down theological statements, might seem to lend credibility to the older scholarship's claim that rationalism and

---

18. van Asselt, *Federal Theology of Johannes Cocceius*, 90.

19. See Paul Guyer, ed., *The Cambridge Companion to Kant* (Cambridge: Cambridge University Press, 1992).

20. For a survey, see Richard A. Muller, *The Unaccommodated Calvin: Studies in the Formation of a Theological Tradition* (Oxford: Oxford University Press, 2000).

21. For example, see Gerald R. Cragg, *The Church and the Age of Reason, 1648–1789* (London: Penguin Books, 1990), 100, 103.

22. Muller, *Prolegomena to Theology*, 1:222.

coldness were creeping into Reformed scholastic theology.[23] But this would be to misunderstand Heidegger's intentions as well as his location in the seventeenth-century academy. The goal of Heidegger's *Marrow*, to which we will turn in more detail in due course, was fully rooted in earlier Renaissance-humanist pedagogy and not in the new philosophy of his day.

Heidegger's generation was responsible for the "full development and codification of Protestant orthodox theology in the face of new adversaries."[24] Despite their many differences, current scholarship contends that there was "a single but variegated Reformed tradition, bounded by a series of fairly uniform confessional concerns but quite diverse in patterns of formulation."[25] Heidegger's contemporaries included many recognizable figures from Reformed church history, including Gijsbert Voetius (1589–1676), professor of theology at Utrecht; Johannes Cocceius from Bremen, Franeker, and eventually Leiden (a theologian, it has been mentioned, whom Heidegger knew and respected a great deal); Francis Turretin (1623–1687) of Geneva; Peter van Mastricht (1630–1706) from Frankfurt-an-der-Oder and Utrecht, who was an almost exact contemporary of Heidegger; and Herman Witsius (1636–1708) of Franeker, Utrecht, and Leiden.[26] These theologians, despite coming from different regions of Europe, nearly all studied at Utrecht, Leiden, Groningen, and Geneva before dispersing to teach at satellite schools as young pastors and scholars themselves and then returning to major universities to replace the previous generation. In part, the nearly identical educational itineraries helped contribute to the overwhelming theological agreement that the Reformed tradition enjoyed, despite controversies that arose from time to time.

Heidegger was primarily a professor and teacher, although he was also an ordained minister. From 1659 to 1665 he taught theology and church history at the University of Steinfurt, a *Landesuniversität* that was part of a network of educational institutions in the Hanseatic region of northwest Germany, about equal distance from other important centers of learning at Groningen and Bremen. During this time he received his doctorate from Heidelberg and participated in a published series of disputations against the errors of the papists

---

23. For example, see Alister McGrath, *Reformation Thought: An Introduction*, 3rd ed. (Malden, Mass.: Blackwell, 2001), 141; and Stanley J. Grenz and John R. Franke, *Beyond Foundationalism: Shaping Theology in a Postmodern Context* (Louisville: Westminster John Knox, 2001).

24. Muller, *After Calvin*, 7.

25. Muller, *After Calvin*, 7–8.

26. There are English translations of a number of key works, such as Johannes Cocceius, *The Doctrine of the Covenant and Testament of God*, Classic Reformed Theology 3, trans. Casey Carmichael (Grand Rapids: Reformation Heritage Books, 2016); Petrus van Mastricht, *Theoretical and Practical Theology*, vol. 1, *Intellectual Prerequisites* (Grand Rapids: Reformation Heritage Books, 2018); Herman Witsius, *The Economy of the Covenants between God and Man*, trans. William Crookshank, 2 vols. (London, 1822).

presided over by Johann Heinrich Hottinger.[27] Upon his arrival in Steinfurt, Heidegger himself presided over and published his own disputations against the papacy in 1660.[28]

In 1665 he returned to Zürich to teach moral philosophy (ethics) until Hottinger's death in 1667, when he assumed the chair of theology. His writing productivity increased from that time, and many of the more than one hundred publications under his name began to appear from 1670. He earned a reputation as a stalwart of the Reformed tradition and became a highly sought-after professor. According to Good, "He received several calls, as to Groningen in Alting's place, and to Leyden in Cocceius' place, which was the most prominent Reformed professorship in Europe. He declined them all."[29] He remained in Zürich instead, working steadily on what would be his magnum opus, the *Corpus Theologiae Christianae* (*Body of Christian Theology*, 1700) and its supporting texts. Before turning to these works, however, it is important to acknowledge the state of the church at the time of Heidegger's activity. This was the age of the Amyraldian controversy, which was disrupting French, Swiss, and other Reformed churches in Europe, which led him to coauthor the Formula Consensus Helvetica with his colleague, Francis Turretin of Geneva.

The Church

The regular ministry of Word and sacrament sustained and strengthened the church during the high orthodox period, and yet the church at the synodical and international level was occupied with a variety challenges and controversies. One in particular emerged from the Reformed academy in Saumur, France.[30] The French Wars of Religion from the 1560s was an extraordinarily difficult time for the French Reformed church, and all the Reformed suffered with her. Under harsh persecution, many Huguenots left France for more peaceful environs, including Geneva and Zürich. Religious peace was only finally established with the Edict of Nantes in 1598. One of its provisions was the legal toleration of Protestant universities, which led to the founding of the academy in Saumur for the training of Reformed ministers. There were several reliable faculty members early on, but over time the school acquired a reputation for advocating a number of controversial positions, led by theologians such as John Cameron (1579–1623), Jean Daillé (1594–1670), and Moses Amyraut (1596–1664). As

---

27. Johann Heinrich Hottinger, *Disputationum historicarum de origine errorum pontificiorum circa s. scripturam prima* (1654), although the young scholar's name did not make the front cover.

28. Johann Heinrich Heidegger, *Disputatio theologica, qua principii religionis papisticae, vicariae infallibilitatis Romani pontificis to alogon demonstrator* (1660).

29. Good, *History of the Swiss Reformed Church*, 144.

30. For a full account, see Martin I. Klauber, *Between Reformed Scholasticism and Pan-Protestantism* (Selinsgrove, Pa.: Sysquehanna University Press, 1994) as well as the highly problematic Brian G. Armstrong, *Calvinism and the Amyraut Heresy* (Madison: University of Wisconsin Press, 1969).

testimony to the influence that a seminary can have, for good or ill, the faculty and graduates (and their writings) circulated among the churches, in many cases causing tension and unrest. Of all the issues, the most alarming—especially in the wake of the Arminian Controversy addressed at the Synod of Dort—was Amyraldianism itself, or "hypothetical universalism."[31] Amyraut's *Brief Testament of Predestination* (1634) caused controversy from the outset, with loud opposition from brothers-in-law Pierre du Moulin (1568–1658) and André Rivet (1572–1651), the latter of whom had been an acquaintance of Amyraut's during his student days.[32] Two years later, Amyraut's *Six Sermons on the Nature, Extent, Necessity, Dispensation, and Efficacy of the Gospel* not only failed to clarify matters but made them worse. This text is likely the point of origin for the "Calvin against the Calvinists" thesis as Amyraut attempted to claim Calvin's legacy and imprimatur for himself by distinguishing his doctrine (and Calvin's, or so he claimed) from the broad confessional consensus.[33] The church responded appropriately by first considering the matter and then asking for advice and recommendations from the international Reformed body. Geneva, Zürich, and the faculties of Leiden and Franeker issued their advisory warnings, and multiple French synods were convened to discuss and censure Amyraut. The controversy, however, came to a boil again when Amyraut's *Brief Testament* was republished in 1658 and a number of Saumur's graduates began teaching Amyraldianism either discretely or openly in the following decades. Some of these graduates, for example, were teaching at Geneva in the 1660s, and the controversy evolved and spread from there.

In the end, the battle over hypothetical universalism was a drawn-out affair, even after Amyraut's death in 1664, and the pastors of Geneva and elsewhere struggled to keep the doctrine of the church sound. According to Martin Klauber, "As early as 1667, Lucas Gernler (1625–75) of Basel wrote to Johann Heinrich Heidegger of Zürich that at least four Swiss towns would support Francis Turretin's efforts to rid the Academy of Geneva of the Salmurian teachings."[34] Two years later, Turretin, still very much concerned, wrote to Heidegger and "suggested the formulation of a new creed for all of Switzerland for

31. Hypothetical universalism, or so-called Four-Point Calvinism, argues that Christ's atonement for sin is hypothetically unlimited in extent, while its efficacy is limited. See Richard A. Muller, *Calvin and the Reformed Tradition: On the Work of Christ and the Order of Salvation* (Grand Rapids: Baker Academic, 2012), 70–106. See also Roger Nicole's classic study, "Moyse Amyraut (1596–1664) and the Controversy on Universal Grace, First Phase (1634–1637)," PhD diss. (Cambridge, Mass.: Harvard University, 1966).

32. Armstrong, *Calvinism and the Amyraut Heresy*, 87.

33. Carl R. Trueman, "Calvin and Calvinism," in *The Cambridge Companion to John Calvin*, ed. Donald K. McKim (Cambridge: Cambridge University Press, 2004), 225.

34. Klauber, *Between Reformed Scholasticism and Pan-Protestantism*, 31.

which subscription would be required" of all ministers.[35] Again according to Klauber, "By 1674, the Swiss Evangelical Diet ordered the creed to be drawn up. Gernler would normally have been the most obvious choice to write the Formula, but he had just died and it was left to Heidegger to compose the initial draft."[36] When Heidegger finished, Basel, Bern, and Zürich adopted the new creed called the Formula Consensus Helvetica almost immediately, with other cantons following in 1676.[37] Geneva delayed its approval until 1679 because of divisions within the faculty and a hesitancy to condemn many French Reformed theologians who were again suffering persecution as the provisions of the Edict of Nantes were being slowly unwound.[38]

Everywhere there were signs of transition, and the theological consensus was relatively short-lived. The Edict of Nantes was revoked by Louis XIV in 1685, and more than 500,000 refugees fled France. In 1687 Francis Turretin died—and with him the confessional impulse of the high orthodox generations. His death arguably marked the "closing of a chapter" in the history of the Reformed church and "the end of an epoch of history."[39] In the next generation, disillusioned sons triumphed against the orthodoxy of their fathers. Louis Tronchin (1629–1705), son of the vigorous Reformed theologian Théodore Tronchin, taught Amyraldian doctrine and fought against the Formula Consensus Helvetica. Jean-Alphonse Turretin (1671–1737), son of Francis Turretin, later oversaw the abrogation of the Consensus. In fact, what began as a controversy over hypothetical universalism and other points of doctrine eventually expanded into a debate about confessionalism itself. Subscription to a confession of any kind was imagined to be an intolerant form of religion in conflict with the modern desire for freedom of individual conscience. Upon being named rector at a Genevan Academy Oration, on January 1, 1700, Jean-Alphonse Turretin even likened confessionalism to a shameful episode in the history of God's people: "The century of the Reformation caused division and schism; the century that we have just finished consecrated these divisions by the formulas of discord; now that we have woken up to a new century, we ought to start it by covering the

35. Klauber, *Between Reformed Scholasticism and Pan-Protestantism*, 32.

36. Klauber, *Between Reformed Scholasticism and Pan-Protestantism*, 33.

37. See Martin I. Klauber, "*Formula Consensus Helvetica* (1675)," *Trinity Journal* 11 (1990): 103–23.

38. For further reading on the aftermath of the abrogation of the Formula Consensus Helvetica, see Jennifer Powell McNutt, *Calvin Meets Voltaire: The Clergy of Geneva in the Age of Enlightenment, 1685–1798* (Surrey: Ashgate, 2013); and David Sorkin, *The Religious Enlightenment: Protestants, Jews, and Catholics from London to Vienna* (Oxford: Oxford University Press, 2008).

39. David C. Steinmetz, "Theodore Beza (1519–1605): Eternal Predestination and Divine Sovereignty," in *Reformers in the Wings: From Geiler von Kayersberg to Theodore Beza*, 2nd ed. (Oxford: Oxford University Press, 2001), 114.

errors of our fathers with a coat of love, and in seeking to unite all churches in the same spirit by the bonds of peace."[40]

Although he served the church faithfully, Heidegger was not unaware of the challenges of defending and teaching the Reformed religion in the late seventeenth century. Yet, even after this controversy, he pressed on with the publication of his life's work, a collection of textbooks of Reformed theology.

An Invitation to Read

Despite the Amyraldian controversy in the background, Heidegger's text presented in this volume was not a polemical work.[41] The world may have raged, but the summary of doctrine is as calm as Lake Zürich on a hot summer day. Coming to terms with the text, it is important to recognize that it is one of three works that must be thought of (if not necessarily read) together as Heidegger's comprehensive contribution to the theology of the Reformed tradition: the *Medulla theologiae Christianae* (1696) or *Marrow of Christian Theology*; followed the next year by the text translated here, the *Medulla medullae theologiae Christianae* (1697) or *The Concise Marrow of Christian Theology*; and finally the major work itself, a large two-volume *Corpus theologiae Christianae* (1700) or *Body of Christian Theology*.

Decoding these titles, we can identify a major text, a summary, and a summary of the summary. It was not uncommon, as in Heidegger's case, for the middle work to be written first, with both the abridgment and the amplified versions to follow in due course. In this way, Heidegger moved from basic definition to elaboration until all could be published more or less simultaneously at the end of his roughly thirty-year teaching career. The texts were meant to work and function together, as Heidegger himself noted, in that *The Concise Marrow* was intended "for the sake and use of beginners" as a "primer and stepping stone" for readers "making progress" to the more advanced works.[42] Furthermore, Heidegger included an in-text notation at the end of each locus with references to relevant sections of the larger *Marrow of Christian Theology*, where one could look for more discussion.

This kind of internal cross-referencing system across the volumes, along with the gradation of texts, ought to alert readers to the fact that Heidegger was working in a very specific genre of writing. Today, we would simply call this

40. Quoted from Klauber, *Between Reformed Scholasticism and Pan-Protestantism*, 144.

41. It should be noted, however, that the *Medulla theologiae Christianae* was equipped with a syllabus of controversial propositions against heterodox agitators such as, as Heidegger lists them, Gentiles, Jews, Muslims, libertines, Socinians, fanatics, enthusiasts, Anabaptists, pseudocritics, Remonstrants, and Lutherans.

42. Heidegger, Dedicatory Letter and "Preface to the Reader."

systematic theology, and it is that. In context, however, Heidegger was employing standard Renaissance teaching methods. As Ann Blair states,

> In the Renaissance schoolchildren throughout Europe were taught to keep notebooks in which they were to record passages from their reading worth saving for memorization and later use. Moral sentences and rhetorical turns of phrase were especially collected in this way (hence the notion of a commonplace as a clichéd expression, most often a moralizing proverb or a rhetorical device), but commonplace books were also used to gather arguments or factual information of interest to the individual or relevant to the discipline under study.[43]

The practice of students in the schools was to prepare notebooks at least in duplicate, if not in triplicate. The first was organized discursively with notes entered organically, more or less in the order encountered in the course of study. In theology, for example, this would involve the preparation of a running commentary or thought journal on an important text, perhaps the Bible or a major theologian. The preparation of the second notebook was where pedagogical issues became especially important. The goal was organization of material "to ensure easy retrieval," promote long-term memorization, and ultimately accomplish a penultimate mastery of content. Thus, material was harvested from the first notebook and rearranged topically (instead of serially) under identifying headings or "commonplaces." Blair continues,

> The proper selection of these headings constituted a central issue for the many authors who proffered advice on commonplace notebooks in the Renaissance, and the assignment of each new passage to the appropriate heading was a critical process for each reader, which could require multiple readings of the text and careful reflection. Some authors recommended copying the same passage or providing cross-references under multiple entries to resolve difficult cases. As for the ordering of the headings, maintaining any system under the constant accumulation of new material, which might require new headings, would inevitably prove difficult; many authors kept track of the headings in a table of contents (listing the headings by order of appearance), or in an alphabetized or semi-alphabetical index.[44]

From this educational trend, the discipline of systematic theology was further developed into the form that is recognizable today. Heidegger's topics or loci, twenty-eight in number, were for the most part very standard Reformed commonplaces, although the rich development of covenant or federal theology

---

43. Ann Blair, *The Theater of Nature: Jean Bodin and Renaissance Science* (Princeton, N.J.: Princeton University Press, 1997), 65–66.

44. Blair, *Theater of Nature*, 66.

along Cocceian lines is also evident. The typical commonplaces include Scripture, God (attributes, Trinity, and works), creation, providence, angels, sin, the law, Christology (person, states, and offices), calling, justification, sanctification, sacraments, ecclesiology, and glorification. The other headings, dispersed throughout, were all covenantal in nature, nuanced and refined, in no way departing from the broad consensus of the Reformed tradition despite some unique areas of emphasis.[45] These loci moved through the different periods of redemptive history to introduce the different economies of the covenant of grace, working from a basic definition to the times of the patriarchs, Moses, and the New Testament. To facilitate browsing and navigation of the text, Heidegger provided a table of contents at the outset (i.e., a list of commonplaces) as well as a Scripture index and, importantly, an alphabetical list of topics in conclusion (which is not translated here).[46]

The Concise Marrow, then, was a teaching tool and should not be understood as an end in itself. Heidegger aimed to provide only "the essence of things in a few words" for the purpose of committing the headings and content to memory, in the first instance, and then use of the volume as a resource to be consulted later.[47] Its relevance and benefit for modern readers today is very much the same. As Heidegger reminded his initial readers, "To be sure, we only know as much as we remember."[48] Although, it could be added, we can also relearn what we have forgotten if we but know where to look for it.

Heidegger also had theological reasons for proceeding with multiple, interactive, and progressive volumes. Scripture itself invites metaphors of growth from a diet of milk to solid food (Heb. 5:13–14), and progress from youth to maturity (Heb. 6:1). The Bible also employs metaphors of body, joints, and ligaments in different ways, and so it is not surprising that Heidegger, like so many of his predecessors and contemporaries, utilized the language of marrow.

---

45. See R. Scott Clark, *Caspar Olevian and the Substance of the Covenant* (Edinburgh: Rutherford House, 2005).

46. Heidegger's trilogy of textbooks is organized according to the same structure of twenty-eight commonplaces. Within each locus, however, the *Concise Marrow* combines subheadings, whereas the *Marrow* and the *Corpus* are very nearly identical. For example, the *Concise Marrow* reduces Locus III, "On the Existence and Divinity of God," from twenty-six separate subheadings in the *Marrow* and the *Corpus* to just twenty. This was accomplished by combining the incommunicable attributes of God's infinity, eternity, and immensity into one subheading, whereas each has its own place in the other editions. Curiously, the *Concise Marrow* adds a subheading, "Spirituality," that is in neither of the other editions. In the same way, the *Concise Marrow* combines the communicable attributes of intellect and knowledge into one subheading, and God's virtues of holiness, uprightness, and goodness (and its species, love, grace, and mercy) into just one subheading.

47. See Ann M. Blair, *Too Much to Know: Managing Scholarly Information before the Modern Age* (New Haven, Conn.: Yale University Press, 2010), 117ff.

48. Heidegger, "Preface to the Reader."

Precisely defined, *medulla*, or "marrow, central core," refers to "the primary or central issues in a body of knowledge," while the broader concept of a *corpus* refers to the whole "body of doctrine held by the church as true throughout its history and developed systematically during the various ages of the church."[49]

William Ames, a teacher himself and similarly the author of a very well-known *Marrow of Theology*, recognized that this overtly pedagogical genre of theology could meet with objections. The text is succinct, matter-of-fact, and entirely without frills. The enjoyment one gets out of it is in the quick accumulation of knowledge, like consulting a dictionary to learn or confirm a fact, instead of committing oneself to a lengthy tome or encyclopedic treatment. But Ames knew well that for some there would be resistance:

> Some people...dislike this whole manner of writing, that is, of placing the main body of theology in a short compendium. They ask for great volumes in which they may...wander about as they will. But I intend this for all those who have neither the ample leisure nor the great skill to hunt the partridge in mountain and forest. Their situation calls for showing them the nest itself, or the seat of what they are pursuing, without ado.[50]

The arguments in favor of a textbook listing definitions, neatly arranged, were essentially practical in nature and not at all obscurantist or unconcerned about cultivating the love of God, as some have imagined. There was an underlying conviction that true piety is best encouraged by increasing the knowledge of God's grace to us in Christ Jesus, especially as grace comes to us covenantally in history. But first steps were important, rather than falling into a "swift stream, carrying with it many kinds of things," as Ames explained.[51] Better to give readers the ability to "catch and hold fast."[52] As another divine of the seventeenth century put it quaintly, changing metaphors: "To have the choicest flowers transplanted out of several gardens into a little parcel of ground, cannot but minister both pleasure and profit."[53] Or better, from Ames again, borrowing from the ancient writer Xenophon, "I wish they would learn from Cyrus that the sight of the sun's rays...shining through a window loses its charm if the window is too

---

49. Richard Muller, *Dictionary of Latin and Greek Theological Terms: Drawn Principally from Protestant Scholastic Theology* (Grand Rapids: Baker, 1985), 189, 84.

50. William Ames, "A Brief Forewarning of the Author concerning His Purpose," in *The Marrow of Theology, William Ames (1576–1633)*, trans. John Dykstra Eusden (Grand Rapids: Baker, 1968), 69.

51. Ames, "Brief Forewarning," 69.

52. Ames, "Brief Forewarning," 69.

53. Samuel Clarke, *Medulla theologiae: Or The Marrow of Divinity, Contained in Sundry Questions and Cases of Conscience; Both Speculative, and Practical; the Greatest Part of the Collected out of the Works of Our Most Judicious, Experienced, and Orthodox English Divines. The Rest Are Supplied by the Authour* (London: Thomas Underhill, 1659), B2.

large."[54] Heidegger was in good company with those who promised in teaching "not to say in two words what may be said in one," and to choose "the key which best opens the lock," even if it be a key of extraordinary simplicity.[55] There was a place for two words and many more, which may be found in Heidegger's *Corpus*.

Thus, if the text before you was intended to provide only "elementary and basic points" and "not the heights of weightier matters," this also implies that Heidegger aimed to introduce his readers to a consensus summary of the Reformed tradition as a whole.[56] There should be no doubt about the influence of other theologians and sources, as this was not only common but encouraged, and did not offend existing standards of citation. Just as Johannes Wollebius of the previous generation provided a summary of Amandus Polanus's enormous *Syntagma theologiae Christianae* (*Body of Christian Theology*, 1609), in some respects Heidegger relied on Jacob Alting (1618–1679) of Groningen, whom he had been invited to succeed, for many of his definitions. This was a debt he acknowledged, merely as one indication of the reality and importance of the communion of saints in the handing down of the faith. As you consult, browse, and read this new translation from a high orthodox theologian, one of the last of his kind, you will no doubt find that Heidegger taught theology out of an academic context, but he did so always *for* and *with* the church.

---

54. Ames, "Brief Forewarning," 70.

55. Ames, "Brief Forewarning," 70. Ironically, scholars have noted with some plausibility that the proliferation of this practice—in other words the use of compendiums to "prepare students for full-scale *systemata*"—may eventually have had the unintended effect of leading "to a decline in rigorous humanistic education" because it "separated the introductory students from any first-hand familiarity with the classics" of literature, the Scriptures, or important authors. Hotson, *Commonplace Learning*, 184.

56. Heidegger, Dedicatory Letter.

The Concise Marrow of Christian Theology

by Johann Heinrich Heidegger

for the sake and use of beginners,
from the recently published *The Marrow of Theology*
abridged here,
to serve as a primer and stepping stone for that text

Zürich
Heinrich Bodmer
1697

Dedicatory Epistle

To the triad of very distinguished theologians
in the renowned Basel Academy,

Dr. Peter Werenfelsius, Doctor of Sacred Theology and Professor of
New Testament, and Minister of the same for the church,

Dr. Johann Rudolph Westenius,
Doctor of Sacred Theology and Professor of Old Testament,

Dr. Samuel Werenfelsius, Doctor of Sacred Theology
and Professor of Systematic Theology,

highly regarded gentlemen, advisors, and friends in Christ.

Men of God, I am neither such a charlatan nor so out of my mind that I think that I can worthily offer you anything. Indeed, this little book, which I am sending into the light under your auspices, is a small foundation and destitute of loftier matters. It was fitting to place before your eyes only matters of a general sort. The book displays not the heights or weightier matters (τὰ βαρύτερα) of theology, but its elementary and basic points. Although such an acknowledgment may appear to lack a certain skill and depth, I nevertheless have several higher purposes for my project. The chief purpose is that it may complete my threefold work—the *Corpus Theologiae*, which, in the process of being published, will appear before your sight, God willing; the *Medulla* of the same, which has already been published; and the *Medulla Medullae*, which is published here. I will employ you as keen judges and experts in theology (θεοδιδάκτοις), for whose approbation above all others I strive in these holy labors of mine.

Indeed, whether I long for the astuteness (ἀγχίνοιαν) or fairness (ἐπιείκειαν) of your judgment or for love of myself in this effort, there is no one who can match you in all these things. Indeed, I know that your godliness, judgment, talent, and vast learning have become greatly esteemed everywhere. For that reason no prudent person who seeks your approval for something will rashly be reproached. I add as proof not only our mutual agreement in our equally honored (ἰσοτίμῳ) faith, but also the great respect with which I have always attended your radiant faces (τηλαυγέστερα πρόσωπα) and always will attend until my blessed death (ἄναλυσιν). Indeed, with that very excellent (τῷ πάνυ), incomparable theologian, Luke Grenler, let us have in view holiness in addition to vast learning, zeal, and the charm of all manners. Alas, he died prematurely! But until the end of his life, this great friend of mine, with whom I shared unity of will and study, corresponded with me very devotedly in letters.

I also have nothing other than holy memories of my longtime friendship with the distinguished and blessed (τοῦ μακαρίτου) theologian Johann Rudolph Westenius Sr., in whom very deep and wide erudition flourished so brightly. I also add your friendship, venerable minister, Peter Werenfelsius, who succeeded that man. Our age rightly elevated you as an ideal theologian, praising your singular godliness, teaching, judgment, prudence, and countless accomplishments. And in turn, I add your friendship, Johann Rudolph Westenius, which I have so far enjoyed and which I will always enjoy. You are most worthy of such a remarkable father, and you are most excellent and distinguished in fame for sacred and Greek literature. I also add your friendship, Samuel Werenfelsius, most worthy offspring of a great father, and very recent successor of the very distinguished and accomplished theologian, the godly Johann Zwinger, who recently died in the Lord. Your succession came about not from any favor due to your father's accomplishments, but truly from your own virtues. The votes of the academy raised you to the position, while all good men praised your talent. But you were appointed and made a colleague more by divine providence than by chance. Therefore, since all this resounds with cheerful congratulations, you understand that the last purpose of my inscription (ἐπιγραφῆς) is nothing else besides congratulating you and affirming that your very holy appointment was made eagerly and swiftly. Certainly the memory of that time has never escaped me—that is, when over twenty years ago you, a very pleasant and sweet guest of ours, decided to communicate with our Zürich Muses. To that end, the proofs of your singular godliness, keen judgment, cheerful disposition, love of learning (φιλομαθείας), and breadth of learning (πολυμαθείας), which you displayed in our presence, delighted us. And indeed, these qualities are neither few nor lacking in you. We already knew that you were full of everything good, which others affirmed, especially your very distinguished guest and friend, Johann Lavater, who is now with the saints (νῦν ἐν ἁγιοις). He was a philosopher in his own league, blameless in holiness of life, and above all a faithful and devoted cultivator of friendship. Certainly we all did not lack fortunate success when God's providential care soon moved you into our very old academy to teach the arts. You fulfilled that duty so favorably, producing so many memorials of your refined and razor-sharp (ὀξυδερκοῦς) talent. As a result, the board of directors (οἱ προεστῶτες) deemed you most worthy not only to make you the replacement of the very distinguished theologian who had died, but also to admit a son as a colleague to his father in the same faculty. Indeed, you are a very rare, eminent, and distinguished example of success. For certainly the sons of other very great men—Scaliger, Heinsius, Vossius, Zwinger, Buxtorf, Spanheim, and Turretin—have carried away greater fame and glory. But it has been granted to very few sons to sit on the same chair and faculty as their father, thereby to join him in the work of the Lord. Therefore, for the very successful father of the same name, I acknowledge that there was no advantage (πλεονέκτημα) given, so that his son might become a colleague, which the latter obtained by virtue of his own exceptional talent. Indeed, I congratulate the whole academy, which recently increased its splendor by giving you this coveted lot. I certainly congratulate everyone from my heart and soul (ἐξ ἄκρου μυελοῦ), and I ask God with eager prayers that, as He has blessed us with both of you, He may preserve your success as long as possible. I pray that the weary age of the father with all of its strength will gradually pass on to the son as a staff and that, increased, it may be mighty and strong again. May you, also, bring your father comfort, honor, and delight as long as he lives. And may you bear on your broad shoulders the very heavy funeral honors according to the plan of your old father with prudence, wisdom, and blessing, when the time comes. And may that most holy triad of colleagues, which passes down the faith for God and the church, abound with an increase of edification, even more than that of the Nazarites themselves until the days of Moses.

Finally, may the whole academy, adorned with these morning stars, be preserved in the beauty of its long-held greatness. Therefore, *venerable men*, you now know the reasons why I was moved to entrust the dedication of my little book to you, displaying your renowned names. It remains for me to say that with many prayers I seek that you may receive this loyalty of mine toward you with equal eagerness. I pray that you will be of the same mind as this testimony of my like-minded (ἰσοψύχος) affection, and that as long as I live among you there will be an even tighter bond of holiness among us. Lastly, I pray that this token of my sincere gratitude and fragrant offerings will be passed down to our posterity.

Goodbye, men of God, and never cease to walk in that pure love that you have long shown me.

Zürich
December 20, 1696

Very respectful of your very regarded and distinguished names,
Johann Heinrich Heidegger

Preface to the Reader

The work is threefold, with which I have brought to an end the late-night labors of many years, with God as my leader and light. The first is *The Substance of Christian Theology* (*Corpus Theologiae Christianae*), which, consisting of two rather large volumes, is beginning to exercise the press. The second is *The Marrow of Christian Theology* (*Medulla Theologiae Christianae*), which recently came to light. The third is *The Concise Marrow of Christian Theology* (*Medulla Medullae Theologiae*), which, now abridging the critical points, is ready to come to light. I have devoted the first for the use of the advanced, the second for those making progress, and the last for beginners. I have so made these works to agree that the last corresponds exactly to the substance of the first, and *The Concise Marrow of Christian Theology* serves as steps of initiation for *The Marrow of Christian Theology* and *The Marrow of Christian Theology* itself in turn for *The Substance of Christian Theology*.

Nothing holds me back from explaining the reasons of this plan of mine in many ways, because I think that it is clear to all, in the instruction of the talented and capable youth of the church dedicated to ministry, that the method must be retained. The easier things in which the foundations and main points of the special faith are contained, having been set out in advance, the more difficult and extensive things have been arranged in order that the youth may advance by steps in the same manner, as with a swift foot, from squadron to squadron (חיל מחיל אל), or having advanced from virtue to virtue, the suitable and apt one may be brought back prepared for the office of teaching in the church.

Therefore, in this *Concise Marrow of Christian Theology* that I now set forth, I have begun the way, in order that, having used what I selected, I may expound the especially necessary things, confirmed by the consensus of nearly all, and to this end: that I might also display the idea of the chief points and heads of truth. Therefore, I delivered the particular definitions, which represent the essence of things in few words, transferred and divided in lines, whether in special words or from many ones that do not at all belong to the theologian, indeed arranging (συντακτηρίου) Jacob Alting, the blessed (τοῦ μακαριτοῦ), whenever I was able to retain them because they are both the most exact of all, his definitions being in harmony with great judgment, and our Zürich School has hence been accustomed to the same for thirty years. I have indeed set forth the assertions of Scripture, on which alone I thus support the mysteries of faith claimed, the testimonies, which I set forth more usefully translated into Latin. I have confirmed and so confirmed in what I was able, with brevity, perspicuity, firmness, and the right order, but most difficult of all these, I did this as a married man. Indeed, I leave it now to the industry of beginners, in order that they may chew on the foundations of theology, rightly and in the order of learning, before all things the definitions and the more distinct testimonies of Scripture, even for themselves. To be sure, we only know as much as we remember. Finally, I leave it to them to return to these again and again, not only as beginners but also when they leave the stage of the beginner, prepared for work (παρόντα ἔργῳ).

LOCUS I

On Theology in General

I. Theology

Theology in general is teaching or a word about divine things. In this sense, the old Greek writers called those who taught a word about divine things *theologians*. And since there can be a word about God or divine things from either nature or revelation, the former comes as natural theology and the latter as revealed theology.[1]

II. Natural Theology

Natural theology is a word about God from nature, taught by the dictation of reason alone. For "what can be known about God is manifest in them, for God has manifested it to them. For since the creation of the world His invisible attributes are seen, having been observed in what has been made, His eternal power and divinity"—not unto the end that they may be saved through such knowledge, but "so that they are inexcusable" (Rom. 1:19–20).[2]

III. Revealed Theology

Revealed theology is teaching about God, reconciling man, the sinner, to Himself in Christ, and in the same right knowledge and godly worship, revealing it through His word for the salvation of man, the sinner, and the glory of God. For "this is eternal life, that they may know You, the only true God, and the one whom You have sent, Jesus Christ" (John 17:3). "We speak out of sincerity, as from God, before the face of God in Christ" (2 Cor. 2:17).[3]

---

1. In the original text, in nearly every section, Heidegger included references to his larger work, the *Medulla*, which is not yet translated. To improve the clarity of the main text, the editor has moved those references to footnotes. *Medulla*, I–IV.

2. *Medulla*, IV–VII.

3. *Medulla*, VII–VIII.

IV. Religion

The knowledge and worship of God comes in the name *religion*, which is the right reason of rightly knowing and piously worshiping the true God. Saint Paul calls it "the knowledge of truth according to godliness" (Titus 1:1) and "zeal for God according to knowledge" (Rom. 10:2). It is marked by that which teaches God from God or His revelation, delivers the means of reconciling man with God, and explains reasonable worship worthy of God, who sanctifies the sinner.[4]

V. Distinction of Revelation

Divine revelation ought to be distinguished by revelation formed from anything whatsoever, not only from the peculiar nature of revelation, which being worthy of God reveals God, but also from the conscience of man, which as the "light of the Lord" (Prov. 20:27) discovers those things that are in himself and in the works of God, conferring with revelation he thinks to be remarkably enlightened, also from the proofs of a thing governed, as well as from predictions that have been proven to occur. But yet conviction depends on the grace of God alone. For "God, who commanded light to shine out of darkness, shines in hearts for the illumination of grace, in the face of Jesus Christ" (2 Cor. 4:6). For although men are ministers in their "watering" and "planting" (1 Cor. 3:6), "through whom we believe" (v. 5), nevertheless their genuine words and purpose are not through themselves.[5]

VI. The Instruction of Reason

Hence, the instruction (*magisterium*) and authority of human reason is not the sure rule of distinguishing revelation. "The unspiritual man does not grasp the things that are of the Spirit of God, for they are foolishness to him" (1 Cor. 2:14). For God "hides" His "mysteries from the wise and reveals them to infants" (Matt. 11:25). And "every thought" ought "to be taken captive for the obedience of Christ" (2 Cor. 10:5).[6]

VII. The Use of Reason

Nevertheless, faith and revelation do not tear down right reason even remaining in the sinner, but rather they perfect it. Indeed, there is no dissonance between revelation and reason regarding either God or truth. For God is not "yes and no" (2 Cor. 1:18). He is "unable to lie" (Titus 1:2); He "revealed" what even can be

4. Likely an allusion to the medieval axiom: *Theologia Deum docet, a Deo docetur, et ad Deum ducit* (Theology teaches God, is taught by God, and leads to God). *Medulla*, IX–X.

5. *Medulla*, XI–XV.

6. *Medulla*, XV–XVI.

known about God naturally (Rom. 1:19); and He "wrote the work of the law on the heart" (2:15).[7]

VIII. It Is Principal or Organic

The use of reason in theology is either principal or organic. It is principal, whereby reason brings out arguments for the faith out of one's own bosom, not only examining the witness about divine things from the light of conscience but also making arguments available for the principles of faith and their trustworthiness (ἀξιοπιστίᾳ), striking down the sophistries of corrupt reason and comparing the natural signification and truth of words and ideas. It is organic in matters that depend on revelation alone, in which reason serves by receiving revelation; by discerning it from what is false, according to the rules of good conscience imprinted on reason by God; by making clear with the help of language and arts; and by comparing a word with words, reason with faith. The use of logical consequences also is brought back to the use that distinguishes, whereby reason elicits and brings in those things that are contained in the strength and vitals of the written Word. Such logical consequences concern faith because the things that are contained in the valor and strength of the Word of God are the very Word of God. Hence, Christ said to the Sadducees, who did not acknowledge the resurrection contained in the valor of the words of God, "You err, not knowing the Scriptures" (Matt. 22:29, 31–32).[8]

IX. It Must Be Known Explicitly and Implicitly

Some things must be believed that have been revealed explicitly, and others implicitly. To believe explicitly is the foundation of faith. The simple foundation of faith is Jesus Christ (1 Cor. 3:11). The complex foundation of faith can be stated in this axiom: Christ is the righteousness or Savior of the one who believes. From this foundation, the fundamental articles of the faith are derived. These must be believed implicitly for all and everyone to be saved, who are comprehended in that foundation or built on it.[9]

X. Theology Is One and Manifold, Not Scholastic or Mystical

Theology is one in the method of its foundation and of that without which it cannot be known. It is varied and manifold in the method of the manner of delivering it and of its external form. This also dictates in a certain order the progress of revelation, history, and the economy of the covenant of grace. It ought to be regulated by the words of the Holy Spirit and also by "comparison

7. *Medulla*, XVII–XVIII.
8. *Medulla*, XIX–XXIV.
9. *Medulla*, XXIV–XXVIII.

of spiritual things with spiritual things" (1 Cor. 2:13) and delivered without the sophistry of human wisdom and philosophical teachings and terms. Hence, the trifle of scholastic and mystical theology, in which there is no use.[10] For scholastic theology depends on heterogeneous principles and a skeptical method. Amusing itself with tricks of terms, the whole serves the interests of the reign of the Antichrist. But mystical theology, the Word of God having been abandoned, attends closely to fallacious inspirations; turns faith into ignorance; overturns love, without which knowledge does not exist; and turns the state of the way into the state of the fatherland.[11]

XI. It Is Imperfect

Whether residing in the delivered system or in the mind as a disposition (*habitus*), theology is imperfect in this life. For "we know in part" and "we prophesy in part" (1 Cor. 13:9). Therefore, it must always be "progressed" (1 Tim. 4:15) and proceed "to perfection" (Heb. 6:1). Moreover, any theology, because of the danger of error, is subject to examination. "Test the spirits, whether they are from God" (1 John 4:1).[12]

XII. It Is Practical

Theology is practical because all its truths either directly command practice, faith in Christ, and love of God or indirectly incline to it in its own strength. "The secret of God is for those who fear Him, even so that He makes known His covenant to them (which must be believed or accomplished)" (Ps. 25:14). "The teaching of truth is according to godliness" (1 Tim. 6:3; Titus 1:1).[13]

---

10. Heidegger might refer to two great approaches to medieval theology and piety, for which we may substitute *rationalist* and *irrationalist*. "Scholastic" here can hardly refer to academic theology per se, since Heidegger himself was an academic theologian who taught *in schola* and who was quite familiar with the distinctions and subtleties of academic theology as practiced by the Reformed, Lutheran, and Roman theologians in the period. The context of the comment makes clear that "scholastic" here is a reference particularly to Roman theologians, most probably contemporary Roman apologists and theologians like Suarez, Molina, and Bellarmine. "Mystical theology" most likely refers to any number of subjectivist approaches to theology that flourished in the period. He might be thinking of Meister Eckhart (c. 1260–c. 1328) or Johannes Tauler (c. 1300–1361), who influenced Luther. Anabaptist theology and piety was marked by the sort of mysticism that Heidegger derides here. Some of the more extreme Pietists (e.g., Jean de Labadie, 1610–1674), a movement emerging in the seventeenth century, also might have been in view.

11. *Medulla*, XXVIII–XXXV.

12. *Medulla*, XXXV.

13. *Medulla*, XXXVI.

LOCUS II

On Holy Scripture

I. Oral Revelation

Revelation was handed down by the mouth from Adam to Moses, especially by four men and sacred heads, *Adam, Methuselah, Shem,* and *Jacob*, the latter of whom always lived with the former, diligently keeping it in their long life and fidelity. After the descent of Israel into Egypt, the end of life having been shortened and the people, on account of awful servitude, having nearly forgotten their God, very eagerly worshipping the abominations of the Egyptians, it pleased God to hand down His Word to guardians of love, in order that the doctrine of the covenant and especially the many ceremonies may be preserved, kept whole, for posterity.[1]

II. Scripture

Hence, *Holy Scripture* was born, which is *the Word of God, with its author being the Holy Spirit, written down by Moses and the prophets in the Old Testament and by the evangelists and apostles in the New Testament, and rendered into the canonical books, in order that it may fully and clearly teach the church about God and divine things as well as be the single norm for life and salvation.*[2]

III. Its Divinity and the Witness of the Holy Spirit

The following powerfully demonstrate that Scripture is the *Word* of God:

- Not only the former *ideas*, which the conscience and reason of man dictate, but also the *manner of handing down* the law from Mount Sinai, out of fire, and
- All the circumcised people present,

1. *Medulla*, I, II.

2. Heidegger italicized this section in the original. Unless otherwise noted, words that appear in italics are italicized in the original. *Medulla*, III.

- Indeed, the gospel through the messenger of the covenant, and
- God descending to earth even manifest in the flesh,
- The *predictions*, the *holy authors* and their work and ingenuity,
- The harmony of its *parts*, the *efficacy of its teaching and speech*, and
- Its *antiquity, propagation, and preservation.*

However, just as the light of the sun is not known except with the light of bodily eyes, so the light of Scripture, as divine, is not known except with the light of spiritual eyes. For it is the "Spirit who bears witness, because the Spirit is truth" (1 John 5:6), not through enthusiasms but "by enlightening hearts, for the illumination of knowledge" (2 Cor. 4:6). "God has revealed to us through His Spirit" (1 Cor. 2:12).[3]

IV. The Office (Ministerium) of the Church

He has given the *office* of the church, which, as the "standard-bearer" (Song 6:10), sustains the standard of the eternal gospel in the world and gives light (φωστὴρ), "to shine, carry about yourself the Word of life" (Phil. 2:15–16). But yet that witness of the church about Scripture is not authenticating (αὐθεντικὸν) and principal but introductory (εἰσαγωγικὸν) and ministerial. For God "does not accept" authentic "testimony from man" (John 5:34, 41). For although the church has the Spirit of God, its inspiration is nevertheless not extraordinary and special but common, which sort of words and deeds do not furnish authority and authenticity.[4]

V. The Holy Writers

The holy writers, "the prophets and apostles" (Eph. 2:20), were few, in order that it may not become vile with the multitude, because it ought to illuminate the corrupted and the poor with religion, "that they may shame the strong and no flesh may boast in the sight of God" (1 Cor. 1:27, 29). Those writing did not impose their "own will" (2 Peter 1:21) as necessity nor occasions of fortune, but the general and special command of God (Matt. 28:19; 2 Tim. 3:16). Moreover, the Holy Spirit inspired them not only in *matters* known (on account of fullness [πληροφορίαν]) and unknown (on account of knowledge that was needed) but also in *words* because it could not be dictated to men ignorant in things known and to upright men in things unknown, apart from the Spirit of God. Therefore, the same were infallible because they were especially inspired by God (2 Tim. 3:16),

3. *Medulla*, IV–VII.
4. *Medulla*, VII–XI.

from above (ἄνωθεν) "followed all things" (Luke 1:3), and "the Holy Spirit led them into all truth" (John 16:13).[5]

VI. The Books of the Old Testament and Their Wholeness

There are books of Scripture, whether of the Old or New Testament. The former are *Moses*, the *Prophets* (historical and such *par excellence* [κατ' ἐξοχὴν]), and the *Psalms* (poetical) (Luke 24:44). All these have arrived to us whole and pure. For the *book of the law*, or the Pentateuch, "was placed by the side of the Ark of the Covenant, in order that it may be a witness" (Deut. 31:25–26). The book of *Joshua* was for the same (Josh. 24:27). The *law of the king* was written by Samuel (1 Sam. 10:25), and analogously (ἀναλόγως) the remaining were also added. Moreover, they have not been corrupted either by Jews, because it was predicted to happen "that the words of God will not depart from the mouth of Israel" (Isa. 59:21), or Christians, because heretics were not able to defile all the codices. And how much less have the whole books been lost, because "not even one jot or tittle" ought to have "passed away from the law" (Matt. 5:18), and otherwise the canon of faith and life would have perished, which opposes the providence of God, keeping watch for the sake of the church.[6]

VII. The Apocrypha of the Old Testament

Since what is of faith has been properly dictated by the canon, the *Apocrypha* (גנוזים) is rightly and meritoriously questionable. For it lacks not only writers inspired by God (θεόπνευστοι), none of which existed after Malachi (Mal. 4:4–5), and divinity throughout, but also authentic tradition, because it was never handed down to the Jewish or Christian church by God.[7]

VIII. The Books of the New Testament

In the New Testament there are five *historical* books, twenty-one *didactic*, and one *prophetic*. They have been written down by those whose names they bear before them in the Greek idiom, although distinct in various dialects, because it was predicted that God would speak with the Jews in a "foreign language" (Isa. 28:11). Saint John established the end for them with that wish, "Come, Lord Jesus" (Rev. 22:20), connecting the time of the book he wrote with the advent of the Lord.[8]

---

5. *Medulla*, XI, XII.
6. *Medulla*, XIII–XIX.
7. *Medulla*, XIX, XX.
8. *Medulla*, XX–XXIV.

IX. The Perfection of Scripture

Scripture of both testaments has perfection (τελειότητα), not only *essential*, of all the articles of faith and life that save, but also *integral*. And it has that *simply*, in the full canon of all the books, and *according to which*, in each and every book in the canon of the Old and New Testaments. For it is *powerful* "to render wisdom for salvation" (2 Tim. 3:15), and "divinely inspired, it is useful for teaching, reproof, correction, and discipline, that the man of God may be perfect, and prepared for every good work" (2 Tim. 3:16–17). Certainly it contains "the whole counsel of God" (Acts 20:27), the "testament" of the Father (Ex. 34:27), "the foundation of faith" (Eph. 2:20), the teaching "of eternal life" (John 5:39, 20:31). Finally, it is simply called perfect (תמימה) (Ps. 19:7). Hence, it does not have need that it may be completed with another word not written, but only what has been *handed down* with the mouth, as specifically distinct by Scripture. For the holy writers of the New Testament "wrote" other things, which "are read" in the Old Testament and are known, corresponding to the types in the thing or truth (2 Cor. 1:13).[9]

X. The Internal Word

Moreover, the Word of God, written with the splendor of the internal writing on the heart, must not be disdained, because the Holy Spirit does not write on the heart something else than what was written and the law inspired by Him. For to Himself He unites the written *Word* (Jer. 31:33), the very thing from the "hearing" of its preaching is "faith" (Rom. 10:17). Otherwise, the norm for testing the spirits would cease and all would go out into madness, and the way to detesting evils would be exposed, as frequently happens.[10]

XI. Its Sense

Nevertheless, Scripture consists not in mere words and characters but in their genuine sense, which is its spirit and form. This sense is singular from the mind of the author Himself, the Holy Spirit, intended by God, its author. This sense is literal or grammatical, depending on particular words or figures, and the scope of whatever passage, and yet consistent everywhere in the circumstances of subject matter. For although the Word of God is "very broad" (Ps. 119:96) and ought not "be despised" (1 Thess. 5:20), the God who speaks in Scripture nevertheless is not double-tongued (δίγλωτος)—the image of the serpent, of "divided lips"—but "simple" and "sincere" (2 Cor. 1:12; 2:17; 11:13), and His "precept" is clear (τηλωγὲς) (Ps. 19:8). The *manner of signifying* ought to be distinguished in that single sense, literal or figurative, and also the *manner of*

9. *Medulla*, XXIV–XXIX.
10. *Medulla*, XXIX–XXXII.

application, when that which the letter signifies, the thing signified being in the middle, is accommodated to another similar thing that must be signified by the decree of God. Hence the sense of Scripture emerges as *composite*.[11]

XII. Its Clarity

The virtue of the sense of Scripture is *clarity, whereby the interpreter plainly and lucidly sets forth the dogmas of faith and those things necessary for life, of his own, without any human authority*. For "the testimony of Jehovah is clear, illuminating the eyes" (Ps. 19:8), the "Word of God" is a "light for the feet, light for the path" (Ps. 119:105). "A lamp shining in a dark place, until the day dawns, and the morning star rises in our hearts" (2 Peter 1:19). For its author is the "Father of lights" (James 1:17). Therefore, nothing in Scripture can be alleged for error, and in it is contained the key of knowledge—Christ and His righteousness. Therefore, if "the gospel" is "veiled, it is veiled to those who are perishing" (2 Cor. 4:3).[12]

XIII. The Interpretation of Matters

But the right sense of Scripture is made clear in the interpretation not only *of matters* in expositions and commentaries, adorned with human work, but also *of the words* in the translations. The norm *of the former* is not human authority or the sense of the Roman Church, but Holy Scripture itself—namely, which is not of its own (ἰδίας ὀπιλύσεως), not flowing from its own movement, and not an "exposition" demonstrated from another source (2 Peter 1:20). Therefore, Ezra and the first people obtained "understanding of the law through Scripture" (Neh. 8:8). For "the things of God no one knows except the Spirit of God" (1 Cor. 2:11), who reveals them in His Word.[13]

XIV. Translations

The *latter* [the words], made in the translations, is also necessary because Scripture ought to be read, investigated, and understood by all. Their norm is the sources or original texts—that is, the Hebrew of the Old Testament and the Greek of the New Testament, with which the translations ought to agree exactly. For although no translation is authentic, because no human translator is inspired by God (θεόπνευσος), nevertheless the translation that is nearer in agreement with the sources is the better one. Therefore, translations of this sort are permitted to be made because the Word of Christ "ought to dwell in their hearts richly (πλουσίως) (Col. 3:16), and they ought to read equally the sources

11. *Medulla*, XXXII, XXXIII.
12. *Medulla*, XXXIV–XXXVI.
13. *Medulla*, XXXVI–XL.

themselves, who know how to, even those who do not know how to, at least to hear them read by others, because blessed is he "whose delight is in the law, who meditates on it day and night" (Ps. 1:2), "who reads and hears the words of prophecy" (Rev. 1:3), and "the Scripture must be searched out" by all (John 5:39) and "known from childhood" (2 Tim. 3:15).[14]

XV. It Is a Canon

Scripture has been given to believers in order that it would be a *rule* and *canon* of faith and life. "Blessed are those who," according to this, "advance the canon" (Gal. 6:16). "We advance to that which we have arrived, in the same canon (τῷ αὐτῷ κανόνι)" (Phil. 3:16). Therefore, we are sent forth to the "law and testimony" as a "canon and rule" (Isa. 8:19–20). For faith and life singly depend on it, as first and quite well known, in order that the divine law may not decline to the right or left. Moreover, it ought not *to be regulated* by the church, because rule and non-rule, canon and non-canon would result.[15]

XVI. It Is a Judge

The same is also a *judge of faith and life* because God, author of faith and life, has spoken the judgment of faith and life in the same, and speaking to the heart of man through the same, He absolves and condemns. Indeed, the voice of this rule and norm is "the living Word, judging thoughts" (Heb. 4:12) and "manifesting truth to the conscience" (2 Cor. 4:2). Moreover, nothing else is demanded in this judgment than that the good may rightly have a good conscience of their deeds and the evil a stinging worm. Absolution is in the former and condemnation in the latter. "The Word, which I have spoken, will judge you" (John 12:48).[16]

XVII. The Church Is Not the Judge

Therefore, there is no *human, personal, authentic, highest,* and *infallible judge* outside of the tested demonstration. For there is "one Lawgiver, who can save and destroy. Who are you to judge another?" (James 4:12). "I am not brought under the power of another" (1 Cor. 6:12). "You have been bought with a price. Do not become slaves to men" (1 Cor. 7:23). "We are not masters of faith" (2 Cor. 1:24). "Why do you allow yourselves to be bound to the dogmas of men in the world?" (Col. 2:20). Certainly a judge of this sort can be neither the pope nor a council. The *pope* cannot be a judge, because revelation did not establish him nor did the authentic tablets or miracles confirm such. Moreover, he is therefore guilty and destitute of all the requirements of a legitimate judge. It cannot be a

14. *Medulla*, XL–XLVIII.
15. *Medulla*, XLVIII.
16. *Medulla*, XLIX.

council for similar reasons, both because elsewhere the church would rarely have a judge and because what a legitimate council is is difficult to know. Certainly it is necessary by divine faith, which is not clearly known where it is led concerning the judge of faith.[17]

XVIII. The Judgment of Discernment

But nevertheless *the judgment of discernment* is given in the world, whereby not only the many assembled but also all believers judge, *discerning* what is true from what is false. And by this the conscience of others is not obligated, but the faith of believers is aligned, in order that they may be "certain" in their "mind" (Rom. 14:5). "You search out better things" (Rom. 2:18). "Be renewed in your mind, in order that you may be able to search out what the will of God is, which is good, pleasing, and perfect" (Rom. 12:2). "The Spiritual man judges (ἀνακρίνει) all things" (1 Cor. 2:15). "I speak as for the prudent. Judge yourselves, what I say" (1 Cor. 10:15). "Two or three prophets speak and the rest will judge" (1 Cor. 14:29). "Test all things. Retain what is good" (1 Thess. 5:21). For that of the salvation of all is of importance, because all "see with their faith" (Hab. 2:4). Neither is the norm of the former judgment the authority or determination of the church, but Scripture, from the very intellect itself, because all are "to test the spirits" since "many false prophets have gone out into the world, and the Antichrist is in it" (1 John 4:1–3), nor could there be another norm of searching out the former than Scripture.[18]

XIX. The Private Spirit

The judgment of discretion, deprived of the reason *of the subject*, and one's own mind (ἴδιος νοῦς), the spirit of each one (ἑκάστου) whether he is a doctor or not a doctor, is "one's own" and private (Rom. 14:5). By reason of the *principal* and *origin* the private spirit is not like the Holy Spirit. For such judgment is not one's own "explanation" (ἰδία ὀπίλυσις) devised nor one's own will (θέλημα) "of men" (2 Peter 1:20–21). Instead, individual discretion is subject to *the Holy Spirit*, the author of Scripture, the One who speaks in Scripture. Indeed, there is for each and every believer a common norm—Scripture. "All these are done by one and the same Spirit" (1 Cor. 12:11). "God has revealed to us (all who believe) through His Spirit" (1 Cor. 2:10).[19]

---

17. *Medulla*, L.
18. *Medulla*, LII, LIII.
19. *Medulla*, LIV.

LOCUS III

On the Existence and Divinity of God

I. The Existence of God

It must be known about God that He is (ὅτι ἐστὶ), what He is (τί ἐστὶ), and who He is (τίς ἐστὶ). *That He is*—that is, the Godhead exists, the first cause of all things, having all possible perfections—teaches the nature of the thing because it is heard by the voice of God, who exists throughout nature. Since the existence of all *other* things is contingent on Him, the rational mind necessarily assents. *That He is* also teaches *thought about God* because it includes His existence, without which there is no God. And it searches for a cause or exemplar, without which there can be no thought, no sort of which can be outside of God Himself, but even the "small stones of the image of God" and "consciousness of God" (1 Peter 2:19) remain in man. It also teaches *things existing in the world*, all of which are from another, to another, or on account of another. For *bodies* are not sufficient to exist in themselves and lack the power of motion, and those that consist without support and that are born from things unaware of themselves must be astonishing. Nor can *spirits*, differing entirely from bodies, be produced by either bodies or other finite spirits, and they cannot be satisfied in any created thing. *That He is* also teaches the *manifestation* of God in *nature* and *the Word*, or revelation, by which nature is more fully set forth and the works of grace and judgment are to be marveled at, and even the future is declared.[1]

II. Divinity

What God *is* is known from His divinity. Although this cannot be defined, because it is infinite, it can nevertheless be circumscribed to a certain extent, and thus it is described through names and attributes in the Word of God, which is *JEHOVAH* or *the most simple Spirit, immense, eternal, supremely living, wise, good, just, free, powerful, and blessed, and He is Father, Son, and Holy Spirit.*[2]

1. *Medulla*, I–VII.
2. *Medulla*, VII, VIII.

III. Names

God does not properly have a name, because He is extraordinary (פלא) (Judg. 13:18). Nevertheless, they are assigned to Him on account of condescension (συγκάταβασιν) since they do not set forth His whole nature but only that which He has willed to be known for His praise. For He is called "I will be" (אהיה) and "Jehovah" (יהוה) (Ex. 3:14) because in Him there is nothing except being (הוית), and *He is what He is*, this Himself, not this and this or not-this. And He is *the One who becomes*; that is, He testifies in His work and deed in Christ that great name because it includes the essence and every perfection of God. Moreover, it is called the "name" and "memorial" of God (Ex. 3:15; Hos. 12:5), proper to God, and is communicable to no creature. Jah (יה), which *He taught* by יאה, signifies divine majesty (θεοπρέπειαν). Elohim (אלהים), because He swears (אלה) to men in covenant and is Almighty (אל) (παντοκρατώρ) (Rev. 1:8). Lord (אדוני), of which sort Christ is in regard to the church. Shaddai (שדי), sufficient in Himself and for all, or devastating (שדד), as He is powerful to create. Elion (עליון), because He dwells in the high place, and is exalted over all. God (θεὸς), because He puts in place (θέσι) all things or watches with sight (θεᾷ). Lord (κύριος)—that is, Jehovah—because among the ancients it was the same to rule (κύρειν) as to be (εἶναι).[3]

IV. The Attributes: Incommunicable

The *attributes* of God are not assigned to God as adjuncts but as essential, because in Him, as Jehovah (יהוה), there is nothing except that He *is* most simple. These are either *incommunicable* or *negative*, removing every imperfection from God, or *communicable* and *affirmative*, affirming His perfection with a certain analogy common to His creatures. The former are independence, simplicity, infinity, and immutability.[4]

V. Independence

Through *independence* God *is and works of Himself and does not depend on another in being and working*. For God is Jehovah (יהיה), and therefore *He is what He is* and does not exist or work from another, because otherwise He would be *what was not*, not *what is*. I am God Shaddai (שדי), sufficient for Myself and others (Gen. 17:1), "the First and Last" (Isa. 41:4), "the Beginning and End" (Rev. 1:8), which sort does not depend on another.[5]

3. *Medulla*, IX–XVI.
4. *Medulla*, XVI, XVII.
5. *Medulla*, XVIII.

VI. Simplicity

It is the *simplicity* of God *through which the divine essence is free from all composition*. For God *is* or "He becomes what He is" (Ex. 3:14). And the One who *is* His own is not another and is not composed even from *being* or *essence*. And since He is *Jehovah*, there can be nothing in Him except being (הוית) first, most perfect and most simple. And since He is one (אחד) (Deut. 6:4), He is clearly indivisible (ἀμέριστος) and absolutely simple. Moreover, He also cannot come outside of Himself into composition, because the Creator and creature "cannot be assimilated" to one another (Isa. 40:18), and the finite and the infinite cannot coalesce into one essence.[6]

VII. Spirituality

God is also a most simple Spirit, clearly invisible and incomprehensible. The "Spirit" (John 4:24) is *most simple* and free from all matter—namely, what is animal. For God, if He does not think, is a mere idol. He is clearly *invisible* (1 Tim. 1:17) since not even man himself ever sees his own mind, and the former could be extended and formed. Finally, He is *incomprehensible* because "the depths of the riches, wisdom, knowledge of God, His judgments are inscrutable, and His ways are unsearchable" (Rom. 11:33), and "there is no examination of His magnitude" (Ps. 145:3). "No one knows the things of God except the Spirit of God" (1 Cor. 2:11).[7]

VIII. Infinity, Eternity, Immensity

There is the *infinity* of God, whereby *He most eminently embraces all perfections without end, manner, and limit*. Zophar said about this, "Surely you will not discover the search for God, will you? Surely you will not discover God Shaddai until perfection, will you?" (Job 11:7–9). "He is higher than heaven, so what do you do? He is deeper than hell, so how do you know? There is no searching out His magnitude" (Ps. 145:3, 4). The former removes from God a beginning *in existence*, end, and succession through *eternity*, through which God "is free from" all "beginning, end, and succession," as God of the world (אל עולם) (Gen. 14:18), "from ages to ages" (Ps. 90:2). He is "the King of ages" (1 Tim. 1:17), simply "eternal" (Rom. 16:26), and "the ancient of days" (Dan. 7:9) in whom "one day is as a thousand years" (Ps. 90:4; 2 Peter 3:8). His infinity also removes Him *from essence* of the same local boundary through *immensity*, through which *the same essence of God is everywhere present and is free from every dimension and local boundary*. For God is not even properly in a place. "Where is a place in which I may rest?" (Isa. 66:1). On the contrary, He is the "Rock" and "Refuge"

6. *Medulla*, XIX–XX.
7. *Medulla*, XXI–XXIV.

(Ps. 18:2) and dwelling place (מעוז) of all creatures, whom "the heavens do not contain" (1 Kings 8:27).[8]

IX. Immutability

Immutability follows from the preceding attributes, whereby *the essence of God is liable to no change, alteration, or passive power.* No perfection can lack what is *most simple*, nor to that degree can the former be changed for the worse or better. "You will change them, and they will be changed. "But You are Yourself" (ואתה הוא) (Ps. 102:27). "I am Jehovah. I do not change" (Mal. 3:6). "Among" Him "there is no change or shadow of turning" (James 1:17).[9]

X. Communicable Attributes: Life

The *communicable* and *affirming* attributes of God are life, intellect, will, His emotions and virtues, and finally, power and blessedness. The *life* of God is that *whereby He both lives, perpetually active in Himself in nature, and is the source of life for others, variously communicating it beyond Himself.* For God is God of the living (אלהי חיים) (Deut. 5:26; 1 Sam. 17:36), the living God (אל חי) (Josh. 3:10; Jer. 10:10), having "the power of an indestructible life" (Heb. 7:16)—that is, eternal, without beginning, end, and variation. And as He lives in Himself, so He gives "life" to others, "breath and all things" (Acts 17:25) since He is the fountain of life (ממור חיים) (Ps. 36:9).[10]

XI. Intellect and Knowledge

The life of God consists of His intellect and will. Everywhere Scripture ascribes *intellect* to God. "Who has known the mind of the Lord?" (Rom. 11:34). "Great is our Lord…there is no end to His intelligence" (תבונת) (Ps. 147:5). Cognition or knowledge and wisdom is in Him. *Knowledge* is that whereby *in a most perfect manner, through His essence and in a single act He simultaneously knows Himself and all things outside of Him, from Him and through Him.* For He knows all not as a man, through the mode of *faculty* and *disposition*, but through His *essence* and in a single act. "Are not the eyes of the flesh Yours? Does man see as You see?" (Job 10:4). He also knows all things *by Himself*, because no one "knows the Son except the Father, and no one knows the Father except the Son" (Matt. 11:27), "who is in the bosom of the Father" (John 1:18), and all things *outside of Him*, because "the eyes of Jehovah attend to and penetrate the whole earth" (2 Chron. 16:9), "all his works have been known by the eternal God" (Acts 15:18), "all things have been manifested and laid before His eyes" (Heb. 4:13). He also "sees

8. *Medulla*, XXIV–XXXI.

9. *Medulla*, XXXI.

10. *Medulla*, XXXII, XXXIII.

the heart" (1 Sam. 16:7). He "alone knows the heart of the sons of man" (1 Kings 8:39), and those things that "ascend into our spirit" (Ezek. 11:5), and finally "what will happen in the future" (Isa. 41:23). For from Him whom all things are and are made, He, being all faithful (παντεπιστήμων), knows all things.[11]

XII. Wisdom

The *wisdom* of God is that whereby *God knows the things that prevail to tell His glory together with their methods.* And it is the controller of all the counsels of God. For God alone is wise (μόνος σοφὸς) (Rom. 16:27) and is "wisdom" itself (Matt. 11:19), which above all has been laid out in Christ, who therefore also came in the name of *wisdom*.[12]

XIII. Will: Signs, Benevolence, Prescriptive, Decretal, Secret, and Revealed

The *will* of God is that *whereby He wills all things from Himself in a single and constant act.* For God "does all that He wills" (Ps. 115:3) through His "will" (Rev. 4:11), "according to the counsel of" His "will" (Eph. 1:11). This is varied: above all are *signs*, whereby He manifests Himself somewhere in a sign, as a command or word, or *benevolence*, whereby He wills, for the sake of His benevolence, that this or that thing exists. The former is more correctly called *prescriptive* and moral; the latter *decretal* and *efficacious*. The former is in whatever is *revealed*, and the latter in what is *secret*. "The secret things are before our Lord God. The revealed things are before us and our children" (Deut. 29:29). The will of *sign*, *prescriptive* and *revealed*, is the rule of our duty. The will of *benevolence, decretal*, and *secret*, is the highest cause of things.[13]

XIV. Emotions

The emotions and virtues of God fall back on His will. There are properly no *emotions* in God, who is impassive (ἀπαθὴς). Moreover, they that are assigned to Him in the manner of human emotions (ἀνθρωποπαθῶς) ought to be understood in the manner of the divine majesty (θεοπρεπῶς), as the act of the will of God, or rather the will itself, having diverse wants (χρέσεις) for its objects. Certain acts concerning man and emotions in man follow, so that God is said *to love*, when He wishes man well and unites him to Himself; *to hate*, when He separates Himself from him; *to be angry*, when He wishes to punish; *to desire, to await*, when He confers gifts that were able to move to obedience; *to fear*, when He anticipates evil; *to rejoice*, when He returns goods to man, gathered

11. *Medulla*, XXXIV–XL.
12. *Medulla*, XL.
13. *Medulla*, XLI–LI.

for His glory; *to be sad*, when He bears witness to the weariness of a troublesome thing; *to repent*, when, His will remaining the same, He changes His work; *to pity*, when He runs to the aid of the miserable. Whatever breathes perfection in such emotions properly agrees with God. Whatever breathes imperfection ought to be abated.[14]

XV. Virtues: Holiness, Uprightness, Goodness, Love, Grace, Mercy

The *virtues* of God are holiness, uprightness, goodness, justice, and freedom. *Holiness* is that whereby in all His words and deeds He breathes nothing except what is divine and of divine majesty (θεοπρεπὴς). "There is no one" at all "who is holy as Jehovah" (1 Sam. 2:2). "He alone" is "holy" (Rev. 15:4). His rule is not only His will but also His nature. *Uprightness* is that through which He is upright and everywhere shows Himself upright in love of good and hatred of evil. "He" is "righteous and upright" (Deut. 32:4). "Good and upright is Jehovah. Therefore, He shows the way to sinners" (Ps. 25:8). *Goodness* is that through which He communicates His goods to creatures. This, with respect to man, especially the elect, is kindness (χρηστότης) (1 Peter 2:3) and is called love of man (φιλανθρωπία) (Titus 3:4). Its species are *love*, whereby He loves Himself beyond others and creatures outside of Him, as entire "charity" (1 John 4:8), and who also "loves when He disciplines" (Prov. 3:12); *grace*, which is that whereby He bestows Himself and His goods on the creature, apart from merit, as gracious God (אל חנון) (Ex. 34:6); and *mercy*, whereby He runs to the aid of the miserable creature, especially sinners, as merciful God (אל רחום) (Ex. 34:6).[15]

XVI. Righteousness: Regulating, Judicial, and Economic

The *righteousness* of God is particular, whereby *He enforces His law in regard to creatures, as His perfection, goodness, promise, and threat demand*. This, regulating tributes to the *Lord* God, is called judicial for a *judge* and economic for a *ruler*. *Regulating* is that *whereby, as Lord, He most rightly orders all things from the law of His supreme and most free dominion*. For He "is righteous in all His ways" (Ps. 145:17). Judicial is that whereby, as judge of the world, He repays rational creatures according to their works. For "He will judge the world in righteousness. The law will speak to the people in uprightness" (Ps. 9:8). He is "judge of the whole world," and "did He not make righteousness?" (Gen. 18:25). The former is essential to God because "He is exalted on account of judgment and is treated as holy through righteousness" (Isa. 5:16), although He enforces it so freely or otherwise. *Economic* or *voluntary* is that whereby God makes use *of the world in governing by exercising judgments, in which good and evil are implicated,*

14. *Medulla*, LI.
15. *Medulla*, LII–LIX.

not to vindicate sin but for an example and correction of the human race, about which God says, "Behold, I will come against you. I will tear away the righteous and the wicked from you" (Ezek. 21:3).[16]

XVII. Freedom

The *freedom* of God is that *whereby for His will He does whatever He wishes in heaven and on earth.* For the will of God is almighty (παντακραταρος), "to whom it is permitted to act concerning His own what" He wishes (Matt. 20:15). For not from another but from Him alone is He settled to act, which is the highest freedom. And yet it is not indifferent, because as God is not indifferent to be, so He is not indifferent to work, understand, and will, and every indifference springs from ignorance.[17]

XVIII. Power

The *power* of God is the *strength of God*, *whereby He can do whatever He wishes in agreement with His nature.* For He is "powerful and frightful" (Deut. 10:17), for whom "all things" are "possible" (Jer. 32:27; Matt. 19:26). For He is also Almighty (παντοκράτωρ) (2 Cor. 6:18; Rev. 1:8). By Himself nothing is impossible for God, but in combination with the rest of His virtues only that is possible for God which can command, call, and make for His glory. For example, He cannot sin or speak or do what is contradictory, which is to lie. Rule (*potestas*) is distinct from power (*potentia*) connected with strength (δικαίωμα) or that *law* of acting, which no one has rightly dared to contradict.[18]

XIX. Blessedness

The *blessedness* of God *is that whereby He, most perfect, is sufficient for Himself for all happiness in Himself.* For He is "blessed" and "the only master" (1 Tim. 6:15), the Blessed One (ברוך) (εὐλογητος) (Gen. 9:26; 14:20).[19]

XX. Glory

The *glory* of God results from all these, *the most beautiful of all the perfections of God and as it were contracted lightening.* For He is God of glory (אל בכוד) (Ps. 29:3), who "does not give" it "to another" (Isa. 42:8).[20]

---

16. *Medulla*, LIX–LXIV.
17. *Medulla*, LXIV.
18. *Medulla*, LXV–LXIX.
19. *Medulla*, LXIX.
20. *Medulla*, LXX.

LOCUS IV

On the True Triune God

I. False Gods

The One *who is* the true God remains to be explained. The Gentiles, "serving the creature rather than the Creator" (Rom. 1:25), "do not know God in the wisdom of God through their own wisdom" (1 Cor. 1:21). The *Stoics*, who seemed very talented, worshiped the whole world and all nature as God. They believed that God is a *divine animal*, from the divine *mind*, which is a fiery body, and conflated it with the earthly *body*, each of the parts of which were divine. *Spinoza* has most recently followed them. He blasphemously devised that *God is identified* as nature and *modified* in infinite thought and extension—namely, such a God that even the devil, had he believed in him, could have been turned into him. But both the *Jews* and *Muslims*, because "they deny the Son," also "do not have the Father" (1 John 2:23).[1]

II. The True God

He is the true God, who revealed Himself in the Patriarchs, Moses, the Prophets, and more fully in Christ. For Scripture, which is the Word of God, demonstrates and confirms such with infallible arguments from creation, providence, redemption, and prophecies. I do not speak only about the astonishing work of the giving of the law, in which God spoke out of fire, but also about the leading out of the people from Egypt, from which Moses confirmed in each work "that Jehovah is God, and there is no other besides Him" (Deut. 4:32–36). I also speak about the grave experience that Elijah took hold of against the worship of Baal. When he appeared, the people exclaimed, "Jehovah is God" (1 Kings 18:39). Indeed, He is the triune God—Father, Son, and Holy Spirit. This great mystery is "not flesh and blood, but the Father reveals it in heaven" (Matt. 16:17). For it is "the mystery of God the Father and Christ" (Col. 2:2).[2]

1. *Medulla*, I–V.
2. *Medulla*, V–XI.

III. He Is One

God is *one*, in most singular unity, and *single*, because there is no other besides Him who is one. "Hear O Israel, Jehovah our God, Jehovah is one" (אחד) (ἕν) (Deut. 6:4). "Who is God besides Jehovah and what is a rock besides our God?" (2 Sam. 22:32). "You are God alone" (לבד) (Ps. 86:10). There is "one God (εἷς θεὸς) for us" (1 Cor. 8:6). Since He is independent, most simple, and infinite, He cannot but be one. And He cannot be the supreme good of man, the first cause and final end of all things, unless He is one.[3]

IV. The Triune Was Recognized in the Old Testament

In this unity (μονάδι) we maintain the Trinity (Τριάδα). The patriarchs knew this mystery from the history of creation (Gen. 1:1, 3, 26), the word of promise (Gen. 3:15), the judgment of Sodom in which "Jehovah" rained "fire from Jehovah (מאת יהוה)" (Gen. 19:24), and the promise made to Abraham in the words, "I will be God for your seed" (Gen. 17:8). But the Israelites knew this mystery from the words, "I will be who I am" (Ex. 3:14)—that is, "I will be God for you" (Gen. 17:7)—and the mention of "sending the messenger" before Moses, "in whose midst was the name Jehovah" (Ex. 23:20–21). This "messenger of presence saved" them (Isa. 63:9), and the promise in the *Sanctifier, Savior, Kinsman Redeemer, Rock, Shield, the God of Israel,* and so on was everywhere, insofar as it was sufficient for salvation. Not to mention, the former was contained in the words of God, "Hear O Israel, Jehovah (Father), our God (Son), Jehovah (Holy Spirit) are one" (Deut. 6:4).[4]

V. Especially in the New Testament

But the mystery of the Trinity was made more clear in the New Testament. For in the baptism of Christ the Father sanctified the Son, having spoken from heaven with the symbol of a dove as the Holy Spirit, coming upon the Son (Matt. 3:17). And Christ commanded to baptize "in the name (with equal authority and invocation of the name) of the Father, Son, and Holy Spirit" (Matt. 28:19). Saint Paul does the same: "The grace of our Lord Jesus Christ, the love of God, and the communion of the Holy Spirit be with you all" (2 Cor. 13:13). Finally, the whole veil having been lifted, John wrote, "There are three, who testify in heaven, the Father, the Word, and the Holy Spirit. And these three are one" in unity of essence, not merely of harmonious will, because all are placed in the same degree of witnesses as self-authenticating (αὐτοπίστων) (1 John 5:7).[5]

---

3. *Medulla*, XI, XII.
4. *Medulla*, XIII–XVI.
5. *Medulla*, XVI, XVII.

VI. The Persons: Their Deity and Properties; Order and Economy

The persons of the Trinity have common deity and each has His own thing (ἴδιόν τι) or special character (*proprietatem*), adjoining which they are distinguished from one another. They are distinguished from one another in a certain order, and each has His own economy. Their common deity is singular, one in number, but it is communicable for each on account of infinity. *The personal properties* distinguish each person from essence and one another. This manner of distinction ought not to be more curiously searched out. For it is sufficient that they are one and another (ἄλλον καὶ ἄλλον) (John 5:32; 14:16). But they do not make another and another (ἄλλο καὶ ἄλλο) as the *tritheists* think, because they are one (ἕν) (1 John 5:7). Moreover, they are not merely distinct in names and relations, as the *Sabellians* insist, because *to be begotten* is of the Son, and *to proceed* from the begetting Father and the begotten Son is of the Holy Spirit. They are not mere names. The *order* of the persons is natural: the Father is numbered the first person, the Son the second, and the Holy Spirit the third. It is a distinction solely *of order and origin*, without regard to difference *of dignity*. For it is not granted that God is more worthy or less worthy, commanding and obeying. Finally, the *economy* of persons consists in that the common works are vindicated by reason of *foundation* and *operation of the mode of the One working* as it were proper to certain persons. They are accustomed to be denominated by those works, as the Father is *Creator*, the Son *Redeemer*, and the Spirit *Sanctifier*. This mode of working outwardly (*ad extra*) follows the mode of working inwardly (*ad intra*).[6]

VII. God the Father: His Character, Deity, and Economy

GOD THE FATHER is *the first person of the Godhead, existing from no one, who begat the Son, His essential image, from eternity*. Therefore, His notion (*notion*) or character is that He begat the Son. "You are My Son. Today I have begotten You" (Ps. 2:7). His deity is unspeakable (ἀνεξαγώνιος). But His *economy* consists in creation and the starting and governing of redemption. For "from Him are all things" (1 Cor. 8:6).[7]

VIII. God the Son: His Character

GOD THE SON is *the second person of the Godhead, begotten from the essence of the Father from eternity*. For He is called *the Son* of God and indeed in power (ἐν δυνάμιν) or in most full power and strength (Rom. 1:4), as His name is very excellent (Διαφορώτερον) (Heb. 1:4). That is to say, whatever is excellent in that name is assigned to Him. And every imperfection of generation, which sort is

6. *Medulla*, XVIII–XXIV.
7. *Medulla*, XXIV.

in His suffering, change, movement, and beginning of existing, is removed from the generation of the Son. For "they went out from eternity" (Mic. 5:2), and He was begotten as radiance (ἀπαύγασμα), the emanation "of glory" (Heb. 1:3) and in an ineffable manner. "Who is the Son that you will have found out His generation?" (Prov. 30:4).[8]

IX. His Deity

The names, attributes, works, and divine worship of the Son confirm His *deity*, being of the same essence (ὁμοουσία) with the Father. The *names* confirm His deity because "the Messenger" is called Jehovah (יהוה), the very "face" of God, distinct from the Father who sends (Ex. 3:2, 4, 7, 23:20), "a righteous sprout, Jehovah of our righteousness" (Jer. 23:5–6), "Jehovah Redeemer" (Isa. 50:1–2, etc.). He is also called God (Θεὸς) sometimes (John 1:1; Acts 20:28), indeed "God blessed over all throughout the ages" (Rom. 9:5), "great God and Savior" (Titus 2:13), "true God" (1 John 5:20), Lord (κύριος)—that is, Jehovah (John 6:68; 1 Cor. 8:6; 1 Cor. 15:47)—and the Word (λόγος) (John 1:1; 1 John 1:1, Rev. 1:2; 19:13). He bears these names on account of eternal generation from the Father, unity with His essence and will, the eternal decree and its execution in Him, and finally the testimony of the whole of Scripture concerning Him. He is of the same essence (ὁμοουσία) as the Father because the following are attributed to Him: "life of God" (John 5:26), "the form of God" (Phil. 2:6), "equality" with God "the Father" (John 5:18), and "unity" with the same (John 10:30). The divine *attributes* confirm His deity because He is *simple*, indeed Jehovah, having the "Spirit of holiness" (Rom. 1:4) and *eternal*, indeed, "not having beginning of life and days" (Heb. 7:3), having the "eternal Spirit" (Heb. 9:14), "coming forth from ancient days" (Mic. 5:2), and "existing before Abraham existed" (John 8:58). This is also the case because He is *immense* and *omnipresent*. For "descending from heaven, He is" also "in heaven" (John 3:13) and "is with us until the end of the age" (Matt. 28:20). He is also *omniscient* because He is the "Wisdom" of God (Prov. 8:1, etc.), "exudes the fear of the Lord" (Isa. 11:3), knowing "what is in man" (John 2:25), indeed "all things" (John 21:17). He is also the *Holy One* and *Sanctifier* of Israel everywhere. Moreover, He is *omnipotent* because "He does similarly (ὁμοίως) as the Father" (John 5:19) and is distinguished as Almighty (παντοκράτωρ) (Rev. 1:8). The *divine works* of creation, providence, and redemption are added. For He is *Creator* because "all things were made by Him, and nothing was made without Him, and the world was made through Him" (John 1:3, 10). "In Him all things were established in heaven and on earth, both visible and invisible" (Col. 1:16). Then the works of divine providence, *miracles*, are attributed to Him because He

8. *Medulla*, XXV, XXVI.

accomplished many miracles by His own power (ἰδίᾳ δυνάμει) (Acts 3:12) and bestowed the power of accomplishing them to others (Acts 3:6). He is also *Redeemer*. "He will be called Vindicator, Redeemer, your Holy One of Israel, the God of the whole earth" (Isa. 54:5). Finally, *divine honor* is also attributed to Him. For the Father "seeks" His "glory" (John 8:50) "and gave to Him the name that is above every name, so that in His name every knee will bow" (Phil. 2:9–10). For He is God of the whole earth and King (Ps. 2:8; 45:2) whom "the angels worship" (Heb. 1:6) and all the godly "kiss" and "trust" (Ps. 2:12) and "honor as they honor the Father" (John 5:23).[9]

X. The Economy of the Son

The *economy* of the Son is that *redemption* is appropriated to Him. For because He is from the Father and lives on account of the Father, He willed to be sent as our Savior and could offer Himself to God the Father.[10]

XI. The Holy Spirit: His Character

GOD THE HOLY SPIRIT is *the third person of the Godhead, proceeding through eternal breath from the Father and the Son*. Therefore, His character is that which *proceeds* and *is breathed* from the Father and the Son, not only internally (*ad intra*), by reason of His person, but also externally (*ad extra*), by reason of creatures. For the Father and the Son create, preserve, save, and sanctify through Him. Indeed, He is "the Spirit" of the Father and "of the Son" (Gal. 4:6; Phil. 1:19; 1 Peter 1:11). "The Spirit will take from Me and will announce it to you. All things that the Father has are Mine" (John 16:14–15). "When I depart, I will send My Comforter to you" (John 16:7).[11]

XII. He Is a Person

The Holy Spirit is a *person* distinct from the Father and the Son. "The Comforter, whom I shall send to you, He (ἐκεῖνος) will testify about Me" (John 15:26). "Today I shall also send another informer (מַגִּיד מִשְׁנֶה)" (Zech. 9:12). "I shall ask the Father, and He will send another (ἄλλον) Comforter to you" (John 14:16). Indeed, He *subsists* because, as another, He is sent by the Father and the Son, and He *lives*, indeed, is "life-giving" (Job 33:4), "regenerating" (John 3:5–6). He also "understands" and wills, "probing the depths of God" (1 Cor. 2:10), and powerfully *acts*, sanctifying. Indeed, "one and the same Spirit, distributing as He wishes, works all these things (even *in the discernment of spirits*)" (1 Cor. 12:11).[12]

9. *Medulla*, XXVII–XXXVII.
10. *Medulla*, XXXVII.
11. *Medulla*, XXXVIII–XLI.
12. *Medulla*, XLI.

XIII. He Is God

The names, the same essence (ὁμοουσία) with the Father and the Son, attributes, works, and divine honors of the Holy Spirit prove His *deity*. The *names* prove His deity, as He is called "Jehovah" (Isa. 6:8 compared with Ex. 17:7; Lev. 16:2; Ps. 99:7–8; Acts 28:25–26; Heb. 3:1; Heb. 9:8), "the God of Israel" (2 Sam. 23:3). He is also called "God," as when it is said that "a lie against the Holy Spirit is a lie against God" (Acts 5:3), and "Lord," according to "The Lord (Jehovah) is the Spirit" (2 Cor. 3:17). Being of the same essence (ὁμοουσία) proves His deity, as when the "Father, Word, and Spirit" are called "one (ἕν)" (1 John 5:7). The divine *attributes* prove His deity because He is *simple*, indeed absolutely *Spirit*. He is *eternal*, as "proceeding from the Father" (John 15:26). He is also *immense*, indeed, existing in heaven and "hell" (Ps. 139:7–8), and in the saints, who "dwell" in His "temple" (1 Cor. 6:19). He is also *omniscient*, as "probing the depths of God" and He who "knows all things of God" (1 Cor. 2:10–11). Everywhere He is *holy par excellence* (κατ᾽ ἐξοχὴν). The divine *works* prove His deity, such as those of *creation* (Gen. 1:2; Ps. 33:6) and *preservation*, because "He restores the face of the earth" (Ps. 104:30). Sometimes He *illuminates, regenerates, sanctifies, seals*, "justifies" (1 Cor. 6:11), and "resurrects" (Rom. 8:11). Finally, religious *honors* prove His deity because "we are baptized" in His "name" (Matt. 28:19) and His "communion" is as equally invoked as "the grace of Christ" and "the love of the Father" for believers (2 Cor. 13:13). Moreover, He equally makes Himself the object of invocation as does *grace* the Son and *love* the Father.[13]

XIX. His Economy

The *economy* of the Holy Spirit is that, as the Final One (*ultimus*) from the Father and the Son, He is Consummator (τελειωτὴς) of the works of creation, providence, and redemption, and *Sanctifier* of those who have been created by the Father and redeemed by the Son. Therefore, He is the *teacher* and *leader* of the faithful. He is a *Comforter* or *Advocate*. He is the Spirit of *grace and prayers* and also *adoption*. He is a *deposit* and *unction*. Everywhere He hears the *seal*.[14]

---

13. *Medulla*, XLII.
14. *Medulla*, XLIV, XLV.

LOCUS V

On the Decrees of God

I. The Decree of God

God advances His kingdom outside Himself, the kingdom having been established in the world, according to His eternal counsel. This comes in the name of *decree*, not as the Vulgate translation everywhere uses decree for a command. Rather, it denotes the thought *delimited* or the *decree* of God about all things. It includes not only the judgment of mind but also the plan of will. Only in this sense is the decree of God the *internal action of God* or *His eternal counsel about future things outside Himself. As He has immutably determined this among Himself, so He infallibly knows it beforehand.*[1]

II. It Exists in That Act of Intellect and Will

Scripture is a witness that such a decree exists, which is Christ (1 Peter 1:20), and that "we are foreknown in Him," being the elect (Eph. 1:4). It also teaches that God "works all things according to the counsel of His will" (Eph. 1:11). Moreover, because foreknowledge is at the same time as predestination (προορισμὸς) (Rom. 8:29), the decree exists with simultaneous foreknowledge and will. In that not only the "mind" (Rom. 11:34) but also the "counsel of His will" (Eph. 1:11) and "plan" (Rom. 9:11) is occupied. Indeed, it so exists in God that He places nothing unworthy of Himself in it.[2]

III. Its Properties

The properties of the decree are that it is *eternal*, because it has been established "before the foundation of the world" (Eph. 1:4; 1 Peter 1:20). It is *one* and *simple* as "the counsel formed concerning the whole earth, and His hand is extended over all the nations" (Isa. 14:26). It is "wise" and "unsearchable" (Rom. 11:33). It

1. *Medulla*, I–V.
2. *Medulla*, V–VIII.

is *free* and *independent* because it is of His mere "good pleasure" (Eph. 1:5). It is *most ample* because all things in time happen according to it. It is *immutable* in the same way that God Himself is. It is *efficacious* because "the counsel of God stands, and He does His good pleasure" (Isa. 46:10).[3]

IV. Its Object and Order

There is no *object* of the decree of God outside of Himself—that is, what cannot properly glorify God. In regard to this it constitutes not only of an *efficient* cause, because God decreed to do whatever happens; it also holds reason of an *exemplar* because not only does it suppose the idea in the mind of God of all perfections, which can come forth—namely, the very essence of God—as intelligence and will, but it is also the very idea (παράδειγμα) or the form fashioned (יצר) of all works outside of God. "As I have fashioned, I shall also do (כאשר יצרתי)" (Isa. 46:11). Nor is the former *general* and *indefinite*, merely of qualities and conditions. Instead, it is *special* and *personal*, of all things and persons, because otherwise a great part of creatures would be independent. And it is also arranged in a certain *order*. It is the sort that is *orthodox*, which reason does not establish but rather the revelation of God, His perfection, and the execution of His counsels.[4]

V. It Is Occupied concerning the End and Means. It Is concerning General or Special Means

The decree of God is occupied concerning the end or the means. The decree concerns *the end of manifesting God's glory*. For "He works all things on account of Himself" (Prov. 16:4), and "He is glorified in the work of His hands" (Isa. 60:21; 61:3). Concerning *the means*, it is general or special. It is *general about all things to be created, preserved, and governed*. It is *special about intelligent creatures to be saved or damned*, which comes in the name of predestination or predetermination (προορισμοῦ). It is commonly used about election, but with its proper meaning about reprobation.[5]

VI. The Predestination of Angels and Men Is Personal

There is predestination of angels or of men, with this distinction: the predestination of angels was made neither of the sinner nor in Christ the Mediator, though the predestination of men was made in Christ, of the sinner, and in respect to the elect. Both belong to persons, not qualities alone. For God did not do away with predestination by decreeing to save believers. But God, as most wise and

3. *Medulla*, VIII.
4. *Medulla*, IX–XIII.
5. *Medulla*, XIII, XIV.

absolute Lord of all, foreordained each of them, their qualities, and persons to their natural and supernatural ends (Rom. 8:29; 9:22).[6]

VII. Election

Election and reprobation are species of predestination. *Election* is a certain *separation*, which happens either properly *in the hand* and *work* through calling in time, or improperly, *in the eternal counsel, determination*, and good pleasure (εὐδοκίᾳ). Election is that *whereby God elected from the corrupted mass certain men, whom He desired before others, in Jesus Christ from eternity. And as He foreordained for the end, eternal life, so also He foreordained for the means to be carried out.* Saint Paul explains in detail the whole nature of this election in Ephesians 1:2–8.[7]

VIII. The Internal Cause of Election

The *principal* cause of election is the triune God. But in the economy of the persons it is simply attributed to the Father (Eph. 1:4). There is the internal, *impelling* (*impulsiva*) love of God toward the Son, whom "He loves" (John 5:20), "gathering us in grace in the Beloved" (Eph. 1:6). Indeed, in this impelling love God the Father "bequeathed the kingdom in the testament" to the Son (Luke 22:29), with which He would seize the will of men redeemed by Himself. Yet the same Son, as Mediator, is not the cause but the means of election—namely, written in the same way, He is the Mediator of the Testament and the Savior of coheirs.[8]

IX. There Is No Cause of Election Outside of God

No cause outside of God has urged Him to elect certain ones. For "while the boys were not yet born, when they had not accomplished anything good or evil, in order that the purpose of God according to election might remain, not from works, but from the one who calls (of the one who calls in His good pleasure [εὐδοκίᾳ]), it is said that the older shall serve the younger, as it is written, 'Jacob I have loved. Esau I have hated'" (Rom. 9:11, etc.). Therefore, God Himself asserts His power, saying "I will have mercy on whom I will have mercy" (Ex. 33:19). Hence the apostle concludes, "It is not therefore of the one who wills or runs, but of God who has mercy" (Rom. 9:16). Indeed, God "predestined us in Him according to the good pleasure of His will" (Eph. 1:5). That good pleasure is soon defined in verse 11: "the plan of God from the counsel of the One who does all things." Election is also made not on account of but rather unto faith and the use of free will after regeneration. "He chose us in Him, in order that

6. *Medulla*, XV–XVIII.
7. *Medulla*, XVIII.
8. *Medulla*, XIX–XXIII.

we might be holy and blameless. He predestined us for adoption through Jesus Christ" (Eph. 1:4–5). "As many as had been appointed to eternal life believed" (Acts 13:48). Finally, God could not have elected from faith or from works foreseen, whether in *Himself*, because He has thus foreseen, as a gift flowing from Himself, or in *man*, because it would thus be a work of free will. Hence, it follows that election is absolute a priori, or without a *cause* in the elect.[9]

X. The Object of Election

The *object* of election is *fallen* man. For such that could be cast away must be saved by God in Christ, Savior "from sins" (Matt. 1:21). Salvation is of Him "who destroys" (Matt. 10:28). Just as *we are chosen* in time and separated "from the world" (John 15:19), so from eternity God elected us or determined to separate us from the world. Indeed, election is an act "of mercy" (Rom. 9:23), which concerns the miserable. Finally, God cast away a group of humans from Himself as the corrupt mass (πηλὸν)—namely, from which alone they can be rendered "vessels of wrath" (Rom. 9:22).[10]

XI. The Subject of Election

There is a certain select number of elect determined by God. "The Lord knows those who are His" (2 Tim. 2:19). "Those whom He predestined, He also glorified" (Rom. 8:30). Moreover, God did not elect each and every man through His *antecedent* will but certain ones through His *consequent* will. For the will of God is one, fixed, efficacious, and immutable, which He always carries out to His end. Furthermore, He elected not all, but selected certain ones. "One is received, another is abandoned" (Matt. 24:40). "Many are called, but few have been elected" (Matt. 20:16). And those few are nearly "infants" (Matt. 11:25), "the foolish and weak of this world" (1 Cor. 1:26), "the poor of this world" (James 2:5), "in order that the wise and strong might be confounded" (1 Cor. 1:27).[11]

XII. Election to Means

Those whom God has chosen for salvation, He has also chosen for the *means* of salvation, *calling* and *justification* through faith in Christ (Rom. 8:30). Indeed, the connection of glory and means is in this decree so that if you displace one of them, election is overturned. For God could not decree it without detriment to His righteousness, so that a sinner is glorified, not atoned for through

9. *Medulla*, XXIV–XXIX.
10. *Medulla*, XXIII.
11. *Medulla*, XXIX–XXXII.

Christ, and not confiding in Him. Therefore, in this sense, absolute election is not a posteriori.[12]

XIII. Certitude of the Same, with Respect to God

Election is sure in regard to not only the God who elects but also man who has been elected. It is sure in regard to the *God who elects* because He has determined a certain number of men, free from increase and decrease, in His eternal and immutable decree. "I know whom I have chosen" (John 13:18). "Those whom He predestined He glorified" (Rom. 8:29). This is also the reason *the testament*, the certitude of *the inheritance* of Christ, the efficacy of *the promise*, the reward of *merit*, the connection of the parts of *grace*, and the administration of its *execution* come to pass. According to these things it is "impossible that the elect be led astray" (Matt. 24:24), because they have been written "in the Book of Life" (Phil. 4:3). It is certain in regard to *man who has been elected* because he can be certain of his election, so much as it suffices for his salvation and consolation. For "they rejoice" because they understand that their "names have been written in heaven" (Luke 10:20). And they render their "election firm" (2 Peter 1:10), which cannot happen without a sense of it. And "the Holy Spirit attests" to the same "that they are sons of God" (Rom. 8:16) and are therefore "elect" (Eph. 1:4, 5).[13]

XIV. Reprobation

Reprobation is that *whereby God decided to leave behind certain men, whom He did not elect, in the mass of corruption, and to eternally condemn them on account of sin.* For Scripture testifies that God "has made the wicked for the day of evil" (Prov. 16:4), "to spurn" some (Isa. 41:9), "to not have pity" (Hos. 1:6; 2:3), "to hold in hatred" (Mal. 1:2, 3), "to abandon" (Rom. 11:7), "to destine for wrath" (1 Thess. 5:9), "to designate for judgment" (Jude 4), and "to write in the earth" (Jer. 17:13). He does this both as absolute *Lord*, arranging man for His will, and as *judge*, decreeing for the sinner just condemnation. He not only *passes over* them, for whom He ordained neither an inheritance in preparation for glory and grace nor the means of an inheritance, but also *ordains to destruction* those whom "He made for the day of evil" (Prov. 16:4), "brought together for destruction" and made "vessels of wrath," establishing means agreeing with this end in the same decree.[14]

12. *Medulla*, XXXII.
13. *Medulla*, XXXIII–XXXVII.
14. *Medulla*, XXXVII–XL.

XV. There Is No Cause of It outside of God, but the Condition Is in the Object—Sin

Reprobation has no cause outside of God, but as equally as election it is dependent on the sole good pleasure of God. For in Romans 9:11, 24 Paul invokes it as equally as election from the most free will and plan (προοθέσιν) of God "the Lord" and self-ruling One (αὐτοκράτορος), who "has mercy on whom He wishes and hardens whom He wishes" (Rom. 9:11, 18). It vindicates not only dominion (*potestatem*) in God, "making vessels for honor or for dishonor from the same mass" (Rom. 9:21), but also the power (*potentiam*) (τὸ δυνατὸν) of demonstrating from His "will" alone—both "the riches of His glory toward the vessels of mercy" and "wrath towards the vessels of wrath, brought together for destruction" (Rom. 9:22–23). Yet it has a *condition* outside of Him in the *object*, sin, apart from which it would not be just in existing in Him. Therefore, the whole human race is opposed to the God who reprobates as "the mass" from which "vessels for dishonor" and "wrath" are possible, which could not be possible without sin. In this sense, reprobation is not absolute.[15]

XVI. Its End and Means

Reprobation, in the same way as election, includes the end and means. Its *end* is the *supremacy* of God—the glory of His power, wisdom, righteousness, most free reign, and dominion. *Reciprocally*, the damnation of the reprobate is just on account of sin. The *means* are separation from Christ and the grace of redemption, omission of calling or at least inefficacious calling, the retention of sins, blindness, and hardness, which final impenitence follows.[16]

XVII. The Canon of the Doctrine of Predestination

The canon of the whole doctrine of predestination is in the words of the apostle who, after handing down the teaching about it, exclaims, "Oh the depths of the riches, wisdom, and knowledge of God! How inscrutable are His judgments, and unsearchable His ways! For who has known the mind of the Lord? Or who has been His counselor? Or who has first given to Him, that He may repay Him? Since from Him, through Him, and to Him are all things. To Him be glory forever, Amen" (Rom. 11:33–36).[17]

---

15. *Medulla*, XL–XLIII.
16. *Medulla*, XLIII.
17. *Medulla*, XLIV.

LOCUS VI

On the Creation of the World

I. The Words of Creation

The general execution of the decree is in creation and providence. *Creare* (to create) is the Latin for *to make something magnificently.* ברא is said in Hebrew, which in its first origin means production of a new thing (חדוש) (Num. 16:30; Isa. 65:17, 18; Jer. 31:22). But the new things are especially those that are made out of nothing (ex nihilo).[1]

II. Definition: Existence

Creation is *the first external act of God whereby in the beginning of time He made, with His Word alone, heaven and earth together with all creatures that are in them, with no pre-existent matter.* "Faith" also recognizes it because "by faith we understand that the world was made by the Word of God, so that what is seen was not made out of things that are seen" (Heb. 11:3). *Reason*, which involves no contradiction, also does not deny it, at least in regard to possibility.[2]

III. Out of Nothing (Ex Nihilo)

No matter preexisted the creation. For the beginning of the works of God was not unformed, eternal matter but uncultivated "heaven and earth" (Gen. 1:1–2). God "made the world by His Word, not from things that are seen" (Heb. 11:3), "calling those things that are not" and thus that did not appear (Rom. 4:17).[3]

IV. God Is the Creator

The Creator of the world is "God" (Gen. 1:1), the same who is "Lord of heaven and earth" (Matt. 11:25). And He is not only the *Father* but also the *Son*, who as Word (דבר) (λόγος) "spoke and created" (Gen. 1:3), "without whom nothing

1. *Medulla*, I, II.
2. *Medulla*, III–VI.
3. *Medulla*, VI.

was made" (John 1:3). For He could not be Redeemer unless He was the Creator, "heir of all things," and the "One who made all things" (Col. 1:15–16; Heb. 1:2). Nor was the *Spirit of God* excluded who, "by hovering over the waters" (Gen. 1:2), maintained them and the earth. By maintaining each "He made them to sprout forth" (Gen. 1:11–12). Need did not impel Him to create, but His most free will, according to which He willed to build a kingdom in the world and to manifest the glory of His wisdom, power, and goodness in it.[4]

V. The Work of Creation Is the World

The effect of creation is the *world*—that is, σύστημα, *the structure of all things created within six days*. Its order teaches that it is one, not many, and that God "made the whole human race to dwell on the whole face of the earth" (Acts 17:26). It is also one from the aggregation of all the parts among each other in order and end. Some created spirit does not preserve and contain it, so unequally abundant in diverse minds and bodies, but uncreated God, author of the same, in "whom all exist, live, and move" (Acts 17:25, 28).[5]

VI. Completion of the World in Regard to Time and Extension

The world has been *completed* in regard to time and extension. It has been completed in regard to *time* because it has a beginning. For all things that have existed (γενέασι) are said to have begun (John 1:3). From this beginning (γενέσιν) He spoke the whole world and the entire course of life (τροχὸν γενέσεως) (James 3:6). "In the beginning God created heaven and earth" (Gen. 1:1). The world has been completed in regard to *extension* because the ends (πέρατα) of the earth are before the eyes, and the airy and ethereal sky is limited to a highest point. And the highest point is not expanded into the infinite, since no body in the world is given infinite action. And in that heaven that God indwells, the term "circle of the world" (חוג) is used (Job 22:14) in the same regard that "circle" (חוג) is attributed to the earth (Isa. 40:22).[6]

VII. It Is Imperfect and Mutable

The world is also imperfect and mutable. It is *imperfect*, because absolute perfection belongs to God alone. It is *mutable* because it began to be, is changed from day to day in its parts, and will perish. "They will perish, and You will remain forever" (Ps. 102:27). Not even "the heavens are in the eyes of God's world" (Job 15:15), which also "will burn" (2 Peter 3:7, 12). And yet the world, an image of an old woman that has brought forth young ones, does not grow old or completely

4. *Medulla*, VII–XI.
5. *Medulla*, XI–XIV.
6. *Medulla*, XIV–XVIII.

waste away with slow decay. For "on the day of the Lord the heavens will perish with noise" (2 Peter 3:10). This does not concur with what has wasted away.[7]

VIII. The Work of Six Days: First Heaven

God created the world in the space of six truly distinct days. And certainly His work was immediate, in a moment, successively rested from. *First* He created "heaven and earth" (Gen. 1:1). The fiery heaven is understood—that is, "the heaven of the heavens" (Ps. 148:4). For air and ether were the work of the second day. And the former heaven is neither God Himself, nor a light emanating from God, nor a space uncreated and immense, but a complete and local body because it contains (δέχεται) Christ (Acts 3:21) and is a "place" (John 14:2). Scripture has not depicted its nature and glory but has reserved it for vision. It has, however, called it "the throne of God" (Isa. 66:1), "the mansion" of the blessed (John 14:2), "the garden of God, Eden" (Ezek. 31:16, 18), and "Paradise" (2 Cor. 12:4). Its *army*, the angels, appear to have been created with the same, because heaven is not called "empty and void" in the same way as the earth (Gen. 1:2).[8]

IX. The Earth and Light

The other work of the first day was the *earth* or the globe of the earth, surrounded with water. Hence it is called "the abyss" (Gen. 1:2). And the earth was void (תהו), cultivated with no inhabitants, without form (קו), and in its adornment, it was also not established (בהו) without strict equality (אבז) (Isa. 34:11), which would agree with the following days. The third work of the same day was *light*. It was not accidents but substance because it was positioned within heaven and the abyss, where darkness was present during the day and absent during the night.[9]

X. The Work of the Second Day: The Expanse, Separation of the Waters from Land, the Foundation of Land

The creation work of the *second* day was the expanse, the separation of the waters from land, and the foundation of land. There was the creation of the expanse (רקיע) "in the midst of the waters, divided waters from waters" (Gen. 1:6–8). It was of the air and ether of heaven. In Greek it is called στερέωμα, in Latin *firmamentum*, not on account of iron solidity but because it was firm (חזק) (στερεόν) (Job 37:18). That is to say, it establishes that it was created by God. The former divided the *lesser waters* in the unadulterated abyss from those that were above the expanse (מעל לרקיע)—that is, from the clouds, which are called

7. *Medulla*, XVIII–XIX.
8. *Medulla*, XX–XXVI.
9. *Medulla*, XXVI–XXIX.

"the waters in the heavens" (Jer. 10:13). "The separation of the waters from the "waters" happened when the "waters" that were "under heaven were gathered into one place," the ocean, and thus "the dry land appeared" (Gen. 1:9). This "dry land" or "earth" was set over the waters. "He established the earth over its foundations, in order that it may never be removed" (Ps. 104:5). "Jehovah Himself established it over the seas, and made it firm over the rivers" (Ps. 24:2). Indeed, elsewhere the foundation of the earth is over nothing (בלימה), about which Job says, "He hangs" the earth over nothing (על בלימה) (Job 26:7), because the whole world, or the sphere containing land and water, hangs in the middle of the air, without pillar or any base.[10]

XI. The Works of the Third Day: Vegetation, Trees, and Paradise

The works of *the third* day are vegetation, trees, and Paradise. God said, "Let there be green vegetation (coming forth voluntarily), and yielding seed (sown), fruit-bearing trees (big and small), bearing fruit (simply bearing fruit or in the act of bearing fruit)" (Gen. 1:11–12). Moses speaks in this manner about Paradise: "God planted a garden in Eden from the East" (Gen. 2:8–9). He attached to that garden a Persian name, Paradise (פרדס). Various things are variously prophesied about its condition. To be sure, He destroyed its flourishing in the flood.[11]

XII. The Works of the Fourth Day: Lights

The works of *the fourth* day were great lights. "Let there be lights in the expanse of heaven, and let them illuminate the earth. And it was so" (Gen. 1:14). These were two: "the greater," the sun, "ruling day," and "the lesser," the moon, "ruling night" (Gen. 1:16). God commanded these to be above *as signs*, *unadulterated memorials* of His infinite power and goodness, *signifying God* as leader of this army, with *foreknowing*, natural, common, and proper use yet with supernatural institution. This sort does not belong to the *Genethliacs* (*Genethliacorum*), because God alone is the One who foreknows the future. There are also natural or instituted *stated times*, certain periods of those in *days* and *years* (Gen. 1:14).[12]

XIII. The Works of the Fifth Day: Reptiles, Birds

The works of the *fifth* day were reptiles and birds. "Let the waters move with the movement of living creatures, and let birds fly above the earth over the face of the expanse of heaven. Therefore, God created the great sea creatures and every living creature that moves in the waters, which the waters produced according to

10. *Medulla*, XXIX–XXXV.
11. *Medulla*, XXXV, XXXVI.
12. *Medulla*, XXXVII–XLIII.

their kind" (Gen. 1:20–21). There שרצ are said by abundance and רמש by treading on the earth. To be sure, Moses does not attribute the rising of the birds to the waters. He only had to say, "Let the bird fly," and so on.[13]

XIV. The Works of the Sixth Day: Animals of the Earth

The works of the *sixth* day were *animals* of the earth and man. God thus said about the former: "Let the earth produce living beings (beasts of the field)" (Gen. 3:1), "beasts of burden (brutish, or domestic cattle), reptiles (which do not walk on the ground but crawl), beasts of the earth (wild), according to their own kind (genuine, not adulterated): (Gen. 1:24, 25). God wished that all these animals be distinct from man in the use of reason and speech.[14]

XV. And Man: Second, the Body and the Soul

Man was the crown of the works of God. God created the rest in the word, "let there be (*fiat*)." He created man with such incitement: "Let us make man for our image, according to our likeness" (Gen. 1:26). "The body" was formed "out of the dust" (מאדמה) "of the earth" (Gen. 2:7). Hence his name was Adam (אדמ) (Gen. 2:19). The excellence of the body is so great that a species worthy of dominion (εἶδος ἄξιον τυραννίδος) shines forth in it. God united the "soul" to the body "by breathing into the nostrils of Adam the breath of life," or the life of the body and soul, and former as if a sign (Gen. 2:7).[15]

XVI. Which Is Spiritual and Immortal

The soul of man was created spiritual and immortal. It was created *spiritual* because "the spirit" was created distinct "from the dust," or from the body made out of dust (Eccl. 12:7; Matt. 10:28). It was created immortal, because it can be destroyed and die neither by itself nor by other secondary causes. For when the body dies the spirit does not also die, but "returns to God, who gave it" (Eccl. 12:7), that it may not be destroyed by God. For He cannot hate and destroy the good. But the soul is honored with reward or punishment for works. "Do not fear those who kill the body but cannot kill the soul" (Matt. 10:28). Manifold reason also confirms that very thing.[16]

XVII. Man Was Created, Immortal

Man was created in body and soul, immediately constant in unity, immortal, wise, just, and holy. He was created *immortal* because, although in regard

---

13. *Medulla*, XLIII.
14. *Medulla*, XLIV, XLV.
15. *Medulla*, XLVI–L.
16. *Medulla*, L–LIII.

to remote power he could have died, he was not underneath the necessity of dying before sin, nor would he die entirely. For only sin imposed on him the necessity of dying. "In which day you eat from the tree, you shall die" (Gen. 2:17). "The wages of sin is death" (Rom. 6:23). "The body dies on account of sin" (Rom. 8:10).[17]

XVIII. Wise, Just, and Holy

He was also created *wise, just, and holy.* Indeed, he was created "very good" (Gen. 1:31), "upright" (Eccl. 7:29), and with the *image* of God (Gen. 1:26), which consists in "the righteousness and holiness of truth" (Eph. 4:24). This righteousness was natural in the first man, not accessory and supernatural, because otherwise his nature would not be morally good and the work not worthy of God the workman, in which He could be glorified. For man could not be without love and desire of Him as the highest good, the upright work of God, immediately made by Him. And concupiscence could not be from God or He could not be good.[18]

XIX. Free

The companion of the righteousness of the first man is *freedom* or *free will*, the former *a faculty of the soul, whereby he freely, willingly, and without any external force chose that, which he perceived, deliberated, and decided to have been chosen*. This was not *indifference* to do good or evil, because it was natural to him to do good, while to do evil was contrary to his nature. And the *freedom* was not *immutable.* For in this way there would have been no place for temptation. For immutability of the will does not belong to nature, but to grace and glory. The freedom was also not *independent*, because in God he was moved (Acts 17:28) and lacked grace not to heal corruption but to preserve integrity, in order to overcome the temptations of the devil. Instead, the *freedom* together with the deliberation of doing good was mutable.[19]

XX. The Creation of Eve; the Institution of Marriage

Adam placed names upon the animals, heavily putting forth proof of wisdom. On that occasion God created a helpmate by the side of him (עזר כנגדו), even "similar" to him, a woman, "from the rib of Adam." And to her, of the nature of man (אישה) (Ἀνδρίδος) (Gen. 2:23, etc.), Adam soon gave the name Eve (חוה) (Gen. 3:20). Moreover, at the same time He established the law of marriage (νόμον γαμικὸν) as indissoluble and only between two people with these words,

17. *Medulla*, LIII, LIV.
18. *Medulla*, LV, LVI.
19. *Medulla*, LVII–LX.

"Therefore let man abandon his father and mother and cling to his wife, and they will be one flesh" (Gen. 2:24).[20]

XXI. The Blessing of Man: His Multiplication through Generation; Alive in the Creation of the Soul; Dominion

God, blessing the same people created equal, said, "Be fruitful and multiply" (Gen. 1:28), tacitly promising in His prolific blessing the increase of the human race. This blessing concerned the whole man, consisting of soul and body, although man supplied the needs from anew (de novo) of neither the substance of the body nor the spirit. This cannot be generated, being immaterial but agreeing with the creature. Instead, it can only be created by God, "placing the spirit in the midst of man" (Zech. 12:1). For by His strength man generates the whole man because the body is so arranged that the soul is united to it. Part of the same blessing is that God granted to man dominion over the animals and fruit of the earth. "Let us make man," "that" even "they may be those who rule over the fish of the sea and over the birds of heaven and over the whole earth" (Gen. 1:26). "Subject the whole earth to yourselves and rule over it" (Gen. 1:28). For before the subjection all things were sufficient (ἀδέσσοντα) and belonged to nobody. After the subjection, nevertheless, anything which, in regard to what could be sufficient, was subject to him without offense to another, he could rule over. As a result, *positive* communion of ownership would never or could never prevail.[21]

XXII. Man the Image of God

In this way God created man "for His image" (Gen. 1:26). The *subject* of this was the whole man, consisting of spiritual and immortal soul as well as body. The *form* of the same was "rectitude, knowledge, righteousness, holiness of truth" (Eccl. 7:29; Eph. 4:24; Col. 3:10), *splendor* following *dominion*, and all blessing and happiness. The subject of the precious image is like assimilation in form on a tablet, and the result of the same is radiance and splendor.[22]

20. *Medulla*, LX–LXIV.
21. *Medulla*, LXIV–LXIX.
22. *Medulla*, LXVIII–LXXI.

LOCUS VII

On the Providence of God

I. Providence

God the Creator is the same *provider* of all things created by Him. For He does not merely watch the things created by Him but provides (προνοεῖται) for them by caring, preserving, and governing them. This is called the *actual providence* of God, *another external action of God whereby the things created by Him are governed.*[1]

II. Its Demonstration

Indeed, God cares and *provides* for all things created by Him, not only in general but also in particular. For "the Lord provides from heaven, regards all the sons of men, and rules over all the inhabitants of the earth" (Ps. 33:13, 14), not observing idly but holding the key and governing all. "My Father works to this point, and I also work" (John 5:17). "In Him we exist, live, and move" (Acts 17:28). "God works all things in all" (1 Cor. 12:6). Nature, the condition of created things, order and harmony, prophecy, the revolution of empires, the benefits and judgments of God, conscience, and conspicuous types most clearly demonstrate the providence of God.[2]

III. Fate and Fortune

Fate, fortune, and chance are opposed to the providence of God. Cicero defines *fate* as "an eternal order and series of causes, in which the cause joined to the cause begets the thing from itself." Some also tie God to this. But this clearly wages war against God's freedom, power, dominion, and kingdom; makes God the author of sin; and overturns prophecy, religion, laws, and miracles. *Fortune*, the mind from heaven having been banished from this world of inconstancy, is thought to turn all things with a blind impetus, which in natural things is

1. *Medulla*, I–IV.
2. *Medulla*, IV, V.

called *chance*. This is pure denial of the one omniscient God, who is the governor of all things.[3]

IV. Preservation

The acts of divine providence are preservation and governance. *Preservation* is that *whereby God sustains and perpetuates the things made by Him, some in the particular, through succession of individualities, but others in the very individualities*. For God "keeps man and beasts" (Ps. 36:6). "You spread out Your hand and they are sated with good.... You send Your Spirit, they are created, and You renew the face of the earth" (Ps. 104:28, 30). "In Him we exist, live, and move" (Acts 17:28), not as in substance but as in the cause that continues to operate all these things and to that degree preserves them. Just as the creatures are out of nothing, are from nothing, and share from nothing, they exist by virtue of God. Thus they further exist, indeed essentially depending on Him.[4]

V. Governance: Mediated, to Which Pertains God's Concursus

The governance of God is an act of the same providence *whereby He orders, directs, and leads all things, every one of every kind, to their ends determined in advance, both means and end*. For God made all things beautiful (יפה) "in their own time" (Eccl. 3:11). "He determined the times in advance and the limits of their habitation" (Acts 17:26). Nothing has been created and preserved by the most wise God except for a certain end. Moreover, God governs all things mediately or immediately. He governs *mediately* through the *ministry of secondary causes*. For "He heeds the heavens, the earth for Him, the wheat, oil and wine on the earth" (Hos. 2:21–22), manifesting not the possession of strength but His power, goodness, and wisdom. God's *concursus* or rather the *work* whereby "He works in all things" (1 Cor. 12:6) pertains to this, as immediate and predetermining cause. Consequently, the action of God and the creature are one dispatch (ἀποστέλεσμα), and God acts in agreement with the nature of secondary causes.[5]

VI. Immediate: Miracles Are Referred to This

His governance is immediate *whereby God works immediately by Himself alone, whether He acts without means, in addition to them, or against them*. Through this He shows that He needs no creatures and that all depend on Him and ought to trust Him alone. *Miracles* are referred to this. They are the *works* of God that

3. *Medulla*, V–IX.
4. *Medulla*, IX–XII.
5. *Medulla*, XII–XV.

transcend all power of creatures. Their criteria are obtained from the substance of the action, the subject and its beginnings, and even the manner of working.[6]

VII. The Object

All things besides God are subject to the providence of God. For angels and men subsist in Him according to *substance.* Men subsist in conception, the giving of life, birth, the whole course of life, and its end. For God has determined the limit of life since there is "a period for man on earth" and "his days are mercenary" (Job 7:1) as it were, and "his days and number of months are determined." God "made limits" to these, which man "does not cross" (Job 14:5–6). This is true according to *quantity*, as the greatest and least things, even "the sparrows" (Matt. 10:29), "the hairs of the head" (Matt. 10:30), and "the hay of the field" (Matt. 6:30) are subject to His providence. It is also true according to *quality* since good and evil as well as crimes and penalties are subject to His providence. Moreover, it is true according to *events*, necessary and contingent, as "a lot" is thrown into the bowl," whose "event is from God" (Prov. 16:33). He also rules voluntary and free actions. For "the heart of a king" is "in the hand of God," who "inclines it to what it wills" (Prov. 21:1), "gives a new heart and a new spirit" (Ezek. 36:26), and "touches the heart" (1 Sam. 10:26).[7]

VIII. The Manner of Reconciling the Providence of God with Free Actions

The manner of reconciling the providence of God with free actions, good and evil, ought not to be sought by reason but by the Word of God alone. This does not show it in the *prescience* of God, because the providence of God is not bare prescience but actual care and a will working together with the act of the mind conjoined (John 5:17; Eph. 1:11). It also does not show it in bare *permission* of evil, because the permission of sin is not bare and of patience but is efficacious and of power, as a species of the will. For God "does" all things "by the counsel of His will" (Eph. 1:11). Moreover, He is introduced everywhere as intervening for sin even in the *general and indifferent concursus of God.* Indeed, those alternatives remove all the providence of God and open the way to atheism, whether we look at God or man. But the foundation of the reconciliation must be sought from the dependence of the creature on God. Moreover, as subordination belongs to Him in being, so also does it in action. For "in Him we exist, live, and move" (Acts 17:28). "From Him, through Him, and to Him are all things" (Rom. 11:36).[8]

---

6. *Medulla*, XV–XIX.
7. *Medulla*, XX–XXVII.
8. *Medulla*, XXVII–XXXII.

IX. The Providence of God concerning Good and concerning Evil

Therefore, the providence of God concerns good and evil. It concerns good according to good pleasure (κατ' εὐδοκίαν) whereby *by Himself He wills, effects, approves, and directs good to a good end.* And it concerns *civil* and *external* goods through *help* whereby as author of nature He freely dispenses, lavishes, and fosters study, industry, imitation, art, and care. It concerns *supernatural* things through *grace*, not common but special, whereby in Christ He confers the qualities of spiritual gifts to the church and individuals to obtain them. These surpass the collective powers of nature and stir up, determine, and lead them into action. It concerns *evil* according to permission (κατ' συγχώρησιν) whereby God *does not will evil or sin. He neither effects nor aids nor approves it, but willingly permits, efficaciously ordains, and justly punishes it.* Indeed, although evil opposes the most holy nature of God, it is nevertheless not removed from the eye of the provident divine will and care. For there is not such a highest evil that it cannot be driven back by the highest good into order. Indeed, God certainly does not thus "tempt" man "to evil" (James 1:13), because God is not willing iniquity (חפץ) (Ps. 5:4) but "permits the lust of the heart, that it may go according to its plans" (Ps. 81:12; Acts 14:16). "He sends" to them "the efficacy of error, that they may believe the lie" (2 Thess. 2:11). Finally, this is His "law, that those who do such things are worthy of death" (Rom. 1:32).[9]

X. The Efficacy of Providence concerning Evil

The efficacy of God's providence concerning sin consists in that which moves and determines the sinner, even joined to the evil qualities contracted by him. He uses that as an instrument, joined to his nature and disposition, to execute His judgments and plans. Otherwise, He does not illuminate his mind with knowledge of the saving truth nor bend his will to obedience. Indeed, He thinks the "same thing" that the sinner "thinks" (Gen. 50:20) with diverse ends and holy thought. He "determines" the evil that men "do," such as Herod, Pilate, and the Jews (Acts 4:27–28), by governing and ordaining their evil actions in a holy manner. "He blinds and hardens" (Ex. 7:3; Isa. 63:17; John 12:40) metaphorically on account of His governance, the occasion of which is similar to an efficient cause. For as the effect is in the established cause, so in that governance hardening follows, not by the force of divine governance but of human malice whereby the sinner is rendered more stiff-necked every day. In this way the sun elicits a bad smell from a dead body with its benign rays. He also "makes to be mad" (Job 12:16–17), not being the author of insanity but depriving light on account of its abuse and opening the way through objects whereby it is snatched from the way and thus striking with stupor. "He makes to err" by permitting

9. *Medulla*, XXXII–XXXVII.

error. "He deceives and seduces" (Isa. 63:17; Jer. 4:10) with His just judgment permitting, so that false prophets may preach false things and men may believe them. "He sends them into the efficacy of error" (2 Thess. 2:11) by removing grace, permitting concupiscence, and provoking the ingenuity of seducers who devise specious arguments (πιθανολογίαν). "He commanded Shimei to curse" (2 Sam. 16:10–11) not through a command properly spoken but through secret direction, through which He did not restrain cursing, and furnished the object that agrees with wickedness, so that he would vomit out the latent malice in the heart. "He impelled David to number" the people (2 Sam. 24:1) without sin, intending judgment. "He stirred up Pharaoh," in order that He "might demonstrate" His "power" in him (Ex. 9:16)—that is, He acted not that He might pour sin into him but that He might consume the experience of His power in him who was corrupt. "He gave the wives" of David to "his son" (2 Sam. 12:11) by wisely and justly governing the impure deed, and directing evil wishes for His glory. Nevertheless, those operations of God concerning evil are something secret, which is known to God alone.[10]

XI. It Does Not Make God the Author of Sin

This efficacy in God's providence concerning evil does not therefore make God the author of sin. For Scripture denies that God is the author of sin and asserts the same efficacy of providence. Moreover, whatever God does and thinks by permitting, ordaining, and vindicating is entirely holy. But perdition (שחת) is from man (Hos. 13:9). They remove all providence of God and religion, who, in order that they may make an offering to the idol of free will, deny God's provident care concerning the free actions of men, even evil.[11]

---

10. *Medulla*, XXXVII–XLV.
11. *Medulla*, XLV.

LOCUS VIII

On Angels

I. Definition and Existence of Angels

In the army of God there are also angels (Ἄγγελοι)—that is, *messengers* who have been sent (מלאכים). They are ministering spirits (πνεύματα λειτουργικὰ) (Heb. 1:14)—that is, *spirits created by God in rectitude, subsisting through Him, endowed with intelligence, will, and power. Some persevere in rectitude and minister for God in the proclamation of His praises and the rule of the world, above all for the church. Others, however, defected from the same, were cast out of heaven, began to suffer punishment, and, as avengers of God's judgment, they will be placed under the punishment of eternal fire after the end of the world.* Scripture testifies that they exist and subsist through Him, and reason argues the same a posteriori, or from their works. Indeed, they are neither accidents of organs nor phantasms, because they were prior to the "foundation of the earth" and man's existence, at least as evil (Job 38:7; Gen. 3:1).[1]

II. They Are Created Spirits

Angels are spirits created in time. They are "spirits" (Ps. 104:4; Heb. 1:14), lacking matter because, as of intelligence, they cannot be material through essence. Moreover, they are not joined to an airy or other delicate body. For delicate bodies are devoid of organs, and without organs nothing can make a spirit united into a body. Angels also do not require matter to subsist. They also were *created* as "the army of heaven" (Ps. 103:21; 148:2) together with "heaven" (Gen. 2:1) and indeed "upright sons" of God (Job 38:7), who are "good" (Gen. 1:31).[2]

III. The Intellect, Will, and Power of Angels

Angels are endowed with intellect, will, and power. Through *intellect* they know *God* in regard to the glory of His majesty, power, and virtues, and *creatures*

1. *Medulla*, I–V.
2. *Medulla*, V–VIII.

among each other, as citizens of the same body-politic—other *minds* and *bodies*, faithful above all to whom "they are sent" (Heb. 1:14). The *foundation* of their knowledge is nature, experience, and revelation. This is the *manner* that they know God: from an inborn idea through other intelligible species outside of themselves. Their *will* was created holy and free, not without affections. These are bare movements of the will in them but are very forceful. Their *power* is natural strength. Indeed, they are "very powerful in strength" (Ps. 103:20), "angels of power" (2 Thess. 1:7). They prevail much over bodies, especially of men, largely over intellect and will. But they do not immediately flow into them but in the mediating body, which also moves. And by moving they act upon the soul.[3]

IV. The Number, Place, Movement, and Appearance of Angels

The number, place, movement, duration, and appearance relate to angels as a whole. *Number* relates to angels because "thousands of thousands minister to Him, and ten thousand times a hundred thousand assist Him" (Dan. 7:10). But the number is known to God alone, and it is not capable of increase or decrease. *Place* relates to angels because they exist in heaven, whether in the air or on earth or in hell, not through extension because they are incorporeal, but in a manner that agrees with their spiritual nature. *Movement* relates to angels because they are sent, ascend, descend, exist, and work only here and only there, locally in bodies assumed. As such, they do not move in the same manner. For they do not so exist in space that they are made equal with it, nor when they leave it and acquire a new one do they divide the middle. *Appearance* relates to angels because they have been sent by God into the earth. They appear in bodies assumed, whether created by God, made through change of matter, or merely in apparent bodies.[4]

V. Good Angels: Their Confirmation

There are good and evil angels. The former "persisted in the truth" (John 8:44) and "retained their proper foundation and dwelling" (Jude 6). But the latter did not do likewise. The former are called "holy" (Deut. 33:3), "angels of Jehovah" (Ps. 103:20), "elect" (1 Tim. 5:21), and "of the light" (2 Cor. 11:14). For standing in the truth they have been confirmed by God in the same. "They always see the face of their Father in heaven" (Matt. 18:10) and "do the will" of God (Matt. 6:10). But they have been confirmed in this way by free will and the grace of God, not by merit.[5]

---

3. *Medulla*, VIII–XII.
4. *Medulla*, XII–XV.
5. *Medulla*, XV, XVI.

VI. Their Ministry

God enjoined to the good angels the ministry and care of faithful men. For they are "spirits of ministry, sent for the sake of ministry on account of those who" will be "heirs of salvation" (Heb. 1:14). The ordaining of this ministry is secret and does not consist of a distinction of hierarchies and orders or of guardianship, in which each is given as a guard to each man. It also does not mean that some are put in charge over the world, and others over the church, empires, and heavenly bodies.[6]

VII. Their Worship, Which Is of Love, Not Servitude, or Is Religious

The faithful owe reverence and cultivation of love and of fellowship to the good angels. For they are messengers of God, sent to us for the sake of our salvation. They are witnesses of holy beauty, which ought to be observed among us with all gladdening modesty and purity, not with fleeting license (Luke 15:7, 10; 1 Cor. 11:10; 1 Tim. 5:21). Pious thoughts must be subject to them, and we must so imitate them that "we do the will of God on earth, as" they "do in heaven" (Matt. 6:10; 22:30). Moreover, since they are our keepers (σύνδουλοι) (Rev. 19:10), they must be cherished in *charity*, not in *servitude*. On that point, they must not be pursued with religious devotion. "You shall worship the Lord your God and serve Him alone" (Deut. 6:13; Matt. 4:10).[7]

VIII. Evil Angels: Their Sin, Number, Penalty of Sin, and State of Immutability

Angels were not created *evil* by God but were made such by their own fault, "not standing in the truth" (John 8:44), "not retaining their foundation and abandoning their own home" (Jude 6). Their *sin* was the sort that did not consist in purity. It was not lust. Perhaps it was pride joined with envy (1 Tim. 3:6). Their *number* is most great because among them are "legions" (Luke 8:30), and they obtain "a kingdom" (Matt. 12:26). "God did not spare those who sinned, but cast them into hell, bound with the chains of darkness, kept for judgment" (2 Peter 2:4). This state of theirs of sin and punishment is absolutely immutable because they can neither rise from the dead nor have a mediator.[8]

IX. Their Knowledge Remains

But yet some knowledge and power remains in them. Indeed, *knowledge* survives in them, not only *natural* though sometimes dull, but also *supernatural*. It is not practical but very obscurely theoretical and is not more than is required to do

6. *Medulla*, XVII–XX.
7. *Medulla*, XX, XXI.
8. *Medulla*, XXII–XXVI.

the commands of God. It is also *empirical*. But none of these penetrates to the knowledge of God, men, or future contingencies. The devil, nevertheless, has "depths" (Rev. 2:24) and "stratagems" (Eph. 6:11).[9]

X. And Their Power

Very great power survives in the same, not only from nature but from the will of God "giving" it (Luke 4:6). For He makes them executors of His judgments. Hence it is limited because nothing appears to allow it over the *heavenly* bodies, and this "power of the air" is attributed to it, or of those that live in the air and on the earth (Eph. 2:2). It is so stretched out over animals and men that it neither generates the former nor has any immediate or all mediate power over the whole external or internal man.[10]

XI. Magic

The mixed bodily and spiritual exercise of the devil is in *magic*, which is defined as *the art of impious men and infidels, belonging to the devil, desiring divine honor, and undertaking to subject to itself the human race, with the power and covenant with the same, intervening with wonders of speech and acts*. This exists even in Scripture, and evil and great works occur in men.[11]

XII. Its Character: Explicit, Implicit

Magic is explicit or implicit. The *former* contracts a covenant with Satan in conceived words and solemn rites. The *latter* is exercised without a solemn covenant, with only the consent of those making a pact together or any exchange with Satan, entered upon and honored by those knowing or imprudent. Indeed, those associating are given association with Satan (חוברי חבר) (Deut. 18:11). The character of each must be discerned. For those who, having abandoned the way that is prescribed in the Word of God and by right reason, fall into other ways and use other means, being eager to know and do what is neither revealed in the Word of God nor has the promise of divine cooperation.[12]

XIII. Specters

The devil also terrifies sometimes through *specters*. "The disciples of Christ said, while walking there, they saw something apparent that is a phantom (ὅτι φάντασμα ἐστι)" (Matt. 14:26). For the devil, as the god of this age who has "power over the air" and over those that are in the air (Eph. 2:2), can fool bodies

---

9. *Medulla*, XXVI, XXVII.
10. *Medulla*, XXVII–XXX.
11. *Medulla*, XXX–XXXIII.
12. *Medulla*, XXXIII–XXXIX.

with human senses that are like men. They can also stir and occupy the bodies of men, ravage the human corpses of the wicked, and harass men with other sensibilities with the judgment of God alone.[13]

XIV. The Kingdom of Satan

Therefore, the devil has, God willing, a kingdom. But it is most miserable, has already been outdated in various degrees, and at some time will be thoroughly abolished. For, in Paradise, God threatened the "crushing of the head" of the serpent (Gen. 3:15), and He soon began to execute the same, having withdrawn the power of victory over the faithful from him. But he will not cease to accuse sin, until one day he is removed and condemned by the blood of Christ (John 16:9, 11; Rom. 8:3). "He was cast outside" (John 12:31), lest he seduce the nations. He established the throne of the Antichrist, from which he is cast off little by little. He will be cast off in greater number until, "with the Beast and Pseudo-Prophet, he is cast into the lake of fire and sulphur" (Rev. 20:10).[14]

---

13. *Medulla*, XXXIX.
14. *Medulla*, XLff.

LOCUS IX

On the Covenant of Works

I. The Covenant of God with Man

God peculiarly deemed man worthy of His friendship. For He is the King and Father of man, and He called the same to *covenant*, offering His closer communion and more excellent goods. But the *covenant of God* is that *pact* with man whereby God, from the eminence that He has, by law and singular goodness makes an agreement on a certain condition for eternal life and seals the same with certain signs even as pledges.[1]

II. Its Existence Is Proven

The covenant of the same manner with God is known more obscurely from nature and more clearly from revelation. It is known from nature because conscience dictates that it is a crime against God for obedience to be stipulated by man. Conscience also dictates that God, as the best and giver of every good, must be loved alone. Moreover, God as the highest good is not loved in vain but reaches delight in the one who loves Him. This also confirms the natural appetite for the highest good. It is known from *revelation*—namely, which is the double covenant, of works and of grace. It mentions the former with the uncorrupted man. The latter began with the corrupted man.[2]

III. The Covenant of Works

The covenant of works is the pact of God initiated with the uncorrupted Adam, as head of the whole human race, in which He stipulated from man perfect obedience to the law. He promised eternal, heavenly life for the same obedience but threatened eternal death for transgression. In turn, man promised perfect obedience to God who stipulated. If he had furnished this, he could have

1. *Medulla*, I–VI.
2. *Medulla*, VI.

expected eternal, heavenly life. Scripture testifies that such a covenant existed with Adam. "They like Adam (כאדם) transgressed the covenant" (Hos. 6:7). Moreover, God established the sacrament of the same covenant: "the tree of life" (Gen. 2:9).[3]

IV. God and Adam Covenanted

They were *covenanted*, God as the Creator, Lawgiver, and Rewarder, and *Adam* as the first man, uncorrupted and head of the human race. For Adam was the "one blood" in which the whole posterity lay hidden (Acts 17:26) and "the first Adam," equally representing those to be born from his blood. "The second Adam" represents the faithful. Indeed, he is a "type of" the one "to come" (Rom. 5:14). And since the remaining words concern the whole human race, it cannot be secluded from the covenant initiated with him.[4]

V. The Legal Stipulation to Obedience

The *duty* of the covenant of works that God stipulated from man is legal obedience. The rule of this was in the law, with which God bound Adam to Himself by oath. For a creature, created for the image of God, and yet bound by no law is inconsistent (ἀσύστατα).[5]

VI. The Law Is Defined: Its Species; Divine, Natural

The *law* in general is the *rule, established by Him, who has the law, directing and obligating the rational creature in actions*. This obligates simply to obedience, and punishment according to it, if obedience to the law should not be furnished. The former is either *archetypal*—that is, *the holiness of the divine nature*, since the natural creature can copy it in life—or *ectypal*, which prescribes to the rational creature according to the archetype. This is divine, either natural or positive. It is *natural* whereby God *in the beginning obligated Adam and in that of the common nature of men, using reason, distributed knowledge of virtue and vice, to do the former and to shun the latter*. This ought not to be judged by its own usefulness or the voluntary law of society, but by love of God and neighbor and natural purity. For man by nature is placed under God the Creator, and he cannot be placed under Him except through the law distributed to the created nature. At the same time, he was created as a social animal, not only with love of himself but also of his neighbor joined to himself.[6]

---

3. *Medulla*, VII.
4. *Medulla*, VIII.
5. *Medulla*, IX.
6. *Medulla*, X–XIV.

VII. The Law of the Decalogue: Explaining Its Rules

Christians have proof of natural law in the moral actions agreeing with the moral judgments of the Decalogue. Its summary is *in the love of God from the whole heart, soul, and strength, and of one's neighbor as oneself.* But the rules of explaining the same must be held: the law is "spiritual" (Rom. 7:14). It is expressed more in commands and prohibitions than in words. Its sense is not the freedom of man but the will of God revealed in His Word. In turn, prohibitions are contained in commands, and its heads are founded not in the mere good pleasure of God but in His natural holiness.[7]

VIII. Positive Law; Prohibition of the Tree of the Knowledge of God and Evil

The law is *positive* that *is placed* in the sole will of God establishing it. In Scripture it comes in the name of a plea (δόγματος) instituted (Acts 16:4; Eph. 2:15; Col. 2:14). The prohibition of *the tree of the knowledge of good and evil* pertains to it. For "food does not commend man" to God (1 Cor. 8:8), nor "is the kingdom of God food and drink" (Rom. 14:17). God had already earlier regarded every tree for food for man (Gen. 1:29). Therefore, the prohibition was positive and fit for testing (πειραστικὸν) because God wished to test man through the former and explore his obedience. Yet that plea was most wise and agreeable to test man from the beginning.[8]

IX. Of Legal Righteousness: The Perfection of Its Parts, of Degrees, of Perseverance

Perfect legal obedience was fittingly born to effect perfect *legal righteousness*, the condition of life. The perfection of this righteousness is threefold: parts, degrees, or perseverance. The *parts* consist in the obedience of the internal and external man, righteousness according to the love of God, himself, his neighbor, and every command. The *degrees* consist in the highest degree of obedience and love, above all of God, "from the whole heart," by which man judges, chooses, and decides "from the whole soul." By this man desires "from the whole exertion and strength" of nature and of the uncorrupted faculties received in creation (Deut. 6:5; Matt. 22:37). *Perseverance* consists in man not changing in parts, degrees, or defects (Deut. 27:26; Ezek. 18:24).[9]

---

7. *Medulla*, XIV–XVII.
8. *Medulla*, XVII, XVIII.
9. *Medulla*, XIX–XIII.

X. The Promise of Heavenly and Eternal Life

The *promise* of the covenant of works was eternal and heavenly life. Its sacrament, "the tree of life," by all means true and eternal (עולם) (Gen. 2:9), was sanctioned for animals and the earthly blessings that he already possessed. In these there was not a covenant (διαθήκη) but an accession (προσθήκη) to the covenant. When Christ, fulfilling the law in our place, merited eternal and heavenly life for us, He obtained the fulfillment of the same law by merit for us. Indeed, God promised something more in the covenant of works than who could be a sharer outside of it. It was not other than the translation into heavenly Paradise.[10]

XI. The Threat of Death

The threat of death is opposed to the promise. "On the day on which you shall eat" from the tree, "you shall die" (Gen. 2:17). This death signifies everything in Scripture that comes in the name of death. Therefore, it is *spiritual*, which is separation from the holiness of God. It is *eternal*, which is separation from the goodness of God. Finally, it is *temporal*, which is the separation of the soul from the body, not only in regard to its temporal blessings but also in regard to the body itself, through dissolution of the union. Indeed, man does not first die when the union of body and soul is dissolved but when it begins to be dissolved through temporal evils and mortality is contracted.[11]

XII. The Confirmation of the Covenant of Works; Reconfirmation; Legal Justification

While God stipulates obedience, man *is confirmed* through the same by promising obedience. In turn, man also could have expected the reward of life from God by *reconfirming*, if he would have obeyed. Hence, *legal justification* was also pending. For "to the one who works reward is imputed from debt" (Rom. 4:4), not on account of the worth of the work but on account of the pact. In it God is not made a debtor to man but to His truthfulness and faithfulness.[12]

XIII. The Sacraments of the Covenant of Works: Paradise and the Tree of Life

The sacraments of the covenant of works were Paradise and the Tree of Life. For Paradise sealed heaven and its delights (Luke 23:43). Indeed, it was not planted in that law, that it may feed the senses alone in appearance and appetite. For all delights (ἡδοναὶ) of the world are nothing except shadows of true and solid goods. Rather, it was planted that, as a sacrament, it might prefigure the

10. *Medulla*, XXIII–XXVI.
11. *Medulla*, XXVI, XXVII.
12. *Medulla*, XXVIII, XXIX.

heavenly mansion. The *Tree of Life*, or "life-giving" tree (Gen. 2:16; 3:22), illustriously offered goods, above all heavenly life and Christ Himself, the author of life. Indeed, it was not for the sake of effecting temporal life or of extending it forever, since it always retained its natural strength. After obedience God would have given immortality without food or drink, and the remaining trees would have been in vain. But it was a pledge of heavenly life, in the way in which the Eucharistic bread is a sacrament of the truly life-giving Christ (John 6:48, 50). For even after the fall it was a symbol of revealing Christ. "I will give to the one who conquers of the tree of life in the midst of the Paradise of God" (Rev. 2:7).[13]

13. *Medulla*, XXX.

LOCUS X

On the Sin of Man

I. The Definition of Sin

The obedience of Adam was interrupted by sin. By force of the term *law*, like an aimless row of cattle, sin indicates transgression, as חטאה and ἁμαρτία signify diversion from the end and scope or missing the mark (ἀστοχίαν) and not laying hold of the scope. Saint John defines it as lawlessness (ἀνομίαν) (1 John 3:4). It is defined more broadly as *a defect of nature and actions in intelligent natures, opposing the law of God and obliging them from the order of divine justice to punishment.*[1]

II. Its Formal Reason

The formal reason of sin consists not in position but in *non-bare privation*. For God is the author of every proper position as such. Nevertheless, if sin is taken *concretely* with its subject, which is nature, disposition, or action, it is something *positive*. For malice dwells in this subject like a bird does in a foreign nest. Therefore, it affects its subject and the mind and actions of madness. It is declared that the same subject thus affects not only privatively (στερητικῶς) but also positively (θετικῶς) (Gen. 6:5; Rom. 7:23). Yet there really is privation, not *pure*, consisting in what (τῷ) is *deprived*, of which sort is death and blindness, which leaves behind nothing of disposition or action. But privation is not *pure*, consisting in what (τῷ) *is to be deprived*, of which sort is sickness, madness, which leaves behind something of disposition or action.[2]

III. The Cause of Sin

The cause of sin is, as such, not an *efficient* evil by itself, but *deficient* from what is good first. The cause of sin is not God, who is "light" and in whom there is "no darkness" (1 John 1:5). Rather, it is the rational creature created by God

1. *Medulla*, I–VI.
2. *Medulla*, VI.

good and free, but which was mutable and hence could exchange its liberty and goodness for servitude and malice.[3]

IV. The First Sin

The first sin sprung from the first man. *The first sin is the disobedience of the first humans, Adam and Eve in Paradise, whereby with the influence of the devil they transgressed the law of God not to eat from the fruit of the tree of the knowledge of good and evil.* For the serpent, or the devil disguised in the skin of a serpent, seduced Eve, and Adam through Eve, to violate the law not to eat the fruit of the forbidden tree. He was skilled with amazing craft (μεθοδείᾳ). Yet the whole blame of the transgression ought not to be diverted to the devil, since Eve herself too lightly admitted the tempter, leaving behind God and her husband and the Word of God, and with primeval simplicity succumbed to the temptation. Adam also allowed himself to be seduced, not by the serpent but by the woman whom he ought to have commanded, so that he also would affect the likeness of God.[4]

V. The Gravity of His Sin

The sin of the first created beings was most grave. For, the *symbolic* law having been violated, they sinned against the most equitable and great Lord with a high hand. The tree of life remained at the same time that they renounced their life. Moreover, they cast off from *natural* law the love of God, themselves, and neighbor, not to mention from the circumstances of place, time, person, and reward.[5]

VI. The Guilt of the First Sin; The Salvation of the First Created Beings

The consequences of the first sin were guilt and punishment. The *guilt* of the one sinning *is an obligation to punishment on account of the fault, by the order of righteousness.* For this is the righteous requirement (δικαίωμα) of God established in the law: "the ones doing this," sinning, "are worthy of death" (Rom. 1:32). And this is that judgment for condemnation (κρῖμα εῖς κατάκριμα) (Rom. 5:16). The *punishment* of the transgression was death, certainly threatened by God. Its proof was not only *spiritual*, the knowledge of nakedness (Gen. 3:7) and concealment from the face of God (Gen. 3:8), but also *eternal*: flight of the sinner from the face of God and expulsion from Paradise (Gen. 3:22–23). Its proof was also *corporal*: misery and toil and mortality coming into being. Yet from these punishments merited by sin, the promise "of the blessed seed" of Eve to crush the head of the serpent came through her—namely, that by

3. *Medulla*, VII, VIII.
4. *Medulla*, IX–XII.
5. *Medulla*, XII, XIII.

believing she became "the mother of all the living" (Gen. 3:15, 20), which also delivered Adam.[6]

VII. Sin Sprung: Original

Sin *sprung* is either original or actual. *Original* sin is defection of all the natural heirs of Adam in his loins and hence the following corruption of nature, which is propagated to each and every one from impure generation. Indeed, there are two parts of original sin: the sin of Adam was imputed to his posterity for condemnation, and it was propagated through natural generation and is therefore inherent.[7]

VIII. Imputed

Original sin *imputed* is *the transgression of Adam, as head of the human race, imputed to the same by the just judgment of God.* For all, having been infected on account of the first human being, are determined infected in the posterity of the same. Without the imputation of his sin it could not be possible that "all have sinned in" Adam (Rom. 5:12) and "die" in him (1 Cor. 15:22). Moreover, the propagation of original sin through generation, or the punishment of the human race, would not be just without the sin of Adam imputed to the same.[8]

IX. Inherent

That *inherent* original sin is what *is propagated through impure generation to all men.* It is called in the original κατ' ἐξοχὴν (par excellence), and in Scripture κατ' ἐξοχὴν ἁμαρτία means sin, indwelling sin (Rom. 7:7–10). God Himself spoke about this: "Every imagination of the thoughts of the heart" of man "is only evil the whole day" (Gen. 6:5), even "from childhood" (Gen. 8:21). For "who will render clean from the unclean? Not even one" (Job 14:4). Hence David naturally first confessed his sins to the source of the same, mounting impure generation. He said, "Behold, in depravity I was brought forth and in sin my mother conceived" me (Ps. 51:5). For "what is born from flesh is flesh" (John 3:6). Hence, it is declared that regenerating "Spirit and water" is necessary for entrance into the kingdom of heaven (John 3:5). "We were by nature (φύσιν) children of wrath, just as the rest" (Eph. 2:3).[9]

---

6. *Medulla*, XIV–XVII.
7. *Medulla*, XVII, XVIII.
8. *Medulla*, XIX–XXII.
9. *Medulla*, XXII, XXIII.

X. Its Essence

The essence of this sin does not consist in the *substance* of man, which good has God Himself as author and preserver. Moreover, Christ Himself could not have assumed this faultiness without sin. Nor does the essence of this sin consist in the *guilt* of sin, because the former is the consequence of the latter. Moreover, it does not consist in *concupiscence* alone—which is part of it, not the whole—nor in *pure privation* or *lack of* supernatural *righteousness owed*. Instead, the essence of this sin consists in *non-pure privation* of natural righteousness owed, indeed lively, active, energetic, and affecting the subject. For "the flesh lusts against the spirit" (Gal. 5:17), "reigns in the mortal body" (Rom. 6:12), and "works evil" (Rom. 7:17).[10]

XI. Parts

Parts of this sin are blindness of mind and will and perversity of affections, which comes in the name of *concupiscence*. This, without agreement of a true name, is also sin because it is devotion to the flesh (φρόνημα σαρκὸς), "enmity against God" (Rom. 8:7), and the mother pregnant with all sins. For "it entices, prolongs, and gives birth to sin" (James 1:14–15).[11]

XII. All Men Are under It, Even the Blessed Virgin Mary, and All the Regenerate until Death

All mere humans are under original sin. Not even the blessed virgin Mary is excepted. For Christ alone was born as "holy," conceived by the Holy Spirit (Luke 1:35), and ought to be "separated from sinners" (Heb. 7:26). That cannot be said about the blessed Mary. Therefore, "in" Adam "all sinned" (Rom. 5:12), and the blessed Mary confessed Christ her Savior (σωτῆρα), certainly from sins. Even in the regenerate it dwells (ἐνοικεῖ) until death (Rom. 7:17, 24) and works actual sins, although it is neither imputed to them, because there is "no condemnation" in them (Rom. 8:1), nor "dominates" them (Rom. 6:12).[12]

XIII. Actual Sin

Actual sin is *vice of internal or external action, emanating from original sin*. Indeed, it is the "act of the old man" (Col. 3:9), "work of the flesh" (Gal. 5:19), and "dead" (Heb. 6:1).[13]

---

10. *Medulla*, XXIV–XXVII.
11. *Medulla*, XXVII.
12. *Medulla*, XXVIII–XXXI.
13. *Medulla*, XXXI.

XIV. Its Species

There are various species of this sin. For it is either *internal*, of the heart, or *external*, of the mouth and work. The latter is graver than the former because it is the accession and consummation of the former. It is either of *omission*, which omits what is commanded in the law, or of *commission*, which commits what is forbidden in the law. There is some commission in omission, the thought of omission. There is also some omission of the duty of the command in commission. It is either *against God* whereby God is immediately offended, as in blasphemy and idolatry, or *against man*, not guilty of a condemning reason. It is either *in one's body*, as when a consort with prostitutes appropriates his members to the prostitute and devil, or *outside it*, where it is otherwise (1 Cor. 6:18). It is either *by itself* when the act forbidden in the law of God is brought to completion, or *by accident* when a good act defects in cause or circumstance. It is either *deliberate*, which is committed with "a high hand" (Num. 15:30), or *shouting*, which singularly provokes the vengeance of God. It is either of *tolerance*, the punishment of which God delays, of *ignorance*, committed by the ignorant through invincible or conquerable ignorance, or of *knowledge*, committed by one who knows prudence. It is either *reigning*, which readily dominates man sinning without light, or *not reigning*, which man resists through the grace of regeneration.[14]

XV. Blasphemy against the Holy Spirit; There Is Lack of Repentance and Pardon

The gravest *sin* of all is *blasphemy against the Holy Spirit*, indeed the "great prevarication" (Ps. 19:8). It is *the thorough denial of the truth of the gospel totally known and opposition to the same not from human weakness but from singular malice and hatred of the same, proceeding from the devil, lacking all repentance and pardon*. Hence, it is called such not in a general sense, in which any sin is committed against the Holy Spirit, but in a singular sense, in which the operation of the Holy Spirit in applying the evangelical promises or illumination is held in the same place in which the works of Beelzebub are. This is evident from the blasphemy of the Pharisees, who refused the proclamation and miracles of Christ concerning the advent of the kingdom of God (Matt. 12:28). It is "lacking" all "repentance and pardon" (Matt. 12:32) because it is unworthy of God to remit sin that is contrary to the most evident notification of the kingdom of God and His righteousness, which incurs an open war once it is known. It is also "lacking" all "repentance and pardon" because, having fallen thus, "they again crucify Christ among themselves and hold it merely for show" (Heb. 6:6).[15]

---

14. *Medulla*, XXXII, XXXV.
15. *Medulla*, XXXV, XXXVI.

XVI. The Penalty of Sin Properly Called; None Is Venial by Itself

The penalty of sin *properly* called is *preceding suffering inflicted on the sinner.* This everywhere is called *death* since there is curse in it. This is also the penalty of original sin, not only of *damnation* but also of *sense* because all of the condemned will indiscriminately "be cast into the fire" (Matt. 25:41). And therefore no sin by itself is venial. "Cursed is everyone who does not remain in all things that are written" (Deut. 27:26). "The soul that shall sin shall die" (Ezek. 18:20). "The wages of sin is death" (Rom. 6:23). But more grave sins also obtain pardon. They obtain it not from the measure of sins but from the grace of God and hence a foreign power.[16]

XVII. The Will of Man Enslaved

The penalties of the established sinner fall in this whole life, and they are connected and innumerable. The *enslaved will of man* pertains to this above all, through which *man the sinner can do some natural and external moral good but nothing spiritual, but is only carried to evil. And yet even with the judgment of a blind mind leading the way, he wills and acts freely and without coercion.* For "the imagination of the thoughts of the human heart are only evil every day" (Gen. 6:5). "Whatever is from flesh is flesh" (John 3:6). "We are by nature children of wrath" (Eph. 2:3) and "dead in sins" (Eph. 2:1). Indeed, man is born of this sort and remains such until regeneration. Indeed, "will the Ethiopians change their skin or the leopard its spots? Even you thoroughly informed (by evil nature) do evil" (Jer. 13:23). "They are slaves of corruption. For from this there is a certain way of life, delivered over to servitude" (2 Peter 2:19). "A bad tree cannot bear good fruits" (Matt. 7:18).[17]

XVIII. Punishment of the Second Life

The punishment of the second life consists in the separation of the whole man from holiness, goodness, and glory, in eternal captivity, and in the special sense of divine wrath "in burning fire" (2 Thess. 1:6–9).[18]

XIX. The Penalty Improperly Called

The penalty of sin, *improperly* and analogically, is the *suffering of the faithful reconciled to God, inflicted not by Him as Judge but as Father, not from the order of justice, but from fatherly love.* Its likeness with the penalty properly called is in suffering, from which human nature shrinks back. Its dissimilarity is in the cause and manner of the suffering. For it is inflicted not by an angry judge, not

16. *Medulla*, XXXVII–XLII.
17. *Medulla*, XLIII–XLVI.
18. *Medulla*, XLVI, XLVII.

for compensation of sin, but for its guarding against and abolishment as well as the testing of faith. "O Lord, do not convict me in Your wrath, and do not try me in Your anger" (Ps. 6:1). "Those judged are chastised by the Lord, lest they perish with the world" (1 Cor. 11:32).[19]

XX. Their Species

The penalties of the faithful are either chastisement (παιδεία) or testing (δοκιμασία) or martyrdom (μαρτύριον). *Chastisement* is that whereby God variously afflicts His children, bearing among them remnants of the flesh, in order that their flesh might be weakened and the vice of the old man abolished. "Those whom God loves He chastises" (Heb. 12:6). The same chastisement is also *testing*, whereby the faith, love, and patience before God of the sons of God grows more in the people themselves being tested (James 1:2–4; 1 Peter 1:6–7). *Martyrdom* is voluntary suffering whereby some faithful heroes of the church are commanded to speak the cause of Christ and the truth by enemies of the same, heartily confess it from the Word of God, and with most bitter crosses are sealed with death itself. In it are fulfilled the "remaining sufferings of Christ" (Col. 1:24), and it is an offering (σπονδὴ) (Phil. 2:17; 2 Tim. 4:6) poured out in the sacrifice of Christ, in which He is stirred up and delighted to help the church.[20]

19. *Medulla*, XLVIII, XLIX.
20. *Medulla*, L.

LOCUS XI

On the Covenant of Grace

I. The Covenant of Grace

The *covenant of grace* follows the covenant of works antiquated by sin, not in regard to the stipulation of duty but in regard to promise or putting together of life. It is *that gracious agreement between God the offended and some men who have offended in which God, from mere good pleasure, awarded righteousness and life to those who believe and repent, with Christ as Mediator. In turn, the latter promise faith and repentance through the grace of Christ, and they obtain the right of expecting righteousness and life from the same.*[1]

II. God and Man the Sinner Covenanted

The parties contracting that covenant are God and man. *God*, having been offended, acts no longer as Creator but as God Omnisufficient (אל שדי) and God of the sinner. *Man*, offending, was determined in the eternal counsel of God not simply but in Christ the Mediator, who reconciles the parties.[2]

III. The Pact with the Mediator

Indeed, God initiated a *pact* of reconciliation with Christ the Mediator. It is the mutual agreement of the Father with the Son whereby the Father stipulated that perfect obedience to the law must be furnished until death by the Son, who was promised an inheritance for the same obedience. In turn, the Son promised that obedience to God the Father, and furnishing in act, He restipulated the right of claiming that inheritance from the same. This is that "counsel of peace" between "Jehovah of armies," the Father and Lawgiver, and "the sprout of men," the Son and Sponsor (Zech. 6:12).[3]

1. *Medulla*, I–V.
2. *Medulla*, V.
3. *Medulla*, V–VI.

IV. The Stipulation of God and the Promise of the Son

In this singular pact God the Father demanded from the Son, as Mediator, vicarious obedience to the law for man the sinner, and the Son promised it in turn. "Behold, I come. In the scroll of the book it has been written about Me, that I shall do Your will" (Ps. 40:7–8). "Where He placed His soul as sacrifice, He will see a seed" (Isa. 53:10). "This commandment I have received from the Father, that I may lay down My life" (John 10:17–18). "He was born from a woman, born under the law (γενόμενος ὑπὸ νόμον)" (Gal. 4:4). Therefore, everywhere Christ comes in the name of advocate and guarantor (ἐγτύου καὶ παρακλήτου) by guaranteeing and promising for another, who receives Him in his faith (Job 33:23; Isa. 38:14; Jer. 30:21; Heb. 7:22). This Sponsor is at the same time called "Mediator" (1 Tim. 2:5; Heb. 8:6), "Testator" (Heb. 9:15, 16), "High Priest" (Heb. 7:26), "Vindicator" (Job 19:25; Heb. 2:16), and so on.[4]

V. The Demand of the Son

The *demand* of the same Son follows the promise. For as God the Father demanded payment from the Son and promised inheritance for paying, so the Son by promising and furnishing it acquired the right to claim an inheritance, the church, a people of His own possession. "Demand from Me, and I will give You the nations as Your inheritance and the ends of the earth as Your possession" (Ps. 2:8). "Surely My judgment is before the Lord, and My works (פעלתי) are a price before My God" (Isa. 49:4). For the promise and obedience of the Son had reason of true merit, even from condignity, for which nothing could be lacking.[5]

VI. The Duty of Man in the Covenant of Grace

In the covenant of grace between God and man, God stipulated from man not perfect obedience to the law but *faith* in the Mediator and *repentance*. Through the former the sinner is grafted to Christ the Mediator, and through the latter he is transferred from false righteousness to a true and good way of life. "Repent and believe in the gospel" (Mark 1:15). For in that covenant, righteousness and life of the sinner is exacted, not from the sinner but from Christ, and this could be seized by faith alone, not by legal obedience. Therefore, only that together with its fruits was able to be commanded as a condition of the covenant.[6]

VII. The Promise of the Covenant of Grace

The *promise* in the covenant of grace belongs to the final good sprout, which is eternal life, and the intermediate one, which is the righteousness of Christ, the

4. *Medulla*, VII–XIV.
5. *Medulla*, XIV.
6. *Medulla*, XVI, XVII.

cause of life. For it is necessary that He save by the righteous requirement of the law (δικαίωμα τοῦ νόμου).[7]

VIII. Which Is Testamentary

This covenantal promise holds reason of testament (διαθήκης), which is *the free disposition of God the Savior about the inheritance of righteousness and heavenly life for those named from certain heirs according to voluntary generation, to be taken possession of without danger of alienation.* It differs from the covenant of grace because it is the cause of the latter and the mere disposition whereby what is commanded in the covenant is awarded to those named heirs. Indeed, it comes in the name either of ברית or διαθήκης because covenant flows from testament, and in respect to the promise it has an implicit testament. Such ratification (κύρωσις) belongs to the covenant of grace, which belongs to the testament.[8]

IX. The Agreement of the Covenant of Grace: Counter-Obligation

The *agreement* (*astipulatio*) of the covenant of grace is that *whereby man consents to God who requires faith and repentance, believes, and repents from his dead works.* This is called "subjection to agreement (ὑποταγὴ ὁμολογίας)" (2 Cor. 9:13). *Counter-obligation* (*restipulatio*) springs from this whereby *the one believing and repenting takes possession of the God of the promised reward and faithfully expects it from Him.* This is that authority (ἐξουσία) of those who believe which "God gives to them, that they might become sons of God" (John 1:12). It is also "interrogation of a good conscience toward God" (1 Peter 3:21) whereby the one who believes and is united to God through faith asks, "Have You not, Jehovah, God our Father, redeemed us, and You are our Maker and the work of Your hands are over us all? Please repent, for we are Your people" (Isa. 64:8, 9).[9]

X. The Covenant of Grace Is Not Universal

Not all people, but only certain persons, are elected into the covenant of grace. This proves all the actions of the covenant because God does not guarantee faith to all but "to those ordained for life" from eternity (Acts 13:48). He also promises life to those "who believe" alone (Acts 10:43), and only the elect believe (Titus 1:1). Moreover, Christ served as Sponsor for those given to Him alone, who also trust only in the God who promises, and expect salvation from Him.[10]

---

7. *Medulla*, XVIII.
8. *Medulla*, XIX, XX.
9. *Medulla*, XXI–XXIV.
10. *Medulla*, XXIV, XXV.

XI. The Sanction of the Covenant of Grace

The sanction of the covenant of grace is carried out in the pact between God the Father and the Son, the death of the Testator, with oath and description of judgment against unbelievers.[11]

XII. And Confirmation through the Sacraments, Which Are Not Bare Tokens of Duty

The *confirmation* of the same happens through *sacraments*, which are *signs and seals instituted by God in which the promise of the gospel about Christ or the covenant of grace between God and men, initiated by the Mediator Himself, is declared, applied, and sealed to all covenanted in sealed form.* Hence, these portray the very covenant of grace, as on a certain tablet, graphically and pictorially (εἰκονικῶς), according to all its actions. They are not bare tokens of duty but are even seals of the promise and foundations of legitimate use in expecting salvation. For the covenant of grace includes all the latter, of which the former are seals.[12]

XIII. They Come from Elements through the Word of God

The sacraments come from elements through the Word of God. "He purified us with the washing of water in the Word" (Eph. 5:26). For the Word is added to the element, and it becomes a sacrament. This word is the institution of Christ whereby He substituted the earthly, bodily, and visible thing for the spiritual, heavenly, and invisible thing, as a vicarious seal and pledge. He also delivered it to be used as a perpetual sign and seal. There are two parts of this word: command, defining the unjustified taking of the sacrament, and promise, declaring its use and efficacy.[13]

XIV. Their Dispensation through Ministers; Their Intention

The dispensation of the sacrament is through ministers of the Word. "Thus let man repute us as ministers and dispensers of the mysteries of God" (1 Cor. 4:1). It belongs to them in this ministry to profess and declare that they cling to the precept of Christ, the author of the sacrament, and that they faithfully wish to discharge them. But their intention is not required for the efficacy of the sacrament, because it depends on Christ alone, offering grace through the Word and sealing it through the sacrament.[14]

11. *Medulla*, XXVI.
12. *Medulla*, XXVII–XXX.
13. *Medulla*, XXX.
14. *Medulla*, XXXI.

XV. The Changing of the Elements

The Word added to the sacrament effects *change* of the elements, not in regard to substance but in regard to relation, which has great power from the institution of Christ to signify, seal, and display grace in legitimate use. Hence also that change effects union between the sign and the thing signified, neither natural nor supernatural, as of parts locally united. But it effects merely what is relative (χελικὴν) because sacramental union is of the same sort as the sacrament. But the sacrament is merely relative, as its formal reason consists in the relation of the sign to the thing signified.[15]

XVI. They Are Not Bare Signs nor Miracles nor Remedies

Nevertheless, the sacraments are not *bare signs*, because they powerfully seal the thing signified and display it in legitimate use. They make pledges absolutely, like letters, tablets, seals, and pledges do. The sacraments are also not *miracles*, because they have nothing uncommon, although there is supernatural signification. They are also not *remedies*, because they have no power, except of signing and sealing. Finally, they are not *causes* of grace, because they are seals of grace and therefore do not effect grace but seal the effect.[16]

XVII. Sacramental Phraseology: Figurative

The sealing of the covenant of grace through the sacraments depends on the truth of the divine promise and the substitution of the sign for the thing signified. This itself, on account of the constancy of the Word of God, is also constant and infallible. Hence it happened that the names of the signs and things signified were repeatedly changed among themselves in the Scriptures, and one was called another. Hence sacramental phraseology in the Scriptures is found to be twofold: one is improper and another is proper and figurative. The latter is more frequent than the former and is twofold: there is one in which the name of the thing signified is attributed to the sign, through metonymy of *the subject*, and another in which the name of the sign is attributed to the thing signified through metonymy of the composite.[17]

XVIII. The End of the Sacraments: Necessity

The chief end of the sacraments is the declaration and seal of the covenant of grace in regard to its stipulation, promise, and remaining acts. The secondary ends are the profession of faith and hope, contract of friendship around the signs of external communion, preservation in the church of the article of faith

---

15. *Medulla*, XXXII.
16. *Medulla*, XXXIII.
17. *Medulla*, XXXIV–XXXVII.

about the death of Christ, and the whole propagation of Christian doctrine. For that reason, there is no necessity of the covenant of grace. For without the *testament* and covenant of grace, there is no "hope in the world" and one lives "without God" (Eph. 2:12). Although the sacraments are of great use, they are not nevertheless absolute and pregnant to the point that those who are deprived of them without their fault perish. For God does not resign His will and grace and our salvation, matters of great importance, to the earthly elements.[18]

XIX. The Application of the Covenant of Grace

The covenant of grace ought to be applied because it is the will of God that His promise may be seized by faith. That application consists in the external promulgation of the covenant and in the internal divine operations. *The external promulgation* is that *whereby it is declared and sealed in the covenanted in this life through the external word, not only of the command of faith and repentance, but also of the covenantal promise.* The word of *command is* "Believe in the Lord Jesus Christ, and you will be saved" (Acts 16:31). The word of *promise* is conditioned: "He reconciled you, if indeed you remain established and firm in the faith" (Col. 1:21, 23). In this conditioned axiom it ought to be applied to each person to indicate the nexus of benefit and duty and to establish confidence and consolation. The internal divine operations in this life are calling, justification, and sanctification of the predestined, and glorification in another life.[19]

XX. The Unity of the Covenant of Grace

The covenant of grace is perpetually and immutably one in matter and substance, which shows all the parties and acts of the covenant of grace. It shows the parties, which hence from the beginning until the end of the same church, God having been offended, man offending, and the Mediator, Jesus Christ, "the same yesterday, today, and forever" (Heb. 13:8). In His "grace" the fathers were "saved" (Acts 15:11). It shows the *acts* because always, even in the Old Testament, He *commanded by stipulating* faith and *repentance* to those to be saved. Even the fathers of the Old Testament believed, as Abraham, to whom "faith was imputed for righteousness" (Gen. 15:6), and the remaining patriarchs, whose faith is preached (Heb. 11:4, etc.). This was faith in Christ, as it is said of this that Moses carried "opprobrium" (Heb. 11:26). He also always *promised* and displayed righteousness and life in Christ. Indeed, "He would crush the head of the serpent" (Gen. 3:15), sealing "adoption" because they were "sons of God" (Gen. 3:15; 6:2; Ex. 4:22), "remission of sins" (Gen. 15:6; Ps. 32:2, 5), "eternal

18. *Medulla*, XXXVII, XXXVIII.
19. *Medulla*, XXXIX–XLII.

life" because God was the "God of Abraham, Isaac, and Jacob" (Ex. 3:6), and "lead them into glory" (Heb. 2:10).[20]

XXI. The Agreement and Opposition between the Covenant of Grace and Works

There is a twofold relation between the covenant of grace and of works: there is one of agreement and another of opposition. There is one of *agreement* because God is the same author of both. The same condition of life, the righteousness of works, must be furnished by man in the earlier one and was furnished by Christ in the later one. It is the same life, eternal and heavenly. There is one of *opposition* because the covenant of grace admitted a Mediator, which the covenant of works lacked. In the covenant of works, righteousness was commanded. In the covenant of grace, it was furnished by Christ. In the former, man was obligated to be justified by works, and in the latter by faith. In the former, law is preached, and in the latter, gospel.[21]

20. *Medulla*, XLII–XLVIII.
21. *Medulla*, XLVIII.

LOCUS XII

On the Economy of the Covenant of Grace under the Patriarchs

I. Diversity of Economy

The covenant of grace is one in regard to substance, diverse in regard to economy, before Christ and after Him. For "testimony" about Christ had proper times (ἰδίους καιροὺς) (1 Tim. 2:6). There was one economy before Christ, from the beginning of the promise (Gen. 3:15) until "the time determined in advance" (Dan. 11:27), and another "of the fullness of times" (Eph. 1:10) under Christ. Moreover, before Christ there was one economy under the patriarchs that ran down to Moses. It was a little bit more free, the sort for infants. There was another economy under Moses until Christ. It was more servile, the sort for children growing into adolescence.[1]

II. The Foundation of the Economy of the Covenant of Grace under the Patriarchs

The origin and foundation of the economy of the covenant of grace *under the patriarchs* is the first promise: "I will place enmity between you and the woman, and between your seed and her seed. The former will crush your head, and you will crush its heel" (Gen. 3:15). The special heads of this promise are that, after sin, friendship with God and enmity with Satan will be renewed through the special grace of God and righteousness of the Sponsor. Moreover, the Sponsor will be the seed of the woman, will suffer death, and will be grasped by faith alone. There are many things that constitute those heads.[2]

1. *Medulla*, I.
2. *Medulla*, II–VI.

III. The Faith of the Patriarchs Held in the Promise: Adam, Eve, Abel, Enoch, Lamech, Noah

The patriarchs were confirmed in this promise through faith. For *Adam*, having heard it, changed the name of the woman into the name of Eve (חוה) because she "became mother of all the living" (Gen. 3:20). *Eve*, begetting Cain, said, "I have acquired man the Lord" (Gen. 4:1). *Abel* "by faith offered a more excellent victim" (Heb. 11:4). Seth having been born, she said, "He established for me another seed for Abel" (Gen. 4:25). *Enoch* "walked with God" (Gen. 5:24). *Lamech* placed the name of Noah (נוח) upon his son, on account of the hoped for "consolation from works" (Gen. 5:29). Finally, *Noah*, a man "righteous and perfect in his generations, walked with God" (Gen. 6:9). God fixed a covenant with him, in which notable signs of his faith in the seed of the woman granted the preservation of the world on account of the seed of the woman, Christ, and the church (Gen. 9:9–10, etc.).[3]

IV. Of Abraham, the Covenant Made with Him; Of Jacob

Above all, there was conspicuous faith in the seed of the woman in Abraham, Isaac, and Jacob. For God professed Himself "their God" (Ex. 3:6). He also made a covenant with Abraham in which it was stipulated by Him that "he would go out from the house of his father" (Gen. 12:1), "would not fear" (Gen. 15:1), and "would walk with God and be pure" (Gen. 17:1). Moreover, He promised *principally* to the same that "in Him" or "His seed" (Christ) (Gal. 3:16) "all nations would be blessed" (Gen. 12:3; 18:18; 22:18). He promised *secondarily* to him that his "seed," above all spiritual, "would be multiplied" (Gen. 12:2; 13:16; 15:5; 17:2, 6; 22:17), to him and his seed "the land of Canaan would be given" (Gen. 12:7; 17:8), and his seed would be set free from bondage to Egypt (Gen. 15:13, etc.). He was confirmed in these promises by faith. "Having been called, he obeyed in faith" (Heb. 11:8–9), and "he believed" (Gen. 15:6). *Jacob* also bore witness to his faith, predicting with the illustrious prophecy "the advent of Shiloh from the tribe of Judah, whom the people will obey" (Gen. 49:8–10).[4]

V. Of Melchizedek, Job, Elihu, Jethro

The promise made to the patriarchs was also advanced outside their families. For Melchizedek was "King in Salem, Priest of the Most High God" (Gen. 14:18). He was "compared" to Christ (Heb. 7:3). Likewise, *Job* of Uz offered sacrifices and his faith in Goel (*Goëlem*) (Job 19:25), as Elihu also clearly bore witness to his faith in the "Messenger, Advocate, and Redeemer" (Job 33:23–24). Finally,

---

3. *Medulla*, VI, VII.
4. *Medulla*, XIII–XVI.

Jethro also offered sacrifices to God, while those came near with Aaron and all the priests of the people "to eat the bread together" with the same (Ex. 18:12).[5]

VI. The Proclamation of the Word under the Patriarchs

The external worship of the patriarchs was conspicuous in the proclamation of the word of promise and the offering of sacrifices. In propagating the proclamation of the Word, their visible piety and longevity, the institution of public assemblies, frequency of revelations, and institution of sacrifices served their interests. Abraham "commanded anew that" his sons and those of "his" house "after him observe the ways of Jehovah" (Gen. 18:19). "In the time of Enosh there began invocation in the name of the Lord" (Gen. 4:26) because "the sons of God," the Sethites, were separated from the Canaanites (Gen. 6:2).[6]

VII. Prophecy

Revelation under the patriarchs was made twofold, private or public. The *public* came to pass in the servants of the Lord in matters of great importance. Those also came in the name of prophets (נביאים). This word authenticated those who rightly perceived the will of God, and to that degree they spoke not their own but God's Word, as the mouth and echo of God, or as the pen in God's writing. There were various modes of this prophetic institution. Nevertheless, all were moved by the Holy Spirit either to speak or to write. Prophecy also had certain marks, from which it was divine. They themselves knew this and persuaded others of it. Divine revelation is known from internal persuasion, the species of the divine majesty, and in the wisdom and holiness of the things revealed. Moreover, others could be persuaded through signs from the prophets, whether in things proclaimed about them, in proofs of mission, or in the event of predictions.[7]

VIII. The Patriarchal Prophets

The patriarchs were also prophets in the same manner. "The seventh from Adam, Enoch, prophesied" (Jude 14–15). Lamech also, imposing his son's name on him, carried on as prophet. Memorable above all is the prophecy of Noah (Gen. 9:26, 28). Moreover, Abraham is distinctly called a prophet (נביא) (Gen. 20:7). Also, all of his death blessings, as well as those of Isaac and Jacob, were prophetic.[8]

5. *Medulla*, XVI.
6. *Medulla*, XVII.
7. *Medulla*, XVIII–XXIII.
8. *Medulla*, XXIII.

IX. The Sacrifices of the Patriarchs

Sacrifices were part of the external worship of the patriarchs. These were also divinely *instituted* because nature does not dictate to offer to God for sin above all, and faith teaches all things to be subject to the dominion of man, the tree of knowledge excepted. They were offered by the patriarchs *in faith* because Abel "offered in faith" (Heb. 11:4), and "without faith it is impossible to please God" (Heb. 11:6). For the patriarchs' sacrifices to God were nevertheless pleasing because He had respect (ישׁוע) for the sacrifice of Abel (Gen. 4:4). But the faith of those sacrificing was demonstrated in the promise of the seed of the woman. Moreover, pleasing sacrifices were offered more freely under the patriarchs. For before the law of Moses, God defined neither a place, nor time, nor persons for which certain sacrifices were to be offered.[9]

X. The Prohibition of Blood

After the flood, He added a prohibition *of blood* to the sacrifices: "You shall not eat the flesh with the soul" or "its life, in its blood" (Gen. 9:4). The reason of the prohibition was ceremonial because "blood" was to be given "over the altar" to "expiate souls" (Lev. 17:10, etc.). Therefore, it was consecrated to God, bearing the exchange of the soul. The sinful body was also equally obligated to be expiated and to be redeemed by Christ at some time. It pleased Him to prefigure the expiation of the blood through the sacrificing of the body and the destruction of the beast. But the expiation of the soul through devotion of the blood, in which is movement of spirits, comes in the name of soul (נפשׁ).[10]

XI. The Sacraments of the Patriarchs: The Rainbow

There were two sacraments of the economy of the covenant under the patriarchs: the rainbow and circumcision. God said to Noah concerning the *rainbow*, "This is a sign of the covenant between Me and you." "I give My rainbow in the cloud, and it will be a sign of the covenant between Me and the earth. When the rainbow is observed, I will remember My covenant, and there will no longer be waters for the flood" (Gen. 9:9–17). Therefore, it was a sign of preserving the earth and likewise the church through the blessed seed of the woman. "This is the water of Noah to Me. I have sworn that I will no longer be angry against you" (Isa. 54:9–10). There is analogy in the wonder between the rainbow and the covenant of grace initiated in Christ.[11]

9. *Medulla*, XXIV–XXVII.
10. *Medulla*, XXVII.
11. *Medulla*, XXVIII.

XII. And Circumcision

Circumcision was *the sacrament of the covenant with Abraham and his initiated seed, in which election to the covenant of grace was sealed in the cutting off of the foreskin in the males. The cutting off of sins through the blood and Spirit of Christ to come was adumbrated in the same.* Its institution exists in Genesis 17:11–15. The whole served the interests of signifying and sealing the covenant initiated with Abraham by God, as the sign of the covenant (אות הברית) (Gen. 17:10). Since that covenant continued the promise of grace, the righteousness and life of the sinner, circumcision of the flesh was required to signify and seal the same, as "circumcision of the heart" (Deut. 10:16) "not made by hand" (Col. 2:11, etc.). "We are the circumcision, who worship God in Spirit, boast in Jesus Christ, and do not trust in the flesh" (Phil. 3:3). The foreskin of the flesh was the old man. Its cutting off was the abolition of the old man and regeneration through the blood of Christ.[12]

XIII. Its Abolishment

Circumcision did not have the same eternal duration as the covenant of grace. For it pertained to the generations (דורות) of Abraham and "of his seed after him" (Gen. 17:9), as long as the generation from Abraham was making a peculiar people, separate from others, and rejoicing in their own power. After that time of expectation, "circumcision avails nothing in Christ, nor the foreskin, but faith working through love" (Gal. 5:6; 6:15).[13]

XIV. The Patriarchs Were Types

Among the patriarchs were several notable *types* of Christ. For example, *Abel*, believing and righteous, suffered death (Gen. 4:5, 8). *Enoch* was taken up into heaven (Gen. 5:24; Heb. 11:5). *Noah* was "comforter from works" (Gen. 5:29) and above all under the "flood and ark of Noah" (Isa. 54:9; 1 Peter 3:20, 21). *Melchizedek* was that "King of righteousness and peace." He was "compared to the Son of God" (Heb. 7:2–3). *Isaac*, who, "in the likeness of Christ," was "received" living from the dead (Heb. 11:19). *Joseph*, thrown into the pit, was delivered from there and made preserver of the paternal family and of Egypt (Gen. 37:28, etc.).[14]

---

12. *Medulla*, XXIX, XXX.
13. *Medulla*, XXXI.
14. *Medulla*, XXXII.

LOCUS XIII

On the Economy of the Covenant of Grace under the Law of Moses

I. The Economy of the Covenant of Grace under Moses: Its Parties

The covenant of grace under the patriarchs, a little freer, changed its face under Moses because of the servitude introduced. In it the parties contracting were "God," as "Savior of the people" (Ex. 15:26), and the "people of Israel," separated from the rest of the peoples and made a peculiar people (סגלה) of God "before all the nations" (Ex. 19:3–6). The latter were for the present "without Christ, alienated from the body-politic of Israel, not having hope, and without God in the world" (Eph. 2:12). Christ was the true *Mediator*, the "Messenger of the face of God" (Isa. 63:9), but Moses was typical, in whose "hand," as mediator (μεσίτου), "the law was ordained through angels" (Gal. 3:19, 2; 2 Chron. 34:14).[1]

II. The Life of Moses

The life of Moses was both private and public. It was *private* for forty years in which, delivered by the midwives and adopted by the daughter of Pharaoh, he crossed over into the royal hall of Pharaoh. And these forty years, advising with flight on account of Egyptian beating, he, tied to the family of Jethro, went across into Midian (Ex. 2:2, etc.). His life was *public* for the remaining forty years when, called by Him who inhabited the bush, he acted as redeemer of the people, king and leader of the people, and prophet.[2]

III. The Law-Giving of the Covenant: Its Twofold Requirement (χέσις)

In the covenant that God made with the people of Israel from Mount Sinai, God stipulated the *law* from the people. He did so first immediately in the ten words promulgated (Ex. 20:1–18). He did so second mediately, from the darkness of the mountain and from the constructed tabernacle, through Moses as a

1. *Medulla*, I–V.
2. *Medulla*, V.

mediator (Ex. 20:21, etc.). This law was distinct from the mere law of faith and is called law because it had something legal mixed that, flowing from the covenant of works, led to Christ. The requirement (χέσις) of that law was twofold: it was *legal* in the *open*, first in the approach and the skin of the words, which by itself was nothing except the *letter*, and *evangelical* in secret, in a hidden and interior sense and kernel of the thing, which was also the promise and Christ, "the end of the law" (Rom. 10:4). For the Decalogue had both strictures of grace and the whole laws in that the terms agreed on were "shadows of things to come, but the body belongs to Christ" (Col. 2:17).[3]

IV. The Cause of Introducing the Law: The Legal and Evangelical Face

The cause of introducing the law was transgressions. "The law was added on account of transgressions, until the seed would come, to which it was promised" (Gal. 3:19). The apostle distinguished the legal and evangelical face of the same (Rom. 10:3, etc.). He distinguished the legal face in these words, "Moses describes the righteousness which is from the law, that the man who does these things shall live in them" (v. 5). He distinguished the *evangelical* face in these words, "Christ is the end of the law for righteousness to everyone who believes. For righteousness from faith speaks in this way: 'Do not say in your heart, who will ascend into heaven?' This is to bring Christ down" (v. 4, 6, etc.). Therefore, its use was double. One use was in regard to the *carnal* Israelites, who were condemned through legal sentences and carnal precepts, as it were with a veil covering their eyes, "lest they could regard the glory of the Lord with a veiled face" as "in a mirror" (2 Cor. 3:15, 18). They were blind and departed from the true sense of the law. The other use was in regard to the *faithful* Israelites, in whom the law with the help of the promise "was a school master for Christ, that they may be justified by faith" (Gal. 3:24). Therefore, the principal stipulation of the Sinaitic covenant was faith and repentance. The proper accessory to that economy was the introduction of the law.[4]

V. The Promise of the Sinaitic Covenant: It Was a Typical Testament

Both the stipulation and the *promise* of the Sinaitic covenant were principal and accessory. The *principal* was of grace, righteousness, and life in Christ. "I am Jehovah, your God" (Ex. 20:2, 5, 7, 10, 12). The *accessory* was of the inheritance of the land of Canaan, as "the inheritance of the Lord" (1 Sam. 26:19; Isa. 47:6), "the land of the Lord" (Hos. 9:3), "the dwelling place of holiness" (Ex. 15:13). For it was a pledge both of revealing Christ in the land and of taking possession of heaven after death. And that promise had the method of "testament," but

3. *Medulla*, VI–XI.
4. *Medulla*, XI–XV.

typically, because it was dedicated by Moses in typical "blood" (Ex. 24:8; Heb. 9:19), he wrote. The heirs of the land of Canaan, with the hope of the true inheritance through Christ, were all in it who would subject themselves to the law of Moses.[5]

VI. The Confirmation of the Same and Restipulation

The confirmation for the Sinaitic covenant was testified by the people in these words: "Whatever Jehovah has spoken we shall do" (Ex. 19:8). These words of homage having appeared, Moses immediately returned to God. But God promised grace to many, distributed on account of hard-heartedness (σκληρακαρδίαν) known to Him. Yet to some He clearly referred the law to Christ, saying, "Who will give this heart among them, that they may fear Me?" (Deut. 5:29). He thereby showed that He alone could give the heart and wished to give it to some. Those became sharers of the promise in the law, as school master for Christ, not by any right of merit or legal obedience and deeds, but by faith alone in the promise held.[6]

VII. The Promulgation of the Covenant Was Made through Moses, the High Priest, and Prophets

The promulgation of the Sinaitic covenant was made through revelation of the Word of God. Its ministers and heralds were Moses, the high priest, and extraordinary prophets. *Moses*, "faithful in the whole house of God, spoke with God mouth to mouth, in appearance, not through enigmas." That is to say, he spoke before His face, without an intermediary, as friend and familiarly (Num. 12:6, 7, 8). The "appearance of God" had been seen, or the ray of divine splendor (Num. 12:8), not in regard to "the face," but "the back side," and it was also a symbol of Christ (Ex. 33:20, 23). He also published the canon of all prophecy. The *high priest* received the oracles of God through Urim and Thummim (Num. 27:21), while God attested that "He is near to His people" (Deut. 4:7). He also attested that the true light (אור), Christ, was to be expected (John 1:4, 5), and true perfection (תמים), in which Christ, loving even His enemies, wished to die for them (Matt. 5:44; Rom. 5:10). The *prophets* above all flourished in great number under the legal economy, and of all of them their "Spirit was the testimony of Jesus" (Rev. 19:10).[7]

5. *Medulla*, XV–XIX.
6. *Medulla*, XIX–XXII.
7. *Medulla*, XXII–XXVI.

VIII. Legal Types

This economy above all was pregnant with *types*. "All these were produced as types for them" (1 Cor. 10:11). "The priests, figures, and shadows of heavenly things were of service" (Heb. 8:5). "The law had shadow of goods to come, not the very image of the things" (Heb. 10:1). These types were either merely *apparent* things, appearances displayed to the prophets, or *real*, manifesting in the thing something even in spiritual history.[8]

IX. Sacraments of the Legal Economy: Passover

The more dignified legal types came in the name of *sacraments*, which were either ordinary or extraordinary. The former were circumcision and Passover. About *circumcision*, see above. *Passover* was *a sacrament of the Old Testament in which the liberation of mature Israel, yet especially redemption through Christ as a victim, and its communion, was signed and sealed in the sacrificing of and eating the lamb.* For concerning the blood of the offered lamb sprinkled on the houses He says, "It will be the blood for you as a sign in the houses in which you were. And when I see the blood I will pass over you (פסחתי), and there will be no plague for death among you when I strike the firstborn in Egypt" (Ex. 12:13). That sign was paschal blood in type. In anti-type or in the truth of the thing, it was Jesus Christ, His Spirit and faith, which, having been found in man by the saving God, moves him to be spared and saved. For Christ is called "the Passover" (1 Peter 1:19; Rev. 5:6, 8), "the Lamb who takes away the sin of the world" (John 1:29). Moreover, one or simple likeness cannot be shown between the paschal lamb and Christ.[9]

X. Baptism through the Waters in the Clouds and Sea; Feast from Manna; Agreement of These with the Sacraments of the New Testament

Saint Paul commemorates the extraordinary sacraments in 1 Corinthians 10:1–5. He commemorates "baptism through the clouds and waters of the sea," in which divine protection in the heat of day and trouble of the journey, as well as the redemption of a people having a type of spiritual redemption and liberation from afflictions that crossed over through death to life, was put in a figure. There was also sacred feast, existing from "manna" (Ex. 16:31), which was *spiritual food* on account of the signification of Christ, who is called the bread of life from heaven to come (John 6:48–50). The sacred feast also existed "from the waters from the rock" as for drink (Ex. 17:1–6; Num. 20:2–11), which "rock" was "Christ" (1 Cor. 10:4). From His side "blood and water flowed" (John 19:34), from which "the one who drinks will not thirst for eternity" (John 4:13). The "bronze

8. *Medulla*, XXVI, XXVII.
9. *Medulla*, XXVIII–XXXIII.

serpent" is added to these, opposed to the fiery serpents. Anyone who looked at the bronze one was healed from the poisonous bite of the latter (Num. 21:8–9). Christ Himself made this a sign of Christ exalted on the cross (John 3:14–15). From these is known the agreement of the sacraments of the Old Testament with the sacraments of the New Testament in regard to the thing signified beyond. Yet they differ in the consummation (τελειῶσιν) of the thing signified.[10]

XI. The Sinaitic Covenant Was of Grace, Not the Covenant of Works: The Economy Alone Was Singularly Distinct from It

It is also clear from these things that have been said that the Sinaitic covenant was the covenant of grace, not of works. For the parties contracting were the same in the covenant of grace: the same principal Mediator; the true Christ; the Messenger of the Covenant; the same sanction through the *blood of the testament*, which was a type of the blood of Christ; and the same evangelical promises. But yet the legal economy had a mixture of the covenant of grace and of derived legal servitude, and thus it differed from the promise before the law and from the gospel after the law.[11]

XII. The Abolishment of the Legal Economy

That economy of the Sinaitic covenant, according to the prediction of God (Jer. 31:31, etc.) and the prefiguring of Moses, the tablets of the law not without a sign of breaking through, was required to be changed and abolished. In this way the advent of Christ abolished it from law (de jure), the sacrifice of Christ having been offered. He also abolished it from deed (de facto) through the preaching of the apostles and the most recent overthrowing of the city, the body-politic, the temple and Levitical worship, in which the land, before holy in which God had "fire and furnace" (Isa. 31:9), was "stricken with a curse" (Mal. 4:6).[12]

---

10. *Medulla*, XXXIII–XXXIX.
11. *Medulla*, XXXIX–XL.
12. *Medulla*, XLI.

LOCUS XIV

On the Decalogue

I. The Difference of the Mosaic Laws: The Decalogue

Some Mosaic laws are moral, others positive. The *former* inform perpetual and immutable customs or duties of men toward God, themselves, and neighbor. The *latter* flowed from the instituted and free imposition of God and were either ceremonial or judicial. The former drew tight in *the Decalogue in few* words, mostly *negatively* rather than affirmatively because the prohibitions were stronger than the commands. They were directed to *each and every one* and for *the future*, authenticated by God Himself.[1]

II. Its Epitome Is Love

Love marks each page of the Decalogue. "Hear, O Israel. Jehovah, our God," Jehovah, "is one. Therefore, love Jehovah your God with your whole heart and with your whole soul" (Deut. 6:4–5). Christ calls that command of the love of God the "first and greatest command," as that other, "Love your neighbor as yourself," He calls "the second, like that," the prior. For the one who loves his neighbor, a thing of God, also to that degree loves God Himself (Matt. 22:36, etc.). Hence, Paul affirms that the whole law is recapitulated in this word: "Love your neighbor as yourself" (Rom. 13:9).[2]

III. Love of God; Love of Neighbor, Even of One's Enemy

God ought "to be loved from the whole heart, soul, and strength (uncorrupted)" (Deut. 6:5). Next to God, one's neighbor ought to be loved, even an *enemy*, because he does not cease to be a neighbor (רע) or of the common pasture (σύαπτος), born from the same "one blood" (Acts 17:26). The law, forbidding "to speak false witness against one's neighbor and to covet the house and wife of

1. *Medulla*, I, II.
2. *Medulla*, III.

one's neighbor" (Ex. 20:16–17), speaks not about one's neighbor as friend alone, but also as enemy. The *love of one's self* establishes the rule of love of one's neighbor. "Love your neighbor as yourself" (Lev. 19:18). For there is a certain licit love of ourselves in which we so love ourselves that we do not hurt but profit ourselves. We are devoted to exist for the glory of God and to promote our salvation. But yet the law commands not equality of love of our neighbor and ourselves, but likeness, consisting in what wishes true goods for ourselves and our neighbor, and procures them for their strength. But yet the order of love is certain: we love God above all, and the love of ourselves is prior to love of neighbor by nature, posterior by dignity, yet both are equal in degree and intention.[3]

IV. The Tables of the Decalogue and Division

The two *tables* of the Decalogue are the ten *words*. There are four *words* of the first table *about not having other gods, not making images, not taking the name of God in vain, and sanctifying the Sabbath.* These pertain to the love of God. The remaining six are of the second, pertaining to love of neighbor. Indeed, the commands *about not having other gods* and *not making images* must not be joined together, because they are different, as the thing and manner of the thing differ and can be violated separately. Nor should the commands *about not coveting the wife* and *not coveting the house of one's neighbor* be divided, because one act of coveting about different objects is occupied.[4]

V. The First Commandment: Its Root and Branches

The first commandment, the prologue, "I am the Lord Your God," having been laid down in advance, forbade to have other gods (אלהים אחרים) "before the face of God" (Ex. 20:2–3). The *root* of this commandment is the denial of native corruption and the stipulation that we acknowledge God as our only God and strength, and love and fear Him. But its *branches* are *to have God*, to acknowledge Him, to love and trust Him, to hope in Him, to fear Him, to conduct oneself humbly before Him, to be sad on account of offense to the divine will, to be happy on account of goods brought together. It is also *to have* one God, not *another*, for whom we confess that one God belongs to Israel, to whom we give our *heart*, and whose "glory we move" (Ps. 106:20). *Finally, we must have the true* God, who is the God of Israel and has declared that He is our Lord God (יהוה אלהי) and is triune.[5]

3. *Medulla*, IV–XV.
4. *Medulla*, XV–XVIII.
5. *Medulla*, XVIII–XXIV.

VI. The Second Commandment

In the second commandment God forbade them "to make for themselves images (סל זתמזנה) and the likeness of those things which are from above in the heavens, and which are beneath in the earth, and which are in the waters under the earth. You shall not craft them," He said, "nor worship them" (Ex. 20:4–5). There the honor and worship, internal and external, natural and instituted, is commanded, and worship in a false appearance, worship of God in an image, and every type of worship of a false god is forbidden. For to have one true God, *to honor and worship* God's majesty and rectitude, humbly to admire and praise His benevolence, to give thanks to Him, *to adore* God, to pursue Him with humble worship of soul and body, and to worship (עבד) (θεραπούειν) Him are fitting to testify submission to Him although through external signs determined for the worship of God. These things of the commandment are the root as it were.[6]

VII. Honor Owed to God, the One True and One True Alone; Magic and Idolatry Opposed to It; Iconolatry; Species of Idolatry

The honor of God is twofold in species: one commanded is owed to Him as the *True One*, and the other as to the *Only True One*. "You shall worship the Lord your God and serve Him alone" (Matt. 4:10; Luke 4:8). Magic and idolatry are opposed to the latter. We have spoken about *magic* above. *Idolatry* is religious "worship" of any "creature" whatsoever "besides the Creator" (Rom. 1:25), through which the "jealous" God is provoked to jealousy or ambition for His name (Ex. 20:5). The law makes unfavorable mention of its better appearance, consisting in the religious worship of *something engraved* or an *image*, whether of true or false divine will, and of any creature, even holy. For "graven images" and their "likeness, which are in heaven, earth, and under the earth" are forbidden. But the true God and the saints are in heaven. Moreover, under the appearance of images of forbidden worship, of all of those things that by nature are not God, religious veneration is forbidden.[7]

VIII. The Third Commandment

The third commandment forbids "to take the name of God in vain (לשוא)" (Ex. 20:7). There the hallowing of the name of God is commanded in general, that such may be held and glorified as the sort that it is. And that is especially through honorific thought and speech about everything that signifies the name of God, through constant sincerity and truth everywhere in words and deeds for Him. For when man speaks he also does something as the image of God, and he ought to act and speak as professing his God. Holy conversation makes

6. *Medulla*, XXIV–XXX.
7. *Medulla*, XXX–XL.

for this (Matt. 5:16; Titus 2:10), as does the confession of Christ in the midst of cross (Rev. 2:13).[8]

IX. Oath: Its Laws and Form

The hallowing of the name of God is also in oath. "You will fear God and swear oath through His name" (Deut. 6:13; 10:20). God Himself confirms the use of swearing oath in His example, "swearing oath by Himself (בו)" (Gen. 22:16). The angel, also "standing in sea and on the earth, having lifted his hands to heaven, swore oath by the One who lives forever" (Rev. 10:5–6; cf. Dan. 12:7). For the "limit of contradiction" of oaths is "for confirmation" (Heb. 6:16). God Himself has determined its laws, "You shall swear oath: the Lord lives, in truth, judgment, and righteousness" (Jer. 4:2). But the external *form* of the same ought to be such that, in whatever words and rites it is furnished, it has this sense: in it God alone is invoked as witness and judge of words and deeds.[9]

X. The Use of the Lot

The use of *lot* is also referred to the hallowing of God's name. But a *lot* is *a petition of the divine testimony for a controversy concerning a merely contingent event to be determined*. Solomon wrote about this, "The lot is thrown into the lap, but its judgment is from Jehovah" (Prov. 16:33). Its use can also occur in the New Testament, not in consultation or divination, but in division when otherwise doubt cannot be removed concerning what is attributed and to whom in an inheritance, goods, honors, burdens, dangers, and so on.[10]

XI. Blasphemy: Its Species

The supreme apex of the profanation of God's name is in *blasphemy*. This is any assertion or insulting deed against God in which His perfection, majesty, and goodness are disparaged. These are various, positive or negative, direct or indirect, immediate or mediate, simple or affected.[11]

XII. The Sanction of the Commandment

The sanction of this commandment is in these words: "Jehovah will not hold him guiltless who takes His name in vain." If indeed he is blessed "to whom sin is remitted and not imputed" (Ps. 32:1–2), he is miserable whom God does not absolve and to whom He imputes sin.[12]

---

8. *Medulla*, XL, XLI.
9. *Medulla*, XLII–XLVIII.
10. *Medulla*, XLVIII.
11. *Medulla*, XLIX.
12. *Medulla*, L.

XIII. The Fourth Commandment

The fourth commandment commands "to keep holy the day of the Sabbath" (יום שבת). The *Sabbath* is rest from work. God commands "to keep holy" and be devoted to the time of that rest by keeping, worshiping, glorifying the holy things of the one true God, and hallowing His name with thoughts and cares. For the Sabbath is necessary to be performed for the Lord (ליהוה), for the grace of the honor and worship of the Lord (Ex. 20:8–11; 31:15). Hence, neither is all cessation commanded, nor that from any work that man takes up for the necessity of his life, but from servile work (מלאכה) (Lev. 23:7).[13]

XIV. The Species of the Sabbath

The species of the Sabbath are diverse. For it is either divine or human. The *divine* is either of creation or of redemption. It is *human* either before or after he obtained sin. *Before* sin God commanded that all time be sacred for Himself (Gen. 2:3). After sin it is moral, typical, or spiritual. It is *moral* whether *perpetual* (that is, the hallowing of all time for the love and worship of God) or *temporal* (that is, cessation from ordinary labors of this life, to be emptied for the public worship of God and attending to a certain and definite time). The freedom from ordinary works was *typical*, as for the impure, instituted by the command of God for every seventh day. It was to be kept most severely, under penalty of death, to signify the rest and consummation of the conscience of the faithful, brought forth by the death of Christ. Christ removed this in His advent. The thing is *spiritual* and properly *evangelical*, signified through the typical rest removed by Christ, and must be kept holy in this life by entering upon the heavenly through consummation. In the fourth commandment the *divine* is commemorated both in the thing *of creation* and in the anti-type *of redemption*. The *perpetual moral* is supposed. The *temporal* is contained under that which is moral and perpetual in that commandment. It is the sanctification of the certain time that the church, the apostles dictating, defined as the Lord's Day. The *typical* is expressed in the type of the freedom of the seventh day, and the *evangelical* is hinted at in the rest of the New Testament.[14]

XV. The Sanctification of the Sabbath Is Privative and Positive or Ascetic

The sanctification of the Sabbath, since it is moral and perpetual and is turned into the Lord's Day in the Christian church, is twofold, privative and positive or ascetic. It is *privative*, consisting in cessation from labors of ordinary vocation, that we may be freer to worship God. It is *positive* or *ascetic*, consisting in the solemn public and private worship of God, which is exercised at a stated time

---

13. *Medulla*, LI.
14. *Medulla*, LII, LIII.

in the congregation of the church and at home. It cannot be gathered very pure other than from the moral worship of the Sabbath day, which sort, having been secluded even in the Old Testament, was typical compared with the worship of God in the New Testament.[15]

XVI. The Fifth Commandment

In the fifth commandment "honor of father and mother," and under this species, of all superiors, is commanded (Ex. 20:12). This duty "of honoring" and, as it is held in Leviticus 19:3, "of fearing," consists in spirit, words, actions, and deeds in which the authority and power of the superiors is taken up.[16]

XVII. Devotion to the Reputation of Neighbor and Oneself

Devotion to the reputation of neighbor and oneself is referred to honor. For it is necessary to look after the opinion of others concerning our honored neighbor and his dignity, not to diminish but to cherish and to preserve by bearing witness to his virtues and even to one's own reputation and life as it were. "For it is better for me to die than that someone renders my boasting empty" (1 Cor. 9:15). The companion of devotion to one's own reputation is *humility* to which *pride* and *envy* or *jealousy*, "in rottenness of bones" (Prov. 14:30), are opposed. But *rash judgment* and *disparagement* are opposed to devotion to the reputation of one's neighbor.[17]

XVIII. Of Honoring Superiors: Obligation of Inferiors Is Determined

Some superiors *without authority* must be honored, such as elders, surpassing all in gifts of soul, body, and sex. Others *with authority* must be honored, put in charge with special calling to rule over others. Some of their duties are mutual, and virtues tied to the same are gratitude, fidelity, subjection, and obedience. But obligation of inferiors to superiors is limited. For "they must be obeyed in the Lord" (Eph. 6:1) and "by those who fear God" (Col. 3:22). Hence, obedience ought not to be blind and untested.[18]

XIX. Eminent Power—Private; Of the Husband, Parents, Masters—Public

Those who stand above with power are either private or public. The *private* are a husband in respect to his wife, parents in respect to their children, and masters in respect to their slaves. *Marital* power is mitigated in equality, *masterly* is

15. *Medulla*, LIV–LX.
16. *Medulla*, LX–LXIV.
17. *Medulla*, LXIV–LXVII.
18. *Medulla*, LXVII–LXX.

merely masterful, and *parental* is mixed as it were. The duties of all the former are mutual. Children above all cannot marry with unconsulted or unwilling parents, because parents "must be obeyed in all things" and are upright and sincere (Col. 3:20). Moreover, parents are commanded to marry their children (Jer. 29:6; 1 Cor. 7:38) and have the authority to rescind the vows of the children named for themselves in ignorance (Num. 30:5–6). The public are leaders of the state or of the church, about which we speak elsewhere.[19]

XX. The Sixth Commandment

The sixth commandment forbids "to kill" and commands *civility* (Ex. 20:13). For man is the image of God, and cannot perish without the will of God. Moreover, since "no one hates his own flesh" (Eph. 5:29), all men are one "flesh" and "one blood" (Acts 17:26).[20]

XXI. The Duties of Civility

The duties of civility or of man consider their own person or others outside themselves. For everybody is held to devote himself to spiritual and bodily duties. Suicide (αὐτοχειρία) especially wages war against this. "Diligently guard your souls" (Deut. 4:15). "No one hates his own flesh" (Eph. 5:29). God Himself joined the soul to the body, to be separated by no one (Matt. 19:6), and commanded the human race to "be fruitful and multiply" (Gen. 9:7). Finally, as the image of God, man is placed under the dominion of God alone. But everybody is also held to preserve the life of his *neighbor*. In this, internal and external duties pertain to him: *internal duties* consist in love of the heart, inclination, and affections, and *external duties* in external spiritual duties of actions, speech, and deeds.[21]

XXII. Homicide

Homicide is above all opposed to humanity *in deeds*. It is the unjust killing of man, which is accomplished without legitimate power, just cause, right order, and judgment. It is twofold: *casual* or *willful*. The former is committed unforeseen (בפתע), "without enmity" (Num. 35:22), while the *latter* is committed from the plan and deliberation of the will, through violence (בזדון) (Ex. 21:14).[22]

XXIII. The Limitation of the Commandment by Public Justice, Defense of Oneself, and War

The commandment about not killing takes a threefold limitation. The first is *by public justice*, which commands to punish the criminal (Gen. 9:6; Ex. 21:23). The

19. *Medulla*, LXX–LXXV.
20. *Medulla*, LXXV, LXXVI.
21. *Medulla*, LXXVII, LXXVIII.
22. *Medulla*, LXXIX.

second is *by the defense of oneself* or *management of blameless guardianship* in which it is lawful for anyone to protect oneself against an aggressor, even in private, if a judge could not be approached before the attack (Ex. 22:2). The third is *by war* in which it is allowed to kill enemies. Although the origin of this is from sin, it can nevertheless be just and legitimate because nature commends the preservation of oneself to all. Therefore, reason teaches us to preserve society for the safety of everyone, whether it happens through judgment or, it having been disturbed, by force. The voluntary divine right confirms this (Num. 10:9, 31, etc.; Joshua 1:6, etc.). Moreover, He bestowed expertise on His heroes of war (Ps. 144:1). Even John the Baptist admitted soldiers to baptism, and to those, having been baptized, seeking "what they should do," he responded, "Strike no one (violently) and be content with your wages" (Luke 3:14).[23]

XXIV. The Seventh Commandment: The State of Virgins, Widows, and the Married

In the seventh commandment *adultery* and in that species of impurity every kind of wantonness and impurity is forbidden, and *chastity* is commanded. Chastity is that virtue *in which the purity of the person is preserved in regard to those things that relate to generation.* It pertains to virgins, the married, and widows. This virtue is so moral that the state of virgins, the married, and widows is morally good and holy by itself, and indeed the state of the virgin and the widow is not more holy than the married. Yet for those who have the gift of continence, the virginal state is more profitable (συμφέρι) on account of necessity, affliction of the flesh, and suitability to serve the Lord (1 Cor. 7:26, 28, 34).[24]

XXV. Marriage; Difference of Blood; Indivisible Union; Divorce

The *marriage* of one man and woman, instituted by divine will, is indivisible union by lawful consent for communion of bodies, propagation of the human race, the society of life, and the sharing of duties for temporal and eternal life. The just difference of blood is required for *lawful consent.* Moses generally defines it in this way: "Let no one be added to the flesh of his own flesh (שאר בשרן), to reveal disgrace. I am Jehovah" (Lev. 18:6). The very lawful union of man and woman ought to be indivisible. For "man" ought to "cling to his wife" since they become "one flesh" (Gen. 2:24). Moreover, each should be among the "covenant of God" (Prov. 2:17). Nonetheless, there can be just causes for divorce: malicious desertion of the spouse (1 Cor. 7:15) and adultery (Deut. 24:1; Matt. 19:9).[25]

23. *Medulla*, LXXX–LXXXV.
24. *Medulla*, LXXXV–LXXXVIII.
25. *Medulla*, LXXXVIII–XCII.

XXVI. Wantonness: Interior, Exterior; Fornication; Adultery; Incest; Impurity against Nature

Wantonness, opposed to chastity, is illicit use of those things that pertain to generation. It is either interior or exterior. *Interior* wantonness is concupiscence of the soul and impure lust that is turned with lust to a foreign flesh, the burning of impure desire, impure thoughts, as well as ardor and fervor toward a foreign flesh. *Exterior* wantonness pours forth from the soul to the body, and affects not only those things that concern the body but also the body itself. Its notorious species include *fornication*, commingling of the unrestrained with the unrestrained. This comes in the name of *dishonor* if there is a violation of an upright lady placed under the guardianship of parents. It also includes *adultery*—that is, when a man unites with or strives after the wife *of another* or a wife after the husband *of another*. External wantonness also includes *incest*—that is, when the nearest blood is polluted with impure commingling. Finally, it includes *impurity against nature*, from which Saint Paul proves that men are inexcusable and by which he asserts that their idolatry must be punished (Rom. 1:24–25).[26]

XXVII. The Eighth Commandment: Ownership—Its Origin, Its Temperament

In the eighth commandment *theft* is forbidden, and tacitly justice and the charity that assigns itself to everyone in external commodities is commended (Ex. 20:15). This justice, to which the injustice of theft is opposed, concerns *mine* and *yours*, and to that extent the ownership of each person is established. But *ownership* or possession of a thing is that right in which the substance of something so pertains to someone that as a whole it does not pertain in the same manner to another. The origin of this is in the words of God: "Be fruitful and multiply, and fill the earth, subject it, and have dominion over it" (Gen. 1:28). This is diametrically opposed to the established sharing of goods. But yet the right of ownership ought to be received with a temperament of piety, extreme necessity, and harmless usefulness.[27]

XXVIII. Acquisition of the Same: Without Contract

Just ownership consists in acquisition and use. The cause of *acquisition* is *title*, which is opposed to one who doubts the justice of possession. Concerning it there are internal and external duties. The *internal duties* consist in no love of money or little love of it, self-sufficiency (αὐταρκείᾳ), management of lust for possessions, and moderate devotion and procurement of them with tranquil industry. The *external duties* consist in the lawful collection and anxious preservation

26. *Medulla*, XCII–XCVII.
27. *Medulla*, XCVII–CI.

of the same. They are lawfully compared in two manners: with contract or without contract.[28]

XXIX. Theft: Its Species; Robbery, Highway-Robbery

The species of unjust acquisition without contract are theft and robbery. *Theft is the fraudulent stealing of a foreign thing, against the will of the Lord*. Hence, the thief is said "to assume the name of God and to lay hands on His power and dominion" (Prov. 30:9). There are various species of it, especially *man-stealing* of persons, *embezzlement* of profane public things, and *robbery of sacred things. Robbery* is violent stealing of a foreign thing against the will of the Lord. It is simulated either in the species of law and lawful power, or it breathes open force in war or in peace. The most atrocious species of this is highway robbery, principally of nations against nations.[29]

XXX. The Acquisition of Goods by Contract, Trade, Lending, Mutual Agreement, Interest

The acquisition of goods is *with contract* when a contract intervenes. The particular species of this include *trade*, acquisition of goods from contract of buying and selling. It is generally infamous on account of abuse, yet it can be lawful. Another particular species is *lending*, whereby the ownership of the good, as a pledge, crosses over in a certain law from the possessor to the moneylender, in which the thing is *mutual* for each and can be engaged in common. It is given with the law that, after an interval, the same amount will be repayed in the same quantity and quality. It was not a crime for the Israelites to receive interest on account of certain reasons (Ex. 22:25) for this. In general, it is lawful to receive interest, if it is moderate, because it is just that someone may think of interest, who has thought of shared non-interest. Moreover, the Israelites could receive interest from foreigners (Deut. 23:19–20).[30]

XXXI. Use of Ownership: Mercy

The *use* of ownership ought to be just. It consists in the right enjoyment of possessions in regard to ourselves and in liberal sharing of them in regard to our neighbor. *Mercy* above all pertains to this. It is that pity and charity with which we suffer together with the wretched person and eagerly pour ourselves out to compensate for his defects. This also comes in the name of *justice* because it is a conspicuous "fruit of justice" and charity (Phil. 1:11).[31]

---

28. *Medulla*, CI–CIV.
29. *Medulla*, CIV–CVIII.
30. *Medulla*, CVIII–CXIII.
31. *Medulla*, CXIII–CXVI.

XXXII. The Ninth Commandment

In the ninth commandment the rule of the tongue is commanded. For in it we are forbidden "to speak false testimony against neighbor" (Ex. 20:16). In Leviticus 19:11 this transgression is called to deny falsely (כחש) and to lie to one's neighbor (שקר בעמיתן). For since the tongue is the witness of the mind, which lies and falsely denies, it is a false witness to its mind, and to that extent *it speaks false witness.*[32]

XXXIII. A Lie

The duty of the tongue consists in devotion to the truth, the method of which consists in the *sentence of speech and of the mind agreeing with the thing*, as the method of a lie in the contradiction of those things. For every lie, even if courteous and playful, is illicit. For as much as one lies he takes away knowledge of the truth, thrusts error into the hearer, and drives out the Holy Spirit, who is the "Spirit of truth" (John 16:13). It connects to the one who lies the error of thought and removes the truth of speech and trust from the one speaking truly. For it is not permitted "to gladden kings through malice and princes through lies" (Hos. 7:3). A lying tongue is an "abomination" to God (Prov. 6:17).[33]

XXXIV. Fidelity, Affability, Urbanity

Truth consists in a simple assertion or promise. The truthfulness of a promise prevails in *fidelity*, whereby we are constantly inclined to keep the trust granted. Useful (χρησὰ) speeches and words also help the truth. Above all is *affability* through which we communicate with others most pleasant (ἥδισα) words, actions, and mutual duties of life and our "speech is in grace and seasoned with salt" (Col. 4:6). Finally, *urbanity* is what preserves moderation in jokes and games.[34]

XXXV. Freedom of Speaking and Taciturnity

The temperament of speech consists in freedom of speaking and taciturnity. We use *freedom of speaking* in bold confession and defense by more freely asserting a rapid movement of speech. In *taciturnity* we so moderate the tongue for the sake of place, time, and persons that we say nothing immoderate, or are silent. "The prudent man will be silent" (Prov. 11:12). "Do not disclose the secret of another" (Prov. 25:9, 10).[35]

---

32. *Medulla*, CXVI.
33. *Medulla*, CXVII–CXXIII.
34. *Medulla*, CXXIII–CXXVI.
35. *Medulla*, CXXVI, CXXVII.

XXXVI. Devotion to the Truth in Judgment

Devotion to the truth is either public or private. The public is in judgment or outside of it. In *judgment* the duty of a *judge* is to test the truth of the matter and to judge according to the truth. The duty of the *accuser* and *defendant* is not to try in judgment unless he is most persuaded of the goodness of his cause. The duty of the *attorney* is to defend uprightly the tested causes of his client, without lies or fraud. The duty of the *witness* is not to speak false testimony against his neighbor, but truly, insofar as it is demanded by the judge.[36]

XXXVII. The Tenth Commandment: Covetousness, First Movements

The tenth commandment forbids covetousness. "You shall not covet the house of your neighbor" (Ex. 20:17). Not any kind of covetousness is forbidden, but the "evil" (Col. 3:5) of the "flesh" corrupted by sin (Gal. 5:16) whereby it desires what is against God Himself as highest good. It is corrupted when a person furnishes other things outside of Him for his end and highest good. Hence, it is called "corruption in covetousness" (2 Peter 1:4). Moreover, it is either habitual and congenital or actual, of which there are various species in regard to manner and object. Προπάθεια or *first movements* also pertain to these, preceding deliberation and consent, because they proceed from defect of the love of God and His image.[37]

XXXVIII. Self-Sufficiency

The prohibition of coveting includes devotion to purity, internal holiness, and above all self-sufficiency (αὐταρκείας). Indeed, it is appropriate to desire nothing more than what God gives and commands to desire. For He alone is author of desiring those things which He has already decreed to give. "Piety with self-sufficiency is great gain" (1 Tim. 6:6).[38]

XXXIX. The Use of the Decalogue

The use of the Decalogue is excellent in regard to the whole man, both the sinner and regenerate person. For the law, whose sum the Decalogue comprehends, was given to the *whole* man, that he may live through it. It was given to the *sinner* that he may have a rule of his duty and acknowledge the justice of his condemnation. It was given to the *regenerate* person that in it he may have a most certain rule for his repentance and sanctification and be led to Christ by its pedagogical strength.[39]

---

36. *Medulla*, CXXVIII.
37. *Medulla*, CXXIX–CXXXIV.
38. *Medulla*, CXXXIV.
39. *Medulla*, CXXXV, CXXXVI.

LOCUS XV

On the Ritual Law of Moses

I. The Ritual Laws of Moses

The positive laws of Moses are ritual or judicial. The ritual laws are called "commands in the terms agreed upon" (Eph. 2:15), terms agreed upon (δόγματα) (Col. 2:14), "carnal commands" (Heb. 7:16). It pleased God to institute them in order that His people may have in them a type of the true goods, and the faithful in the New Testament may more readily receive the Messiah prefigured in these characters. They differ from the rites of the patriarchs because the judicial laws were merely ecclesiastical and typical. Moreover, the Mosaic rites were servile and pedagogical.[1]

II. Their Bodily Exercise, Public Rites, Sacrifices, Sacrificial Cakes

The bodily exercise of the Mosaic rites came to be distinguished from the spiritual significance. The *bodily exercise* is that whereby the external actions of the body ought to have been yielded to the precept of God, and these were either public or private. The *public rites* concerned things and persons. The *things* were either sacrifices or things without sacrifice. *Sacrifices* in general were *offerings* that were offered before the altar in order that they might be consumed concerning the same rite instituted by divine will. These were either gifts (מנחות) or sacrificial cakes, or victims (זבחים). Sacrificial cakes were taken up from the firstfruits or a tenth of the barley or wheat, so that a meal was made from them. These were offered with or without libation of wine.[2]

III. Victims

Victims were offerings made to God at the altar from animals, which were alive, to represent something spiritual. There were four kinds: *whole burnt offerings*,

1. *Medulla*, I–VII.
2. *Medulla*, VII, VIII.

peace offerings, *expiatory offerings for sin*, or the same *for guilt*. It was peculiar to the expiatory victims that vicarious punishment was inflicted on them.[3]

IV. Sacrifices for Families, for Society

The Paschal sacrifice for each of the Hebrew *families*, the *whole society*, and the thing born was a young bull and he-goat. Times were stated by a yoke, which were sabbatical, monthly, yearly, Passovers, Pentecost, of trumpets, of expiation, and of tabernacles.[4]

V. Rites Fit for Sacrifice (θύσιμοι), Sacred Fire

Rites fit for sacrifice (θύσιμοι) were the leading of the sacrificial animal to the altar, movement toward blows of the ritually clean victim, placing on of hands, prayers, slaughtering, sprinkling of blood, removal of hides, dissection of the victim, making offerings, and the burning and slaughtering of some. *Sacred fire* makes for this, which, having descended from heaven, burned up the sacrifices.[5]

VI. Sacred Atoning Elements Not Offered

Some sacred atoning elements not sacrificed were appointed as things appointed for sacred use *without sacrifice*. These include the tithe, offerings, and money for expiations or half a shekel, with which someone was obligated to redeem his head.[6]

VII. The Place of Sacred Worship: The Tabernacle, the Time

Place and time fell on sacred matters. The *place* was indiscriminate before the construction of the tabernacle. After its construction, it was bound to the tabernacle, the fixed seat of which was in Shiloh, and in that profaned Jerusalem. There were two sanctuaries of the *tabernacle* itself: the *outer* of the priests, and the *inner* or innermost, the holy of holies. Its *atrium* was adjacent to the entrance. Solomon very majestically built up the temple in Jerusalem for imitation of the sacred things of the tabernacle. There were stated *times* for worship: daily, weekly, monthly, yearly—called the *solemn observance and feast of Jehovah*—and of the fiftieth year with the conspicuous name *Jubilee*.[7]

VIII. Persons: Prophets, Priests, Levites, Nazarites, Rechabites

The *persons* were certain men, whose ministry God willed to use for the governance of His church. The extraordinary ones were *prophets*. The ordinary ones

---

3. *Medulla*, IX–XII.
4. *Medulla*, XII, XIII.
5. *Medulla*, XIV, XV.
6. *Medulla*, XVI–XX.
7. *Medulla*, XX, XXI.

were *priests*, set up for men among them, which were to be led by God. Among them was the *high priest*, the one above all of those consecrated, and the *Levites*, who ministered to priests and the tabernacle. Among the persons were also *Nazarites* who, consecrated to God by vow, abstained from wine and intoxicating drink, did not shave their heads, and did not go among the dead. And there were the *Rechabites*, who did not drink wine because of their paternal institution. They neither built a house nor kept land, and they dwelt in tents.[8]

IX. Private Ceremonies: Clothing, Food, Legal Purity, Purifications

Private ceremonies consisted in the clothing of all, food, legal purity, and purifications for its violation. In *clothing* some items were to be diligently avoided and others to be made. For fringes (ציצת) were commanded to be worn on the corners of vestments (Num. 15:38–39). In *food* they were to abstain from the use of animals and fish, which the law declared impure and unfit for sacrifice, even the blood and fat. There was *legal purity*, and the impurity that opposed it concerned generation, edible things, sicknesses (especially leprosy), death, and above all the corpses of dead men. Various *washings* were set in opposition to these species of legal impurity. There were also purifications (καθαρισμοὶ), above all for people who had leprosy and had handled a corpse, through *waters of shame*, made from the ashes of a ruddy cow.[9]

X. Spiritual Significance of the Rites

A *spiritual significance* is added to the bodily exercise of these ceremonies. All the former rites had a mystery, without which they could not have been obeyed from faith or have pleased God. Indeed, the spiritual things signified the heavenly things—Christ, the gospel, the kingdom of Christ—from the instruction of God. Moreover, they could have or ought to have been searched out with an analogy or certain likeness to the compared promise of the seed.[10]

XI. The Mystery of Offerings in General

All the *offerings* bore the figure of Christ, His supreme purity, and death. Indeed, Saint Paul compares all the kinds of the victims with the one sacrifice of Christ, "of the one coming to do the will of God"—namely, the type with its anti-type (Heb. 10:5–10).[11]

8. *Medulla*, XXII–XXVII.
9. *Medulla*, XXVII–XXX.
10. *Medulla*, XXX.
11. *Medulla*, XXXI.

XII. In the Species of Sacrificial Cakes

Sacrificial cakes or offerings from inanimate things were figures of Christ, as "the fruit of the earth" (Isa. 4:2), "the Bread of life" (John 6:48), fire "with salt" and the salt of afflictions, "to be eaten" with true faith (1 Cor. 11:24, 26). They were also figures of the sufferings of the church that, as *firstfruits*, flow alongside the sacrifice of Christ.[12]

XIII. The Pick of Animals; Of Whole Burnt Offerings; Of Peace Offerings; Of The Victim for Sin and Guilt, for the Whole of Society; Rites; Sacred Fire

The pick of animals means that sins may not be blotted out with the blood of cattle. It also means that the strength of some animals, such as the ox, he-goat, sheep, turtle-dove, and dove, are found in the sacrifice of Christ. The *whole burnt offering* signifies the passible Christ and was burnt up by the zeal of God. The *peace offering* has the same signification with its best for God, offering itself to be eaten by us. *The victim for sin and guilt* signified the vicarious death of Christ for sinners, performed to satisfy God for sins. The victims *for the whole society* signified as with a *yoke* the time of the death and resurrection of Christ and the yoke of His worship. *The lasting of a week* signified the greater celebration of worship. *The new moons* signified the renewal of all things. Rites fit for sacrifice (θύσιμοι) signified the voluntary offering of Christ, His death outside of Jerusalem, ascension into heaven, and eating by faith. *Sacred fire* clearly adumbrated the acceptance of the sacrifice of Christ and the divine love of the same.[13]

XIV. Of Things without Sacrifice: Of the Firstborn, the Firstfruits, the Tithes; The Curses; The Money for Expiation

The things without sacrifice also signified something secret: the *firstborn* above all, Christ, "the firstborn of all creation" (Col. 1:15), His inheritance, and the firstborn elect. The *firstfruits* signified the same. They included the firstfruits of those who were asleep, who were raised from the dead, and even Israel. Through Israel, as the remaining firstfruits, the Gentiles were sanctified in the promised seed of Israel. The reasonableness (ἐπιείκειαν) of *the tithe* expressed the spiritual things of God in those governing carnal things and the elect chosen out of the world. The *curses* expressed the devotion of those who are outside of Christ. They expressed His expectation in the equitable and small *money for expiations*, which established the redemption price of the faithful.[14]

---

12. *Medulla*, XXXII.
13. *Medulla*, XXXIII–XXXVIII.
14. *Medulla*, XXXVIII.

XV. Tabernacles and Temples; Of Stated Times; Of Feasts—Of the Passover, Omer, Pentecosts, of the Tabernacles, of the Trumpets, of Expiation, of the Sabbatical Year, of Jubilee

The *sacred places* also had the pregnant mystery. For the *tabernacle* and the *temple* foreshadowed Christ to come in the flesh, to dwell among men as Propitiator, to enter into heaven through His own flesh that was broken, and to unite the church militant and triumphant. But the *stated times* that were conducted among them were also full of the mystery. For the *feasts* and their *parts* were "shadows of things to come, the body of which belongs to Christ" (Col. 2:17). We wrote above about the mystery of the Passover. *Omer*, or a *handful* of grain falling on the day after the Sabbath for that feast, represented that Christ would rise again on the day after the Passover and that the firstfruits of those who rise again would come. The *firstfruits* of harvest, *the bread of raising*, offered in the feast of *Pentecost*, represented the apostles consecrated on the same day of Pentecost. The feast *of tabernacles* represented the last state of the church in which, having left the earth and the world behind, she aspires to the heavenly Canaan alone. The feast *of trumpets* represented the year of good pleasure in which the new King was to be received with a joyful shout. The feast *of expiation* represented *expiation* of the faithful through the blood of Christ and the entrance of Christ into heaven together with His own blood. It also represented the exile of hardened Israel until the time of their expiation in regard to the he-goat *Azazel*. *The Sabbatical year* above all represented desertion of the land of Canaan, to be abandoned by the faithful, in order that the church may cease to be there. The *Jubilees* represented Christ as the Lamb (for that יובל was proclaimed in the horn of the lamb or ram), bearing the sins of the world and proclaiming freedom.[15]

XVI. Of the Persons: As of Aaron and the Priests, the Levites, the Nazarites, the Rechabites

The persons, administrators of the ceremonies, were not void of the mystery. For *Aaron* and the remaining *priests* had a certain likeness to Christ in vocation, consecration, and priestly office. The priestly office was typical of Him, Christ, truly and properly called. The mystery was also in the orders of the priesthood because Aaron symbolized Christ the true priest. Since He will always live to intercede for us, He certainly lacks nothing vicarious, but rather "has made" all the faithful "priests to God and the Father" (Rev. 1:6; 5:10). *The Levites*, ministering to God in varied order, symbolized the faithful of the New Testament under one High Priest, Christ. *The Nazarites* symbolized Christ separated from sinners and the concern for willing obedience of the faithful. *The Rechabites*

15. *Medulla*, XXXIV–XLIII.

symbolized the faithful, "placing a nest on a rock" as it were (Num. 24:21) and spurning the world.[16]

XVII. Of Private Ceremonies: Clothing, Food, Legal Impurity, Purifications, and Baptism on Account of the Dead

Finally, the *private* ceremonies also signified something secret. For the *clothing* laws foreshadowed the simplicity, equality, worship of God alone, and remembrance of the law. The *food* laws foreshadowed sin that existed but was not yet expiated, the impurity of the Gentiles, and expiation for souls to come. *Legal impurity* concerning *generation* foreshadowed the corruption of nature. It concerned *diseases*, above all leprosy, which foreshadowed the inmost impurity of sin, commingled with the external species of purity. It concerned *dead flesh*, above all *the corpse* of man, which foreshadowed the nature of man who, while sin had not yet been expiated, was impure and guilty of death. *Purifications* or legal *washings* foreshadowed true *purification* through the blood of Christ (Heb. 1:3; 1 John 1:7), "clean waters," and the *Spirit* of God (Ezek. 36:25). The waters of shame and baptism for the dead foreshadowed the resurrection of the dead above (1 Cor. 15:29).[17]

XVIII. The Abolition of the Ceremonies

All these ceremonies were abolished through the advent of Christ. For the shadows withdrew for the body and the figures for the truth. In many ceremonies there was also "remembrance of sin" (Heb. 10:3), while its expiation had not yet obtained. Moreover, there was not consummation in those signs, because while they endured, "a station in the former tabernacle" was required (Heb. 9:8). The sanctuary was closed by a veil as it were, into which the high priests alone were allowed to enter only once per year. The nature of the ceremonies, predictions, the dignity of the Messiah and priests, and the destruction of the temple brought about the same abolition.[18]

---

16. *Medulla*, XLIII, XLIV.
17. *Medulla*, XLV–XLIX.
18. *Medulla*, L, LI, LII.

LOCUS XVI

On the Judicial Law of Moses

I. Judicial Laws: The State of the Republic

Moses not only ordered the church but also the republic with saving instructions from the command of God. These are related to have been received by reason of God being their singular author. For He did not so much confer prudence on Moses to relate civil laws as did He dictate civil and religious laws to the same with His most holy mouth. Indeed, the state of the Israelite republic was not human, but divine and theocratic, serving as a prelude to the spiritual kingdom of Christ under the New Testament.[1]

II. Its Persons: Magistrates, Temporary Magistrates

The judicial Mosaic laws concerned persons and things. The persons were *magistrates* or subordinates. All *magistrates* were subject to another, God, also their civil king, and were temporary or perpetual. The *temporary ones* included *Moses*, highest commander of the people after God, and *Joshua*, his successor. They also included *judges*, summoned by divine will after the things of the people had been called together, and *kings*, demanded by the people but against the will of God and with improper auspices. Of these there was also a twofold law: one was commanded by divine will (Deut. 17:14ff.) and another by despotic human will, predicted by Samuel (1 Sam. 8:11–19).[2]

III. Perpetual Magistrates, Master of the Sanhedrin, Inferiors

The *perpetual* magistrates were the judges or Sanhedrin, and they were either superior or inferior. The *highest* was the master of the Sanhedrin or the assembly of seventy men of the elders of Israel, instituted by the plan of Jethro (Num. 11:16, etc.). This continued, as it is clear from 1 Chronicles 19:8–9, Ezekiel 8:11,

1. *Medulla*, I–V.
2. *Medulla*, V–VIII.

and the history of the New Testament, although not without interruption. The *inferior* assembly of the cities consisted of twenty-three judges and three districts. For the same the magistrates were also to be referred to as *chiefs of the tribes of Israel, prefects, and the called of society.* Various *scribes* served their interests.[3]

IV. Subordinates

The *subordinates* were derived either from birth or from strangers. The *former* could invoke the fathers Abraham, Isaac, and Jacob. The latter, springing from other nations, united themselves to the Israelites: strangers either of *righteousness*, admitted into the church by baptism, circumcision, and offering, or of *dwelling*, tolerated by certain laws in the republic. Of those derived by birth mentioned above, some were *free* and others were *slaves*—mercenaries, not possessions. The strangers were of the latter sort.[4]

V. Judges, Capital Punishments, Non-Capital Punishments, Quasi-Punishments, the Law of the Zealots, and the Avenger of Blood

The cases of the subordinates were treated by the public judges. Punishments were also inflicted on guilty parties. These included *capital punishment*; pure *stoning*; *burning* through tin or liquefied lead, thrust through the mouth into the vitals; the *sword*; *strangulation*; and *hanging of the dead*. They also included *non-capital punishments*, like *retaliation* (not Pythagorean but analogical), *flogging*, *fine*, *restitution*, *sale*, and *exile*. Added to these were *quasi-punishments*: *overthrow*, divine exclusion from the communion of the church, and *curses*, human separation from communion of the same church. The punishments also included the *law of the zealots* who, inflamed with divine zeal and fortified with no human power, avenged crime, and the *avenger of blood* who, fortified with divine authority, could kill a murderer.[5]

VI. The Reasonableness (Ἐπιεικεία) of the Mosaic Punishments

The Mosaic punishments did not lack their reasonableness (ἐπιεικείᾳ). Indeed, many appendages of the Decalogue depended on the same equity and justice as the Decalogue itself and were guardians of the Decalogue as it were. Yet some, like the penalty of death, decreed for a person who ate blood (Lev. 17:14) and the daughter of a priest who prostituted herself (Lev. 21:9), after the type involved ceases, lose the particular reason of equity.[6]

---

3. *Medulla*, VIII–XI.
4. *Medulla*, XI.
5. *Medulla*, XII–XVI.
6. *Medulla*, XVI.

VII. Judicial Matters: Ecclesiastical

Judicial *matters* were ecclesiastical, economic, or political. *Ecclesiastical* matters concern the religion or goods of the church. The laws concern *religion*, removing all impediments to divine worship. These include laws "about not constructing a pillar" or "a statue" (Deut. 16:22), not establishing a "distinguished, engraved stone" (Lev. 26:1), and not planting a "grove next to the altar of the Lord" (Deut. 16:21). The laws concern the *goods* of the church, in which priests and Levites were granted claim to the possession and enjoyment of their own goods.[7]

VIII. Economic Laws, concerning Marriages

Economic laws concerned marriages, inheritances, and similar things. Those concerning *marriages* required puberty of contracting persons, respect of blood, and communion of religion. They permitted a petition of divorce. They required drinking for the woman of suspect chastity on account of jealousy. They determined a manner for exploring the virginity of a spouse. They also decided about who oppressed a spouse in the city or field or who polluted an accosted or seduced virgin.[8]

IX. And Inheritances

Inheritances were goods of a dead person, which legitimate heirs inherited. The inheritance of goods of the dead was fivefold: *of sons*, who, as their heirs, inherited the paternal and maternal goods; *of the father*, and *from the side*, when the inheritance for the dead person, children not existing from the offspring of either sex to the father, or of his dead person falling back to the neighbors; *of the brother* leading the brother; of the *husband* or *hence man*, who inherits the goods of the dead wife; and of the *imperial treasury*, inheriting the goods of the dead national enemy. There was a *right of the interim possession* or *of the redemption* of inheritances over the Hebrews. The neighbor of the same blood was held to redeem those that had been sold.[9]

X. Political Laws: Concerning Peace, concerning War

Political laws pertained to peace or war. The former are principally about not making covenants with devoted Canaanites. They required wages to be paid to laborers. Compassion toward the poor and wanderers, even beasts themselves, was required. Concerning the ox and donkey in the plowed field, they were not to be yoked. Concerning the young goat in the milk of the mother, it was not be cooked. There were also laws of peace concerning measures, weights, and so on.

7. *Medulla*, XVII.
8. *Medulla*, XVIII–XXII.
9. *Medulla*, XXII–XXIII.

Laws *of war* prescribed the method for taking up the same, conducting it, and completing it.[10]

XI. The Use of the Judicial Laws in Regard to the People of Israel, Abolished through Christ

The *use* of the judicial laws was fourfold in regard to the Israelite people. For it pleased God not only to rule the people of Israel with this norm of political law but also to separate them from the remaining peoples with the singular command of those laws, lest they be implicated in their impiety. He also did this to induce Israel with these public laws to pursue His wisdom, goodness, and righteousness, and to foreshadow to them the kingdom of the one Christ in this form of theocratic rule. After Christ was furnished for them, this singular form expired. For the duration of the Lawgiver (τοῦ מחוקק) is bound until the advent of Shiloh (Gen. 49:10). Moreover, the city of Jerusalem, the sanctuary, and the people, to whom the laws were affixed, also had to be cut off after the Messiah was cut off.[11]

XII. The Use of the Same in Regard to the Christian Republic

Outside this singular *form*, in regard to matter some of these laws were mutable and abrogated, though others are perpetual and must be imitated by the Christian republic. The mutable laws should be recognized from what was mixed with the types or accommodated to the Jewish body-politic in a singular manner, or from what was singularly adapted to the inborn character and nature of the Jewish people. The *perpetual laws*, which unite the duties commanded in those laws with common notions, are conformed to the commandments of the Decalogue and serve to confirm the same. They establish love and justice among men, conformed to what is in the divine mind, and some are repeated in the New Testament.[12]

---

10. *Medulla*, XXIV–XXVIII.
11. *Medulla*, XXIX–XXXI.
12. *Medulla*, XXXI–XXXV.

LOCUS XVII

On the Person of Jesus Christ

I. The Teaching concerning Jesus Christ under the New Testament

Jesus Christ "is the same yesterday, today, and forever" (Heb. 13:8). This "yesterday" was from eternity and also in the Old Testament, as we have already seen. This "today," or "in the fullness of time" (Gal. 4:4–5), sent by God, born from a woman, and made man must be seen next in succession. Before all things we will speak about His *person*, *state*, and *office*.[1]

II. The Definition of Jesus Christ

Jesus Christ is *the Son of God*, *made flesh* in time or *born* God-man (θεάνθρωπος) *from His mother the virgin Mary through conception by the Holy Spirit. He is also the Messiah and Savior of the human race, promised* to the fathers *and fulfilled in time. The holy evangelists describe His birth, life, death, resurrection, and ascension into heaven. We wait for Him, returning from heaven, to come as judge of the living and the dead.*[2]

III. The Incarnation of the Son

The incarnation of the Son of God, or the sending from heaven to earth and manifestation in the flesh—predicted, promised, and variously foreshadowed in types in the Old Testament—was fulfilled in the fullness of time. For "the Word became flesh" (John 1:14). "God appeared in the flesh" (1 Tim. 3:16). "When the fullness of time came, God sent out His Son, born from a woman, born under the law" (Gal. 4:4). "He was born from the seed of David according to the flesh and appointed Son of God in power according to the Spirit of Holiness" (Rom. 1:3–4).[3]

---

1. *Medulla*, I.
2. *Medulla*, II.
3. *Medulla*, III–V.

IV. God and Man: Born through the Conception of the Holy Spirit from a Virgin, Betrothed and Always a Virgin

The same God-man (θεάνθρωπος) is *God* and *man* in the same person. We have spoken about His *deity* above. He is also *man*, consisting of "flesh and bones" (Luke 24:39), "similarly, as children, a sharer of flesh and blood" (Heb. 2:14). He has a rational "spirit" (Luke 23:46) and "will," distinct from the will of the Father (Matt. 26:39). In this He is God consubstantial (ὁμοούσιος) to the Father and man consubstantial to us. He received His *divine* nature through eternal generation and His *human* nature from the Blessed Virgin Mary through conception by the Holy Spirit, who "furnished a body" for the Son (Heb. 10:5), "came over" Mary, and "overshadowed" her (Luke 1:35). For He was due to be born and born from *a virgin*, according to Isaiah 7:14: "Behold a virgin will hold in her womb and bring forth a son, and (each one) called His name Emmanuel." But although a virgin, she was nevertheless *betrothed* to Joseph, lest the Son, being "of illegitimate birth, not be admitted into the congregation" (Deut. 23:2) and thus be prevented from the function of His office. "Not coming together with" him (Matt. 1:18), she was therefore a virgin before birth and in birth. For, in order that He may be holy, He had to be born "not from blood and the will of flesh and man" (John 1:13). Indeed, it was settled against Helvidius that, even after birth, she was always a virgin.[4]

The Act of the Conception of Christ: The Formation of the Human Nature[5]

There were three actions of the conception of Christ by the Holy Spirit: the formation of the human nature, sanctification, and assumption of the person into unity. *The formation of the human nature* is *that whereby, with that strength of the Holy Spirit without the intervention of a man, He was formed from the blood and substance of Mary*. For Christ is the seed of the woman (זרע אישה) (Gen. 3:15), "the fruit of the womb" of Mary (Luke 1:42), "born from the seed of David"—namely, through Mary (Rom. 1:3). He is pronominally (ἀντονομαστικῶς) called Son of Man (בו אדם) (Ps. 8:4) to designate something singular in the

4. Helvidius (fourth century) denied Mary's perpetual virginity in response to the growing ascetic movement. Jerome (c. AD 345–420) responded in *Against Helvidus On the Perpetual Virginity of the Blessed Mary* (c. 383). Many of the sixteenth- and seventeenth-century Reformed and Lutheran theologians followed Jerome rather than Helvidius on this point. On patristic opinion, see J. B. Lightfoot, ed., St. *Paul's Epistle to the Galatians. A Revised Text with Introduction, Notes, and Dissertations*, 4th ed., Classic Commentaries on the Greek New Testament (London: Macmillan and Co., 1874), 253–90. *Medulla*, V–IX.

5. In the original this section appears as a distinct unit, but it is enumerated as IV, just like the section prior to it. I removed the number but left the heading in bold. This preserves the original numbers of the remaining chapters of this *locus*.

species of the sons of individual men. And the genealogy of Christ made from Adam through David also demonstrates that.[6]

V. Sanctification of the Same

His *sanctification* is *that whereby in conception itself He was free from all original sin, to which Mary was liable, and was separated and preserved from the same by the strength of the Holy Spirit.* The angel said about this, "Because He is born from you, holy, He will be called the Son of God" (Luke 1:35). For otherwise, "what is born from flesh is flesh" (John 3:6).[7]

VI. His Assumption into Unity of Person

Finally, His assumption of the flesh into the unity of the person is that whereby the Word (λόγος), the Son of God, in the very moment of formation and sanctification, assumed human nature, destitute of proper substance (ὑποστάσεως), into unity of person. For "the Word became flesh" (John 1:14). "Christ took the form of a servant" (Phil. 2:7) and was the "seed of Abraham" (Heb. 2:16). Hence, one and the same substance (ὑπόστασις) and one person exists of the Word (λόγου) assuming the flesh and the flesh assumed.[8]

VII. Union of Natures: Its Manner

Union of the two natures in the one person of Christ follows this assumption, the full manner of which is a mystery. But that synodical exposition of faith in the Council of Chalcedon rightly settled it: according to assumption (κατ᾽ ἄρσιν) in Him, which was made unchangeably (ἀτρέπτως), indivisibly (ἀδαιρέτως), and inseparably (ἀχωρίστως), and according to setting down (κατὰ θέσιν) in Him, both natures *come together into one person and one hypostasis.*[9]

VIII. Communication: Non-Mutual, Made of Human Nature, and That of Eminent Grace and of Habitual Graces

A certain communication follows from the union of the natures. This is either unilateral or mutual. The *former* is the communication of the grace of human nature by the Word (λόγῳ), made on account of personal union. This is either of eminent grace or of habitual graces. It is *of eminent grace*, in which human nature, as the flesh of the Son of God, is eminent over all creatures. "You have crowned Him with glory and honor" (Ps. 8:5; Heb. 2:7). It is *of habitual graces*, in which the Word (ὁ λόγος) conferred incomparable but finite qualities to

6. *Medulla*, IX–XV.
7. *Medulla*, XV, XVI.
8. *Medulla*, XVII.
9. *Medulla*, XVIII–XXI.

Himself in the flesh. "God has anointed You, Your God, with the oil of happiness over Your sharers" (Ps. 45:7). For *He received* much more than the church did: "the Spirit beyond measure" (John 3:34). The perfection of these graces did not begin with the beginning of the union itself. Instead, it increased little by little not only in the soul but also in the body. For "wisdom made progress" (Luke 2:52), "increased, and was made powerful in the Spirit" (Luke 2:40). And His body, at first passible (παθητὸν), became impassable (ἀπαθὲς) after death.[10]

IX. Mutual Communication of Properties (Communicatio Idiomatum)

Mutual communication is of the proper qualities, office, and operations. It is *of the proper qualities* whereby *the qualities of each nature united are communicated to the person.* Through it the person from each nature, indeed having each and leading through each, *is designated.* But also those things that are of each nature concerning the person designated by both are proclaimed. "The Son of Man, who is in heaven, descended from heaven" (John 3:13). "God purchased the church with His own blood" (Acts 20:28). "They crucified the Lord of glory" (1 Cor. 2:8). That communication is *real* in respect to person, *verbal* in respect to natures, in neither of which did He divert His qualities into another. For the proper qualities of one nature could not be communicated to another, except both were destroyed. Nor are all or some communicated. *All* are not communicated, because eternal or infinite flesh is neither proclaimed nor can be proclaimed. *Some* are not communicated because all the qualities of God cohere in an undivided union and are God Himself. Therefore there are none. But some of the proper qualities are called non-acting upon (ἐνεργητικὰ). Others are called acting upon (ἐνεργητικὰ), not in themselves but in regard to effects and us. Therefore, the latter are proclaimed about the same, and the former can, too.[11]

X. Communication of Office and Honor

Communication *of office and honor* is that whereby Christ, on account of the union of natures, is Savior and Mediator according to each nature and has possession of the honor of each but with a distinct reason suitable for each. The result of His office from each nature, dependence of each nature on operations, and the unity of worship or adoration bring about this communion. The latter, on account of the mediatorial office, is directed to the whole Christ the God-man (θεάνθρωπον).[12]

10. *Medulla*, XXI–XXV.
11. *Medulla*, XXV–XXVIII, XXXVI.
12. *Medulla*, XXVIII.

XI. Of Operations or Results

Communication *of operations* or *of results* is that whereby the works of Christ the Mediator, accomplished by both His natures, are assigned to the same, and each does what is proper to it with communion of the other. Where there is the person who works (ὁ ἐνεργῶν), there is the active beginning (τὸ ἐνεργητικὸν), both natures of Christ, the working (ἐνέργεια), the efficacious operation of each nature, and the work (ἐνέργημα) produced in that action, which is the result (ἀποτελεσμα), and the work is called the God-man (θεανδρικὸν). The latter results are all the mediatorial works of Christ, attributed to Christ in the concrete and abstract.[13]

---

13. *Medulla*, XXIX.

LOCUS XVIII

On the State of Jesus Christ

I. The State of Emptying

The state of Christ is twofold: one of emptying and another of exaltation. The state *of emptying* is that *whereby He, although He was in the form of God and it was not foreign to Him to be the image of God, emptied Himself, in the likeness of man, taking the form of a servant. While He was thus found in disposition, as man, He humbled Himself and furnished obedience to God to the death of the cross* (Phil. 2:6–11). The former is of deity, concealing majesty, and of humanity taking up final servitude unto death.[1]

II. Its Beginning and Progress: His Private and Public Life

The *beginning* of the emptying of Christ prevailed in His conception and birth in which "He took the form of a servant" (Phil. 2:7), "was made under the law" (Gal. 4:4), and *progressed* in His whole life. His life was either private or public. The *private* was not only of childhood but also of *adolescence*. One see marks of voluntary emptying; although being God-man (θεάνθρωπος) as it were, He immediately took the form of a servant, "called servant of Israel from the womb" (Isa. 49:1–3). Moreover, He endured shameful poverty (Luke 9:58). Moved with love toward His parents, it is manifest that He did not abstain from miracles (John 2:3–5). Fear of death and waiting for His calling troubled Him. Finally, "He offered pleas and supplications" for the salvation of the church (Heb. 5:7, 8). He undertook the auspices *of public* life in the thirtieth year of His life, beginning (ἀρχόμενος) then (Luke 3:23), namely, "to proclaim the gospel" (Luke 3:18) after John ceased to preach.[2]

1. *Medulla*, I.
2. *Medulla*, II–VIII.

III. The Time of the Public Ministry, Passover Death

The time of the public ministry of Christ was three and a half years, the exact space of four Passovers. This famous Passover above all was the final crucifixion (σταυρώσιμον), or what brought death. For that humiliation (ταπείνωσις) fell on Him whereby Christ, "humbling Himself, obeyed God unto death, even the death of the cross" (Phil. 2:8). This was the final degree of His emptying. It was exacted chiefly on the final two days of His emptying.[3]

IV. Its Celebration; The Institution of the Eucharist; Struggle in the Garden

In the fatal two days before all things Christ celebrated Passover with His own, on the day "on which it was necessary" (Luke 22:7). To that degree this was anticipated by the Passover of the Jews, but lawfully (νομίμως). He instituted in the eating the memory of Himself, the true Lamb, now to be sacrificed, in the Eucharistic Supper, to arrange for the Paschal Lamb, to be remembered most religiously (Matt. 26:26, etc.). The fatal passion itself began soon after His struggle (ἀδημονίᾳ) in the garden (Luke 22:44). For there He struggled "to the point of shedding blood" (Luke 22:44) because the ancient serpent had begun to bite into His heel. Hence, there was that "struggle of soul" (Isa. 53:11) on account of which He was "poured out like water." "His heart became like wax, melted in the middle of His entrails" (Ps. 22:14).[4]

V. Betrayal by Judas, Crucifixion

In this last struggle Christ was thus handed over by Judas, "a man of peace in whom He confided, pursuing Him with his own heels" (Ps. 41:9). He offered Himself to the priests. Hence seized, He came into the power of the Jews and the Gentiles, by whom He was condemned in *judgment* to the punishment of a *wooden* cross. "Hanging" from the cross was according to the "curse" (Deut. 21:23). Indeed, while He died for us, He had to become "a curse," to "redeem us from the curse of the law" (Gal. 3:13).[5]

VI. Hanging There on the Cross, Some Things Preceded His Death

While Christ was hanging on the cross, some things preceded His death and some followed it. Those that *preceded* it included what *others did to Him* with a hostile spirit, what *He spoke* on the cross, and what the Father did to glorify Him. These are generally *sevenfold*. Among them is the fourth, which He shouted with a loud voice and as "one roaring" (Ps. 22:2): "My God, My God, why have You

---

3. *Medulla*, VIII–IX.
4. *Medulla*, X, XI.
5. *Medulla*, XII, XIII.

forsaken Me?" (Matt. 27:46). In these words there is nothing of despair, because He bore witness to His faith with the words "My God." Moreover, the remaining words are of the nature of sinlessly enduring the depth of divine wrath and the hidden face of God because of foreign sins, not His own. The sixth word was Τετέλεσται ("It is finished") (John 19:30)—everything that lied on Me as Sponsor. Finally, the Father also began to glorify Him while He was hanging on the cross: "during the sixth hour darkness came over the whole earth until the ninth hour" (Matt. 27:45; Mark 15:33), proof of the darkened Sun of righteousness and the atrocity of the crime.[6]

VII. Others Followed It

Three things followed the death of Christ on the cross. For "the veil of the temple was torn into two" (Matt. 27:51) as testimony that the way to heaven had been opened, to be tread with all trust after the flesh had been broken. There was attempt *to break His legs* but with no success, because He was already dead. This was so that it may be clear that He is the true Lamb, whose bones were not to be broken. Finally, His "side was pierced, from which blood and water poured out" (John 19:34), in order that it may be clear that an end was placed on the legal pouring out of blood in the purity of His obedience and the purifications in His bloody sufferings.[7]

VIII. The Burial of Christ

After this, Christ, who had been removed from the cross, was *buried*, Nicodemus and Joseph of Arimathea attending to the work. For He was not only to be vanquished on the cross *of crime* but also "to be buried with the rich" or in the grave of the rich (Isa. 53:9). In this way the curse was to be removed, the truth of the death of Christ demonstrated, and death to be conquered in its outermost place of refuge.[8]

IX. Descent into Hell, Sufferings of Soul

The descent into hell follows burial in the Apostolic Creed, which was not reproduced by the Athanasian Creed. It is analogous to Scripture because one was obligated to "descend into hell" who was obligated not "to remain in hell" (Ps. 16:10). From the use of Scripture it properly means the state of persevering in the grave, not without the likeness of the triumph of death. Analogically it means the infernal sufferings and vexations that He sustained in His soul. For He endured infernal sufferings not only in the body but also in the soul. His "soul"

6. *Medulla*, XIV–XVII.
7. *Medulla*, XVII.
8. *Medulla*, XVIII, XIX.

was "saddened" (Matt. 26:38), "disturbed" (John 12:27), and His "will" was afflicted" (Matt. 26:39). The struggle between His soul and conscience with the terrors of death (Ps. 22:2–3; 69:2–3) also confirms that His distress (ἀδημονία) was *until death*. Otherwise, He would not have satisfied His promise to endure vicarious punishments.[9]

X. The State of Exaltation

The state of *exaltation* is that whereby He *was exalted to the highest and ineffable glory*. For He was not only obligated to be made less (ἐλατοῦας) than "the angels" but also "to be crowned with glory and honor" (Ps. 8:5), "to be justified" (1 Tim. 3:16), "to be brought to perfection as Head of life" (Heb. 2:10), "to be exalted, to be exalted above others," and thus to claim for Himself "the name above every name" (Phil. 2:9–10). Thus He is properly exalted as *man* and improperly as *God*, bringing to light in the fullest brightness His majesty in the glory of human nature.[10]

XI. Resurrection from the Dead

The degrees of exaltation are the resurrection from the dead, ascension into heaven, and sitting at the right hand of the Father. "He rose from the dead on the third day," on the first of the Sabbaths or of the Sun, "beginning to wash" (Matt. 28:1). He rose through the "efficacy of the strength of the power of God" (Eph. 1:19), the Son "raising" the "temple" for Himself (John 2:19) and the Father "taking up" His "soul" for His "power" (John 10:18). To Him the former is attributed everywhere. For, by raising the Son as Judge, He released and justified the same, together with those given to Him. "He rose again," indeed, "on account of our justification" (Rom. 4:25).[11]

XII. Its Truth

The truth of the resurrection of Christ is uncontested (ἀνεξαγώνιος). For there are more testimonies of those who saw Him living again, with the exception of all men. For there were many, indeed five hundred at the Council of Galilee (1 Cor. 15:5–6), and they had no reason to make up stories. Rather, if Christ had not risen again, they would not have made up stories, to look out for their lives. Moreover, the enemies of Jesus assigned a guard to the grave. Neither could the guards show the corpse to the former or attempt to substitute another in its place, nor did they protest that it had been removed by force, nor were they punished on account of wrongful guardianship. He was also obligated to rise

9. *Medulla*, XX–XXV.
10. *Medulla*, XXV–XXX.
11. *Medulla*, XXX–XXXIV.

again "according to the Scriptures" (1 Cor. 15:4; Ps. 16:10; Isa. 53:10). Persevering memorials of the same were instituted: the Supper by dying and about to rise again, and baptism by having risen again.[12]

XIII. His Apparitions

Having been brought back from the dead, He did not immediately enter into heaven, but being "visible" for forty days, "He spoke about those things that pertained to the kingdom of God" (Acts 1:3). The apparitions were nine in number. Four were made to individuals or to a few—that is, to Mary Magdalene, to two brothers going to Emmaeus, to Simon Peter and James. The remaining *five* were made to many in Judea while Thomas alone was absent; in Jerusalem to the same while Thomas was present; in Galilee to Peter, Thomas, Nathaniel, the sons of Zebedee, and others; and in Galilee to the eleven apostles. Finally, He appeared to more than five hundred brothers at the council and at Bethany to the eleven apostles. After wishing them farewell, He was carried away into heaven.[13]

XIV. Ascension into Heaven

The ascension of Christ was both reception on high (ἀνάληψις) (Mark 16:19; Luke 24:51) and ascension (ἀνάβασις) properly (Eph. 4:8–9). The former is attributed to the Father and the latter to the Son. The *Father* received Him on high, the *Son* ascended in His own strength. Yet it was the one will of both. But the *Father*, by receiving Him on high, as now to be crowned, justified Him. The *Son*, ascending, showed that He is the Son, and by right, power, and merit entered heaven. He entered heaven as "home," of which He was the "Lord" (Heb. 3:5–6), as Mediator and go-between of salvation. Moreover, He ascended into the heaven of heavens, made "more exalted than the (visible) heavens" (Heb. 7:26). Since the former heaven is the *place* and *mansion* of Christ and of the blessed on high (ἄνω) where Christ ascended, having been lifted up from the earth, it follows that the ascension was local.[14]

XV. Its Truth

The truth of the ascension of Christ into heaven hangs on the predictions (Deut. 30:11–12; Ps. 47:5; 68:19) and the testimonies of the eleven apostles, eyewitnesses (αὐτόπτων). There was no suspicion toward those who labored. For they would not wish to bring about their death and so many calamities on themselves by making it up. Stephen and Paul saw Him in heaven, who had ascended there

12. *Medulla*, XXXIV, XXXV.
13. *Medulla*, XXXVI–XXXVIII.
14. *Medulla*, XXXVIII, XXXIX, XLI–XLIV.

and dwells there. He brought the Spirit of Christ, sent according to promise; His kingdom that He rules in heaven; and the whole Christian religion.[15]

XVI. Sitting at the Right Hand of God

Having entered into heaven, *He sat down at the right hand of God*. For "God" the Father "placed" Christ, "risen from the dead, at His right hand in the heavens above" (Eph. 1:20) according to the prediction, "Jehovah said to My Lord, 'Sit at My right hand, until I place Your enemies as a footstool for Your feet" (Ps. 110:1). Indeed, although God, as Spirit, properly has neither right nor left, the right is nevertheless assigned to Him in likeness. That is of power (δυνάμεως) (Luke 22:69), "of throne" and glory (Heb. 8:1), or signifies His "power" (Isa. 62:8), the instrument of which is the right or "honor" (Ps. 110:1). Conceding to the right is a sign where not simply the right is assigned to Him but *sitting at the right*. Such belongs to Christ; namely, this signifies His supreme glorification and all that He merited with His obedience as Mediator, which He did and accomplished for His glory and the salvation of the church. The former agrees with Christ according to both natures: as *God*, improperly in regard to the manifestation of glory, and as *man,* properly and really in regard to the comparison of the new glory that His obedience merited.[16]

15. *Medulla*, XXXIX, XL.
16. *Medulla*, XLIVff.

LOCUS XIX

On the Office of Jesus Christ

I. The Cause of Christ Being Made Incarnate and Emptied; The Office of Christ

The cause of the Son of God having been made incarnate and emptied was grave. It was none other than that, the office of Savior having been taken up, "He may save sinners" (1 Tim. 1:15) for the glory of God. But the office of Jesus Christ is mediation (μεσιτεία) of the same, *mediation between God and men, which He voluntarily undertook from the will of the Father, for men, sinners, given to Him, to save and reconcile to God. He alone completed it according to both natures.*[1]

II. The Name of Jesus

The names and properties declare the nature of this office. His special *name* is Jesus (Ἰησους), imposed on Him by the angel. Mary "will give birth to a son, and you shall call His name JESUS (ΙΗΣΟΥΝ). For He will save His people from their sins" (Matt. 1:21). That was also put on Him in circumcision (Luke 2:21). As Bernard aptly said, "There were also others in Judea who had the name Jesus, in whom one glories with empty names. For they neither shine, nor feed, nor heal, but our Jesus is the Savior of His people from their sins." This also agrees with God alone. "I am a righteous God and Savior (ומושיע), and there is no other besides Me" (Isa. 45:21).[2]

III. And of Christ

The same Jesus also came in the name of Christ (משיח) or the *Anointed One* because He was anointed to the office of saving in His mediation or was appointed not through external anointing but internal and spiritual. That was not only *eternal* because He was appointed to the office, "anointed from eternity" (Prov. 8:23),

1. *Medulla*, I, II.
2. *Medulla*, III–VII.

but also *temporal.* It was done partly in the inhabitation of deity in the flesh, to be engaged with the office of Mediator through the gifts bestowed on Him, about which He is Christ. "The Spirit of the Lord Jehovah is over Me because the Lord has anointed Me to announce the gospel to the gentle" (Isa. 61:1). Moreover, it was done partly in the demonstration of deity dwelling in the flesh and of the royal dignity assigned to Him, according to those words of Peter, "God anointed Jesus of Nazareth in the Spirit (after having been poured out at Pentecost) and in power (of divinity or in divine works)" (Acts 10:38). "I have anointed a king over Zion, the mountain of My holiness" (Ps. 2:6).[3]

IV. The Cause of Mediation Is the Triune God; Christ Is Mediator according to Both Natures

But there are more things expressed in these names that declare the nature of the office of Christ. Certainly the *cause* is *commonly* and indivisibly the whole Holy Trinity. Moreover, all persons of the Godhead are *singular* in regard to the manner of working. God *the Father* by sending the Son, *the Son* by undertaking and accomplishing His office, and *the Holy Spirit* by anointing the same and conferring gifts on Him. Christ is Mediator according to both natures. For it is *human* work to proclaim the gospel, to pray, to suffer, and to die. It is divine work to address and immediately "reveal" the will of God from the bosom of the Father (John 1:18), "to sanctify a victim" (Matt. 23:19), "to hear the prayers" of all (Rev. 8:3), and to protect the church in His own power (John 10:28). But the same work of Mediator, which is of the sort "to purchase the church with His own blood" (Acts 20:28), "to cleanse from sins" (1 John 1:7), "to save" (Matt. 1:21), and "to reconcile" (Rom. 8:11), is the result or God-man (θεανδρικὸν) work.[4]

V. Mediation Consists in Reconciliation of Parties; He Is Mediator by Merit and Is Efficacious and That in Both Testaments

The mediation of Christ consists in the reconciliation of parties. For "all things" are from God reconciling (ἐκ θεοῦ καταλλάξαντος) us to Himself through Jesus Christ, "just as God was in Christ, reconciling the world to Himself, not imputing their offenses to them" (2 Cor. 5:18–19). But it is the same to reconcile as to receive into grace (χαριτούειν), which God "did in His love" (Eph. 1:6). For in that which God receives us, as pleasing to Him, in the same He reconciles us to Himself. That manner of reconciliation is that by which Christ removed the enmity between God and man by His blood and restored friendship between both. He furnished that in the merit of His death and the unbroken efficacy

3. *Medulla*, VII–XI.

4. *Medulla*, XI–XVI.

of merit, certainly both in the *Old* Testament, future merit and the efficacy of merit always being present, and in the *New* Testament, merit and efficacy being equally present. He did so more fully in the latter.[5]

VI. The Threefold Office of Christ

The office of Christ is threefold: prophetic, priestly, and kingly. For He became for us "Wisdom" (as Prophet), "Righteousness" (as Priest), "Sanctification" (as King, author of internal holiness and heavenly glory), and "Redemption" (which is executed in the former parts) (1 Cor. 1:30). The natural lack of man, corrupted by sin, also required that very thing. For the prophet removed *ignorance*, the priest *alienation from God*, and the king *weakness* of drawing near to God.[6]

VII. The Prophecy of Christ

The PROPHECY of Christ is that whereby *He fully and plainly revealed to us the will of God concerning our salvation, immediately disclosed to Him*. He discharged those things not only in the Old Testament as the "Angel of Jehovah, speaking" (המדבר) (Isa. 52:6), "speaking to that one" (פלמוני המדבר) (Dan. 8:13), but also above all in the New Testament, when God "in the last days spoke through His Son" (Heb. 1:2) according to the prediction, "prophecy from your midst, from your brothers, just as I, Jehovah your God will stir you up. Hear Him" (Deut. 18:18–19). For the prophet is not only made but is born because He "comes above from heaven" (John 3:13) and in Him "treasures of wisdom and knowledge have been hidden" (Col. 2:3). "The only begotten Son, who was in the bosom of the Father, has made Him known" (John 1:18).[7]

VIII. Legal and Evangelical Prophecy

The prophecy of Christ was both legal and evangelical. It was *legal* whereby He preached the true righteousness of the law, apart from which the Savior could not be known. Therefore, in explanation, the former was not established in the proper measure of a new law of works. For the Lawgiver was not properly called the author of a new law of works, as there was no new God of Israel or new object of worship (Σέβασμα). It was above all *evangelical* because "He was sent to preach the gospel to the humble" (Isa. 61:1). Therefore, the gospel is called "the teaching of the Lord" (Acts 13:12), "the testimony of Christ" (1 Cor. 1:6), and "salvation," which "began to be declared by the Lord" (Heb. 2:3).[8]

---

5. *Medulla*, XVI–XIX.
6. *Medulla*, XIX.
7. *Medulla*, XIX–XXIV.
8. *Medulla*, XXIV–XXVII.

IX. Its Tenor; The Duties of a Prophet

Indeed, before all things He preached "repentance and the drawing near of the kingdom of heaven" (Matt. 4:17). For the kingdom of God drawing near demanded *repentance* or change of plan and conversion from false righteousness to acknowledgment of the true—that is, "the heart of the fathers" (Mal. 4:6) and the "sense of the righteous" (Luke 1:17). Elsewhere faith is also joined with repentance (Mark 1:15) because the first work of repentance is no longer *to believe* the promise but *the gospel* in which "righteousness is revealed from faith to faith" (Rom. 1:17). Whatever Christ spoke toward sinners concerning saving grace and mercy must be referred to the same. Moreover, that proclamation was above all efficacious because "He spoke not as the scribes but as having power" (Matt. 7:29), to the point that He "pierced" His hearers (Mark 1:22; Luke 4:32). For, as a faithful witness, He spoke those things that He heard in heaven, the conscience of men attesting to Him.[9]

X. Its Confirmation through Miracles

Christ also confirmed His proclamation through various and many miracles. These were both true and divine. They were *true* because the first people who produced them shrunk back from frauds and lies so that they could not even be cast to dissemble for a brief time the profession of faith by any instruments of torture, not even death itself. They were *divine* because they were made known neither naturally, since diseases could not be cured by word alone and the stinking dead be raised by natural power, nor could they have been made known by an evil or good spirit. They could not have been done so by an *evil* spirit, because He would thus be an enemy and destroyer of His own kingdom (Matt. 12:24–25). They could not have been done so by a *good* spirit, because the raising of the dead—the obedience of the whole of nature, heaven, the earth, and the sea, furnished for the testimony of only His command and will—testifies to a higher cause. Moreover, God did not *tempt* the people of Israel through the miracles of Christ, because Christ did not advise apostasy from the God of Israel. Whatever He did, He did according to the prophets in that time in which they were required to happen and in which the people were required to be seduced by the formerly predicted Pseudo-prophet. Finally, the miracles had teaching as companion, which was required of a great prophet.[10]

XI. And through the Example of His Life and Death

Christ confirmed His teaching not only in miracles but also in the *example* of His life and death. He confirmed it in the example of His *life*, decreeing "to

9. *Medulla*, XXVI–XXX.
10. *Medulla*, XXIX–XXXV.

learn" from Him, because He is "gentle and humble" (Matt. 11:29). For Christ is the archetype of all obedience and righteousness. He confirmed it in the example of His *death* and *martyrdom* because He was "a faithful witness" (Rev. 1:5), and in His death His exemplary (מוסך) patience was conspicuous. Being innocent, *He endured* unjust judgment *without contradiction*.[11]

XII. The Priesthood of Christ

The priesthood of Christ is that whereby *He, as established priest by the Father,* through *obedience of emptying Himself to the point of the death of the cross, perfectly satisfied God for our sins and with the same constantly intercedes for us*. For the name of Priest was clearly assigned to the Christ to come. "Jehovah swore oath, and He will not take it back. You are a priest forever according to the order of Melchizedek" (Ps. 110:4).[12]

XIII. The Condition of Christ the Priest Was External and Internal; Functions of the Same

The condition of Christ the Priest was external and internal. It was required to be *external* to spring from the tribe of Judah (Heb. 7:14), not to be called according to the law of the carnal commandment (Heb. 7:16–17), and by swearing oath to be established eternal Priest (Heb. 7:21–22). It was *internal* that He was required to be "a holy Priest, without sin, unpolluted, separated from sinners, raised over heaven" (Heb. 7:26). The *functions* of Christ were also distinct from the functions of the Aaronic priesthood (Heb. 7:27–28).[13]

XIV. Christ Himself Was the Victim and Expiatory: Its Parts

The *victim* of the priesthood of Christ was Christ Himself. For "He offered Himself" (ἑαυτον) (Heb. 7:27; 9:14). Moreover, the victim was principally *expiatory*. For Scripture assigns to Him the putting away (ἀθέτησιν) of sins (Heb. 9:26) and propitiation (כפר) (ἱλασμὸν) (Dan. 9:24). Therefore, according to the type of the expiatory victims there were parts of the sacrifice of Christ: voluntary offering of Himself to death, death itself, and representation of the victim in heaven.[14]

XV. The Voluntary Offering of Christ to Death

There is the voluntary offering of Christ to death whereby above all He sanctified Himself and devoted Himself to God to death both for favor with God and

11. *Medulla*, XXXV.
12. *Medulla*, XXXVI.
13. *Medulla*, XXXVII–XLI.
14. *Medulla*, XLI, XLII.

the power to unite with men. "For them I sanctify Myself," freely, willingly, not against His will (John 17:19).[15]

XVI. The Death of the Same

The *death* of the same had this same power, in order that through it sins might be expiated and God satisfied for the whole. For God willed to save some, and unless sin was expiated, He could not save. But only obedience unto death could expiate sin.[16]

XVII. This Was Expiatory and Vicarious, and Had True Reason of Satisfaction

Indeed, the death of Christ, in the same way as the typical expiatory victims, had reason of vicarious punishment and expiation. "He established His soul as a price of satisfaction" (אשם) and "took away the sins of many" (Isa. 53:10, 12). "He was made sin for us" (2 Cor. 5:21) and a sacrifice "for sin" (περὶ ἁμαρτίας) (Rom. 8:3). "Seventy weeks have been decreed to expiate iniquity" (לכפר עון) (Dan. 9:24). "Our failures You expiate" (תכפרם), blot out, and obliterate them (Ps. 65:3), as You are Yourself through ransom the price of redemption (λύτρον, ἀντίλυτρον). Redemption (כפרה) (ἀπολύτρωσις), a familiar word to the writers of the New Testament (Rom. 3:24–25; 1 Cor. 1:30), agrees with such (פדות) of the thing produced through expiation. The power of ransom (λύτροῦ) (Matt. 20:28) and of the price of redemption (ἀντιλύτρου) (1 Tim. 2:6) are also attributed to the blood of Christ. The particles "for" (ὑπὲρ) and "in exchange" (ἀντὶ) do not have meager force (Matt. 26:28; Rom. 5:8; Gal. 3:13). Since Christ is said to "have been made a curse" for us (Gal. 3:13), He thereby endured the curse of the law, the cursed death, on account of taking our sins on Himself. Reason attests to the same satisfaction of Christ of the old types, above all the sacrifices, because by bearing the exchange of others, they bore and expiated their sins.[17]

XVIII. The Death of Christ Also Has Reason of Merit

The death and whole obedience of Christ has reason of *merit* properly called in regard to us, as *satisfaction* in regard to God. For all the conditions of merit from condignity agreed with Him because His works of obedience flowed from His own, works of the God-man (θεανθρώπου). Moreover, they were not owed but did have proportion with the good, which followed from them. Therefore, He came in the name of the righteous requirement of the law (δικαιώματος)—that

15. *Medulla*, XLIII.
16. *Medulla*, XLIV.
17. *Medulla*, XLV–LI.

is, for the sake of justification (αἰτίας δικαιώσεως) or "righteousness" meriting life (Rom. 5:18).[18]

XIX. Christ Died for the Elect Only

Christ died for the same ones for whom He made satisfaction. But these are the elect only. For since the death of Christ had reason of vicarious punishment and to that degree Christ offered Himself for those whom He died and satisfied God in whole, they could certainly only be the elect for whom Christ died. For He made satisfaction for the elect only, reconciled only them to God, and expiated their sins alone. "We judge that, if one died for all, all died" (2 Cor. 5:14). This is also clear from those passages in which the death of Christ is called אשם, λύτρον, ἀντίλυτρον, κατάρα, and so on, which signify substitution in the place of another. But only the elect, Christ dying, are deemed dead, because they alone have died and been expiated in Christ, who died for them, and obtain righteousness and life. For "who has died has been justified from sin" (Rom. 6:7). Moreover, since Christ also procured the Holy Spirit and faith for those for whom He died, only the elect obtain it. Therefore, He died for them alone. For that reason Scripture says that Christ died "for many" (Matt. 26:28), for "His people" (Luke 1:68), for "His sheep" (John 10:11). He did not indeed die more for *the seed of the serpent* than for the *serpent* himself. It is added that for those for whom Christ died He also interceded, but not *for the world* but only for those whom "the Father gave" to Him (John 17:9). Finally, He pursued them with greatest love for whom He died (John 3:16; Rom. 5:16). But He "hates" the reprobate (Rom. 9:13).[19]

XX. Representation of the Victim in Heaven and Intercession

The victim of sacrifice, offered and slaughtered on earth, is *represented* in heaven. For Christ "entered into heaven, in order that He may appear before the face of God for us" (Heb. 9:24). He always lives to intercede for us" (Heb. 7:25; Rom. 8:34). "If anyone has sinned, we have an advocate with the Father, Jesus Christ the righteous" (1 John 2:1). This intercession, not general but special, and not doubtful but efficacious, consists in the undertaken protection of the faithful with God. For He is a παράκλητος—namely, an *advocate* or *patron* of another person, who leads the cause for the other person.[20]

---

18. *Medulla*, LI–LVI.
19. *Medulla*, LVI–LIX.
20. *Medulla*, LIX–LXII.

XXI. The Kingdom of Christ

The KINGDOM of Christ is that *whereby He governs His church by His Word and Spirit and protects and preserves it against enemies.* For everywhere Jesus was predicted to be *King.* "I have anointed My King in Zion, the mountain of My holiness" (Ps. 2:6). "A son has been born to us. A son has been given to us, and rule has come upon His shoulders. And His name has been named Wonderful,… Prince of peace" (Isa. 9:6). "Exult greatly, daughter of Zion. Behold your righteous King will come to you" (Zech. 9:9). "The Lord God will give to Him the throne of David, and He will reign over the house of Jacob, and there will be no end to His kingdom" (Luke 1:32–33). "I am King. For this I was born, and I have come into the world to give testimony to the truth" (John 18:37). For Christ, by His death, purchased "a peculiar people and inheritance" (Ps. 2:8; Isa. 53:10; 1 Peter 2:9) who, by the same as King, ought to be separated from the world, rendered into one body of the church, enriched with gifts, kept and protected in laws, and made complete in eternal glory.[21]

XXII. It Is Mediatorial, Spiritual, and Heavenly

The kingdom of Christ is *mediatorial*, distinct from the essential manner, because its King is Savior and Mediator, and it is *spiritual* and *heavenly.* "My kingdom is not from this world" (John 18:36). "For this I have been born," in order that I may be King, "and I have come into the world to give testimony to the truth" (John 18:37). That is to say, God is the first truth, He did all things for His glory by teaching righteousness and demonstrating it through obedience, the law is true and promises life to the one who obeys it, and the true promises are in Him as well as the true covenant, begun by Him as Mediator. The "scepter" of His kingdom is the "Word" of truth, which "goes out from Zion" (Ps. 110:2; Isa. 2:3) and "is written on the heart" by the Holy Spirit (Jer. 31:33). Those who obey Him are "from the truth" (John 18:37) and love the truth. That kingdom "did not come" with "pomp" (παρατηρήσιν), but it is "within" (ἐντος) (Luke 17:20–21). Those who believe in Christ have "righteousness, peace, and happiness in the Holy Spirit," and they are in the "kingdom" of Christ. Therefore, it is distinguished as the kingdom "of heaven" (Matt. 3:2; 4:17) because all in it are heavenly, and as long as the faithful are on earth, its roots are in heaven and its fruits are blooming on the earth.[22]

XXIII. It Consists in Governance and Defense of the Faithful

The kingdom of Christ is administered in governance and defense of the faithful. *Governance* is either external or internal. The external is brought about in

21. *Medulla*, LXII, LXIII.
22. *Medulla*, LXIV–LXX.

the *word* of law and gospel (Ps. 110:2). *Internal governance* is brought about by the illuminating and regenerating Holy Spirit. *Defense* is that whereby He powerfully protects and preserves His people against their enemies. For in power His church is a burdensome stone on all peoples, to which, whoever burdens themselves, will be burned by burning.[23]

XXIV. It Is Eternal

The kingdom of Christ is also *eternal*. For its king is the "Father of eternity" (Isa. 9:6). His "throne is forever" (Ps. 45:6). "His kingdom will have no end" (Luke 1:33). But yet the economy varies. For both those things that prevailed in the Old Testament ceased and those that prevail in the New Testament will cease. For "it is necessary to reign until He puts all His enemies under His feet" (1 Cor. 15:25). But the economy of the second life, all enemies having been put away, "God will be all in all" (1 Cor. 15:28) and will rule the church with His immediate operation under her King, Head, and Spouse, which will never cease.[24]

XXV. Christ Is the Messiah; The Advent of the Messiah

The same Christ the King is Messiah (משיח) or *anointed* King. Many things confirm that He was promised in the Old Testament and fulfilled long ago. For those things that were required to precede His advent according to prophecies—Moses above all, and the signs of the times after the return from Babylon, like the "multiplication of the people," being enriched and spread even in the increase of Idumaeans (Deut. 30:1, 6)—came to pass before Jesus fulfilled them. All those things that were required to exist at the advent of the Messiah, such as the "Scepter, the Lawgiver from the midst of the feet of Judah" (Gen. 49:10), the "temple" (Mal. 3:1) or the later house, the "glory" of the Messiah "to be fulfilled" (Hag. 2:7–9), "Damascus" or "the Head of Judah" (Isa. 7:8–9), "having power (משלים), the priests, rulers of the people" (Isa. 49:7), the "land" of Canaan as the "peaceful land" of the Jews (Isa. 7:16), "the holy city, vision, sacrifices, offerings" (Dan. 9:24, etc.), exist no longer but passed away long ago. Above all, the point of time indicated by Daniel 9:23ff., the "seventy weeks" of prophetic things—that is, determined in the course of 490 years—and "over the people" of Israel, hence by assembling and increasing the spread of the Word "to restrain transgression, end sin, expiate depravity, bring in eternal righteousness, seal the vision and prophecy, and to anoint the Holy of Holies," put to an end, expired long ago.[25]

23. *Medulla*, LXX.
24. *Medulla*, LXXI–LXXIV.
25. *Medulla*, LXXIV–LXXIX.

XXVI. Jesus the Messiah

There is no other Messiah who arrived than our *Jesus*. For another who came could not be demonstrated. Moreover, those things that were required to precede the advent of the Messiah and exist during the advent, and indeed the point of time sealed by the angel to Daniel, agree exactly with our Jesus. Finally, when Jesus arrived, those things were *seen* and *heard*, which were required *to be heard* and *seen* according to the prophecies. With this argument Jesus demonstrates that He is the Messiah (Matt. 11:4–6). They did works that *had been seen* and *were seen*, not only He, but also His apostles, which God gave "as signs and omens" (Isa. 8:18). He began to perform them in heaven through His benefits and judgments and did not cease to perform them. Things *had been heard* and *were heard* that were required to be heard: the gospel preached to the poor, and above all the proclamation of the resurrection from the death, the ascension into heaven. This was not without the added strength of witnesses, eyewitness (αὐτόπτων), of circumstances and works, the pouring out of the Holy Spirit on believers, the inheritance of the Gentiles given, and of the same kingdom promoted to that point. It is supported not only by the *prophecy* of Christ and the apostles that became clear in the event and daily became clearer, but also by the *parallels* between those things that the prophets preached and the gospel narrative tells us about Jesus.[26]

26. *Medulla*, LXXIXff.

LOCUS XX

On the Economy of the Covenant of Grace under the Gospel

I. Jesus Was Required to Be Proclaimed to the World: The Gospel

Jesus the Mediator, Prophet, Priest, and King, was required to be proclaimed to the world. For "there is one Mediator between God and men, the man Christ Jesus, who gave Himself as the price of redemption, as a testimony for His own times" (1 Tim. 2:5–6). This testimony comes in the name gospel (Ἐυαγγελίου) par excellence (κατ᾽ ἐξοχὴν), which is defined as the joyous announcement of the new covenant and testament of grace whereby through and on account of Christ manifested in the flesh He suffered, died, was resurrected, and glorified. Under the condition of repentance and faith and of rightly giving the same, consummate remission of sins, adoption, freedom, peace, regeneration of the Spirit, and eternal life are promised and given. It was proclaimed by the forerunner of Jesus, John the Baptist, Jesus Christ Himself, the apostles, and witnesses of Christ's resurrection.[1]

II. Christ Is Proclaimed as Mediator of the New Testament: The New Testament

Jesus Christ is proclaimed in the gospel as "Mediator of a better and New Testament, enacted on better promises" (Heb. 8:6; Matt. 26:28). But *the New Testament* is that *part of the plan of God which He, having abolished those things that were added to the promise until the time of correction, willed to become known in the new dedication and confirmation of the eternal testament of grace through the blood of Christ. Finally, it became known in the giving of better promises to execute in the last time in Israel and through the proclamation of the gospel in the world.* This is not that typical old (but true and eternal) testament of grace, yet in regard to economy *new*. For it succeeded the old typical one as pure, purged from types and the law, and was newly dedicated. God spoke about this: "Behold, the day will come,

1. *Medulla*, I–VI.

says Jehovah, and I shall cut a new covenant (חדשה ברית) with the house of Israel and with the house of Judah,... This is the covenant that I shall cut with the house of Israel after those days, says Jehovah. I will give the law in their midst, I will write it upon their hearts, I will be as God for them, and they will be My people." (Jer. 31:31–35). "I will establish an everlasting covenant for you. You will remember your ways and hide in view of shame when you receive your elder sisters for the younger. I will give them to you as daughters and not from your covenant. I will establish My covenant with you, and you will know that I am Jehovah" (Ezek. 16:60–61).[2]

III. The Economy of the New Testament: Its Law Is the Law of Faith

The New Testament has a peculiar economy, administered in the "fullness of times" (Eph. 1:10), "at the end of the ages" (1 Cor. 10:11), and "at the last hour" (1 John 2:18). Its law is the law of "obedience to the confession in the gospel of Christ" (2 Cor. 9:13), which the apostle calls the "obedience of faith" (Rom. 1:5). This is not commanded in a new law but in a new testimony, to which the law itself fittingly commands belief from the one to whom it has been revealed. That confession is "in the gospel of Christ" because in it alone is the "love and goodness of God toward men" revealed. There are three foundations of this: the pure *wisdom* of the gospel, because in the proclamation of the gospel "the grace of God abounds in all wisdom and prudence" (Eph. 1:8); *agreement with the prophetic Scriptures*; and *piety* and its fruits. For "the saving grace of God shined forth on all men, teaching us to live temperately, righteously, and piously in this age, having denied all impiety and impure desires" (Titus 2:11–12).[3]

IV. It Is not a Law of Works, nor Does It Commend Counsels of Evangelical Perfection, Monastic Vows

Therefore, the law of the gospel is not properly a law *of works*, nor does it even commend *counsels* of evangelical perfection from the commands of faith or works, distinguished and demonstrated, not commanded; mandated, not commended. For if the gospel is taken *properly*, it does not exist except in the doctrine of faith. Or if it is taken *broadly*, it does not commend counsels of faith or necessary precepts of morals. Add to that that the counsels either pertain to the perfection of the love of God or do not pertain to it. If *they do pertain* to it, it is understood that they are commanded, not demonstrated, and mandated, not commended. If *they do not pertain* to it, they are neither good works nor praiseworthy, but must be rejected (ἀπόβλητα). Above all of this sort are monastic vows, the apex of counsels, which disagree much with the gospel and much more with its perfection.[4]

2. *Medulla*, VI–X.
3. *Medulla*, X–XVI.
4. *Medulla*, XVI–XX.

V. Christ Added No New Commandments to the Law

Nor also did Christ under the gospel introduce new commandments not comprehended in the law of Moses. For nothing more perfect is given than the law of Moses, and "He did not come to abolish the law but to fulfill it" (Matt. 5:17). Nor did He add some to all the commands of God for perfection and pertaining to the angelic worship of God under the New Testament for the same reason.[5]

VI. The Promises of the Gospel

The gospel above all has excellent promises into which the very law of faith is brought to apply them, announced with the joyous proclamation to the one who believes. In this sense *the law of faith*, since it is brought into those more excellent promises, is proper to the economy of the gospel and the New Testament. Furthermore, those are most excellent promises. They are the greatest and costly promises (Μέγιστα καὶ τίμια ἐπαγγέλματα) that "the divine power bestowed" on us "in the knowledge of Him who calls" (2 Peter 1:3). "He is the Mediator of a better testament which is enacted with better promises" (Heb. 8:6).[6]

VII. Rules for Understanding the Promises

There are two rules to understand the promises of the New Testament. *First*, Scripture reckons diverse benefits of the covenant of grace equally to the economy of the New Testament. If they did not fall on the sons of God in the Old Testament, although they did, it was because they did not fall on them in the same degree, measure, and perfection. Therefore, those benefits ought not to be understood simply but economically, not in regard to the thing (τὸ ὂν) but in regard to the manner (τὸ ποῖον) of the thing. *Second*, Scripture attributes to the New Testament the consummation of Christ and the faithful. For as Christ "was made perfect through sufferings" (Heb. 2:10), so the faithful "were made perfect as one" (John 17:21, 23).[7]

VIII. The Difference between the Promises of the Gospel from Those Made before Christ

It is a consequence that the benefits proper to the New Testament, such as the display of righteousness, redemption, justification, remission of sins, the Spirit of promise and adoption, revelation, wisdom, trust, love, fear of God, freedom, peace, the inheritance of the Gentiles and communion with heaven, joy, even external worship and its ministry, and the seal of grace may be said to differ from those that, under the promise either pure or mixed with legal servitude,

5. *Medulla*, XX.
6. *Medulla*, XXI.
7. *Medulla*, XXII.

the people of old enjoyed on the earth. Those alone could not obtain perfection (τελειώσιν) that had not yet been perfected through the sufferings of Christ. For "the law perfected nothing but the introduction of a better hope, through which we draw near to God" (Heb. 7:19).[8]

IX. The Times of the Economy of Grace under the Gospel

The economy of the covenant of grace under the gospel had "its own times" (1 Tim. 2:6). These were of *preparation*, hence beginning from Christ, or of *ratification*, made in the death of Christ, or of deadly *execution*, joined with the case of the republic of Israel. Hence, the Scriptures begin the kingdom of heaven only from John the Baptist (Matt. 11:12–13) by reason of *preparation*, only from the resurrection of Christ (Matt. 26:29) by reason of *ratification*, and only from the cutting off of the Jews (Luke 9:27) by reason of *execution*. Concerning the boundaries of each economy a certain mixture of each prevails.[9]

X. The Proclamation of the Evangelists

In all those times the proclamation of the evangelists prevailed. For witnesses and heralds of the words and deeds of Christ, above all of His death and resurrection, clothed with strength from on high, were necessary to discharge that testimony wisely. These are *evangelists*, heralds of Christ present and about to die or having died and in heaven, sitting at the right hand of God. The apostle establishes that this sort ought to have been sent (Rom. 10:13–17) with a twofold testimony of Scripture: one of Joel, "And it shall be that everyone who calls on the name of Jehovah will be saved" (Joel 2:32), and another of Isaiah, "How beautiful in the mountains are the feet of those proclaiming peace, proclaiming goods (טוב), who make them to hear salvation, who say, 'Your God has been made King'" (Isa. 52:7). And already earlier David said, "The Lord gives speech (first he announces the gospel by dying and what was done). Good heralds are many armies" (Ps. 68:11).[10]

XI. The First Herald: John the Baptist

The first herald of the gospel after the prophets fell silent was *John* the Baptist: the "messenger will make the way free before the Lord coming to His temple" (Mal. 3:1), "Elijah (in the spirit of Elijah)…to convert the hearts of the fathers to their sons and the sons to their fathers" (Mal. 4:5–6), "a voice of one crying out in the wilderness" (Isa. 40:3–6).[11]

---

8. *Medulla*, XXII–XLI.
9. *Medulla*, XLI.
10. *Medulla*, XLII.
11. *Medulla*, XLIII.

XII. Parts of His Ministry; Proclamation of Repentance, etc.

The parts of the ministry of John were the proclamation of repentance, testimony concerning Christ, and baptism. Indeed, before all was his *proclamation of repentance*, "turning the hearts of the fathers to their sons and the sons to their fathers" (Mal. 4:6). Moreover, it was efficient, lest He "shame Abraham" and others of his "sons" (Isa. 29:22). He was saying, "Repent, for the kingdom of heaven is near (be converted from false righteousness to true, from evil works to good, to the promised King…and bear fruit worthy of repentance" (Matt. 3:2, 8). Such presented his *testimony concerning Christ*: "This is the one about whom I was speaking, who comes after me but was made before me because He was before me" (πρῶτος μου) (John 1:15). "Behold, the Lamb of God, who takes away the sins of the world" (John 1:29). He sealed both his proclamation of repentance and his testimony concerning Christ with *baptism*. "He appeared baptizing in the wilderness and preaching baptism for the remission of sins" (Mark 1:4). Christ also wished to be baptized with this baptism to "fulfill all righteousness" (Matt. 3:15).[12]

XIII. Christ the Herald of the Gospel

After John, Christ was the same herald of the gospel, who is its Lord. For God "spoke in His Son in the last days" (Heb. 1:1). "Salvation began to be declared by the Lord" (Heb. 2:3). His advent itself was the Word of existing salvation. On the cross He shouted, "It is finished" (John 19:30), and brought back from death, He conversed with His disciples about the gospel.[13]

XIV. The Apostles Heralds of the Gospel; Their Inauguration

From the same *apostles* appeared heralds of the gospel who were sent out. Christ deliberately chose these, future allies, companions, ministers, witnesses of His words and deeds, above all of His resurrection from the dead. "But God raised Him on the third day and gave Him to appear not to all people but to witnesses chosen by divine foreordination (προκεχειροτονημένοις) for us, who ate and drank together with Him after He rose from the dead. They commanded us to preach to the people that He has been appointed by God as Judge of the living and the dead" (Acts 10:40–42). Hence Saint Peter defines an apostle as "a witness of the resurrection" (Acts 1:22), and Saint Paul would prove his apostleship by saying, "Am I not an apostle? Did I not see Jesus Christ our Lord?" (1 Cor. 9:1). They were sent in order to preach this gospel "to every creature" (Mark 16:15) but in their order, and to discharge that office of herald happily, "clothed with power from on high" (Luke 24:49). Moreover, they were required to be

---

12. *Medulla*, XLIV–XLIX.
13. *Medulla*, XLIX.

anointed with sacred oil, or the Spirit of their Head. This anointing came in the name "of the baptism of the Holy Spirit" (Acts 1:5) and followed in the feast of Pentecost when, with the symbol of flaming tongues seizing them, the gift of tongues and wisdom to utter the great things of God followed (Acts 2:1–4).[14]

XV. The Prerogatives of the Apostles

The prerogatives of the apostles, baptizers of the Holy Spirit, were not few nor to be disdained. The *principal* prerogative was that they were witnesses of the death and resurrection of Christ, universal heralds of the gospel, and infallible in public proclamation and writing. "The Holy Spirit will teach you, and He will make you to remember all that I have said to you" (John 14:26). "He will lead you into all truth" (John 16:13). "It will be given to you in that hour what you shall speak. For it is not you who are speaking but the Spirit of the Father who speaks in you" (Matt. 10:19; Luke 12:12). The *accessories* were the following: the keys of the kingdom of heaven were promised to them in a singular manner (Matt. 16:18, 19; John 20:23), they bestowed the Holy Spirit by the laying on of hands (Acts 8:19; 19:6); accomplished signs for punishment of the faithful and unfaithful even by coming with a rod (1 Cor. 4:21; 5:3, 5); preached efficaciously as always having the Holy Spirit (Acts 2:41); were affixed to no place, although to a certain "canon and line" (2 Cor. 10:13–16); and were without successors (ἀδιάδοχοι). Finally, the apostleship had signs: "patience, signs, wonders, and virtues" (2 Cor. 12:12).[15]

XVI. The Seventy Disciples; Prophets; Evangelists; Pastors and Teachers

After the apostles were established, other heralds of the gospel were also sent, such as the "seventy disciples" (Luke 10:1–2). To them it was as equally said as to the apostles: "The one who hears you hears Me" (Luke 10:16). There were evangelical "prophets" (Eph. 4:11) who, although not apostles, nevertheless had common gifts among them, so that they could explain the prophecies and relate hidden things (1 Cor. 14:1). There were "evangelists" (Eph. 4:11) who expounded the history of Christ and the apostles, endowed with singular gift and grace, either in speech or writing or in both, either as eyewitnesses (αὐτόπται) or those who "pursued all things above accurately" from other eyewitnesses (αὐτόπταις). There were "pastors and teachers" (Eph. 4:11) about which we speak below.[16]

---

14. *Medulla*, L–LIII.
15. *Medulla*, LIII–LVIII.
16. *Medulla*, LVIIIff.

LOCUS XXI

On the Grace of Calling

I. The Beginning of the Grace of Christ Is Calling

As God blessed us from eternity, electing us in Christ, so according to His eternal grace in Christ He has "bestowed grace" (ἐχαρίτωσε) on us in a manifold manner (Eph. 1:4, 6). The beginning of this grace is from *calling*, which is the *voluntary favor of God whereby He so summons and draws to the communion of His grace and glory the elect from eternity—redeemed through Christ in time, by nature sinners, many simple and ignoble—by His supernatural and omnipotent power, through the external proclamation of the Word and the Holy Spirit. He creates anew and regenerates them, and at the same time gives them faith in Christ, and through it unites them to God. As a result of God calling in this way, they are infallibly led into and reach His communion by right.* For temporal "election" itself (John 15:16; 1 Cor. 1:20), corresponding to the eternal, is similar to that calling whereby God "calls generations from the beginning" (Isa. 41:4), "calls from the womb" (Isa. 49:1), "calls and brings in" (Isa. 48:15), and "calls things that are not" (Rom. 4:17).[1]

II. It Differs from Common Calling

Clearly, common *calling* is of another kind that is also of those who are not "elect" (Matt. 20:16). For they are not so called according to the plan and testament of God, as heirs written in it. Instead, they are called according to the righteousness and economy of God whereby He tolerates them in the external communion of the elect, convicts through the Word concerning His goodness and their malice, and it provides no excuse for parents. These are not called immediately by God, who moves the heart, but mediately by men who strike the ears. Their hearts are not penetrated and, having been called in such a way, they are not brought in but are abandoned in their misery. Finally, they are called not on account of themselves but on account of the elect, in whose midst they dwell.

1. *Medulla*, I, II.

They do not prevail at discerning these human heralds. This itself is nevertheless not universal, because external calling through the Word has "proper times" (1 Tim. 2:6) and "a measure of rule" or "line" of mission (2 Cor. 10:13, 15).[2]

III. The External Means of Calling the Elect

The calling of the elect happens through means, of which kind are the works of nature, the longsuffering of God that "leads to repentance" (Rom. 2:4), and above all that "Word which is proclaimed to us" (1 Peter 1:25) by which alone God is restored as friendly to the sinner. For this there are three things in the Word: testimony, command, and promise.[3]

IV. The Compelling of the Holy Spirit Is Most Joined with Those

But the calling of the elect through the Word is most joined with the internal compelling of the Holy Spirit, the principal means of calling, and there is no profit without it. For it carries the ears of the natural man, dead in sin, who "neither has eyes to see nor ears to hear" (Rom. 11:8; Isa. 6:9). Moreover, without the Holy Spirit "writing" the Word "on the heart" (Jer. 31:33), there is nothing except "the letter that kills" (2 Cor. 3:6). Therefore man preaches the same Word, and the Holy Spirit writes it on the heart "by opening the heart," so that the Word of God made known may be received and loved (Acts 16:14).[4]

V. The Efficacy of the Operation of the Holy Spirit Who Calls

The operation of the Holy Spirit through the Word preached externally is neither natural nor moral and mediate, but supernatural, immediate, omnipotent, and most efficacious. For so great is the efficacy of the Holy Spirit writing the Word of God on the heart that He subjects man and his will to God through love, makes him willing from not willing, drawing near from fleeing, and "willing" from resistant (Ps. 110:3), in order that God may give to them the Spirit of wisdom and revelation…that they may know what is the hope of their calling, the riches of glory, the supreme greatness of His power toward us, who believe according to the working of the strength of His power which He exerted in Christ when He raised Him from the dead" (Eph. 1:18–19).[5]

VI. No Sufficient Grace of All Called Is Given to Obey Freely

Therefore, the grace of God common and sufficient for all is not given to the man called. Therefore, from two disposed in the same manner, one called is

2. *Medulla*, III, IV, VI, VII.
3. *Medulla*, V.
4. *Medulla*, VIII–XI.
5. *Medulla*, XI–XVIII.

freely converted by cooperating, and another renders the same power of grace ineffective by dissenting. For after the fall, Scripture strips all from the will of man, and whatever good comes about refers to grace received in whole. Next, the calling and conversion of man the sinner comes in the names and actions of "the creation of a pure heart" (Ps. 51:10), "generation, regeneration that is from above and from Spirit and water" (John 3:5; 1 Peter 1:3), "vivification and raising again," as from the dead (Eph. 2:1, 5–6). All are unfit for these things, whether from themselves or from common grace. Moreover, the very calling and conversion of man proceed from the infinite power of God who acts omnipotently. For in it is the "supreme greatness (ὑπερβάλλον μέγεθος) of the power of God" toward us who, having been called, "believe," not from one's own faculty but "according to the efficacy of the strength of the power of God which He worked in raising Christ from the dead" (Eph. 1:19–20). Finally, all called by God are drawn, and they do not come to the Son unless God the Father draws them. "No one can come to Me, unless the Father who sent Me draws him, and I will raise him on the last day" (John 6:44).[6]

VII. The Work of Calling Is Regeneration: Its Parts

Regeneration is the work of divine calling. This *second birth* and rebirth (παλιγγενεσία) is as it were to have been born again. "God regenerated us according to His great mercy to living hope through the resurrection of Jesus Christ from the dead" (1 Peter 1:3), "regenerate not from corruptible seed but incorruptible through the living Word of God, and remaining forever" (1 Peter 1:23). Its parts are *the putting off of the old man and the putting on of the new man*. "In order that you may put off the old man who is corrupt according to deceitful lusts, be renewed in the spirit of your mind, and put on the new man who was created according to the righteousness and holiness of truth" (Eph. 4:22–24). These both prevail in each part of the old and new man, soul and body. For the *oldness* of the *exterior* man is in vain thought, pleasure of the spirit, and according to that the action of the body. The *newness* of the *interior* man is not only of spirit but also of body, speaking with a true mouth, doing right things, and pleasing God through the members of the body.[7]

VIII. The Causes of Regeneration: Its Seed

Christ unfolded the causes of regeneration: "Unless someone is born from water and Spirit, he cannot enter the kingdom of God" (John 3:5). There water is merit or obedience, righteous requirement (δικαίωμα) through the blood of Christ, which on account of purity and the power to purify comes in the name "of

6. *Medulla*, XVIII–XXI.
7. *Medulla*, XXI, XXII.

water" (Ezek. 36:25; Heb. 10:22; 1 John 5:8). "Spirit" is the Holy Spirit to whom regeneration is economically appropriated. He is in and remains in the regenerate, just as part of the substance of the parents remains in the children, and is therefore joined with "pure waters" (Ezek. 36:25). But the "seed" of the same is the *promise* of God, as the "incorruptible Word" (1 Peter 1:23), and the *example of faith*. "Abraham received the sign of the righteousness of faith, in order that he may be father of all who believe in the foreskin of faith" (Rom. 4:11–12). For the confession of the word and hope is the image of the seed in which some "brought forth" (ὠδίνουσι) others (Gal. 4:19), and as "fathers brought them forth in Jesus Christ through the gospel" (1 Cor. 4:15).[8]

IX. The Imperfection of Regeneration

Regeneration is imperfect in this life on account of the surviving flesh that remains to struggle. For the regenerate not only have the "Spirit against the flesh," but also the "flesh lusting against the Spirit, so that they do those things that they do not wish to do" (Gal. 5:17). The struggle of Saint Paul with the flesh most clearly proves this (Rom. 7:14ff.). "If we say that we do not have any (indwelling) sin, we deceive ourselves and the truth is not in us. If we say that we have not sinned (in act), we make God a liar and the Word of God is not in us" (1 John 1:8, 10). For it is of interest to the glory of God that His "power be made perfect in our weakness" (2 Cor. 12:9), that He be exalted, and that man, conscious of his weaknesses, be humbled.[9]

X. Calling Is the Giving of Faith

Calling is being brought to God and His communion. Furthermore, there can be no communion with God except in Christ, nor can one be in Christ unless he seizes Christ by faith. Therefore, calling is the giving of faith—namely, through which the one who is called responds to the one who calls.[10]

XI. Faith in General and What Is Common

Faith improperly and passively received is, in general, persuasion concerning the truth of the divine testimony. The former is legal or evangelical. *Evangelical faith* is common and proper. *Legal* or *historical faith* consists in the knowledge of Christ and theoretical and general assent. It is either "dead" (James 2:26) or *living* in some degree *for a time*, indeed joined with feeling and a certain joy. To that extent it is temporary (πρόσκαιρος) or *miraculous*, which is persuasion about a miracle to be performed that proceeds from singular and hidden divine revelation.[11]

---

8. *Medulla*, XXIII–XXVII.
9. *Medulla*, XXVII–XXX.
10. *Medulla*, XXX.
11. *Medulla*, XXXI–XXXIV.

XII. The Proper Faith of the Elect

The *proper* faith of the elect is defined as *not only certain knowledge but also trusting apprehension of Christ the Redeemer and His saving benefits as those are offered in the Word of the gospel and sealed in the sacraments, whereby each believer adjudges and applies them to himself.* For it is called "the faith of the elect," joined with "the knowledge of the truth, which is according to piety" (Titus 1:1), the substance (ὑπόστασις) and representation "of those things which are hoped for" (in mind through knowledge [*notitiam*], assent [*assensum*], and trust [*fiduciam*]), and demonstration (ἔλεγχος) "of those things which do not appear" (to the mind, to apprehend and trust what has been done) (Heb. 11:1).[12]

XIII. The Divine Disposition (Habitus) Is Infused: The Cause of Faith

This faith is not acquired in work alone or in the exercise of actions, but the divine disposition (*habitus*) is infused. *Disposition* is infused because believers "have (ἔχουσιν) faith" (Mark 11:22; 1 Tim. 1:19) and hence are designated as the "faithful" (πιστοὶ) (Acts 10:45; 16:1). This designation expresses "steadfastness" (στερεότητα) (Col. 1:23; 2:5), insofar as faith "dwells" in them. It is *divinely* infused because faith is "a gift of God" (Eph. 2:8), and it is equally infused in some. Moreover, the Holy Spirit Himself, who is the "Spirit of faith" (2 Cor. 4:13), "is poured out" (ἐκχεῖται) on us (Rom. 5:5). For the *cause* of faith is not man the sinner but the merit of Christ, who is the "Head and Perfector of faith" (Heb. 12:2). It is the working of the Holy Spirit whereby "believers are sealed" (Eph. 1:13). He is "the Spirit of faith" (2 Cor. 4:13).[13]

XIV. The Object of Faith

The object of faith is either general or specific. The *former* is the testimony and revelation of God concerning anything. The *latter* is Christ alone, the Redeemer, and His benefits. That is *personal*, Christ as Prophet and Redeemer, whom God commanded "to hear" and in "whom to believe" (Matt. 3:17; 17:5; John 3:36); *verbal*, the gospel in which Christ and His benefits are revealed; or *real*, that which Christ reveals in the promised and displayed gospel, such as to believe for salvation. Christ with all His benefits was "made wisdom from God, righteousness, sanctification, and redemption" (1 Cor. 1:30), "crucified" (1 Cor. 1:23), and "salvation" for the sinner (Heb. 2:3), and there are "better promises" in the New Testament (Heb. 8:6).[14]

---

12. *Medulla*, XXXIV.
13. *Medulla*, XXXV–XXXVIII.
14. *Medulla*, XXXVIII.

XV. Into Which Faith Is Brought by Applying It

Faith is brought into this object by apprehending it and applying it to itself. For the promise of grace in Christ is set forth as determined, not indefinite. "I will be your God and the God of your seed after you" (Gen. 17:7). This promise was required "to be firm for the whole seed" (Rom. 4:13, 16), which, unless it was empty, Abraham and his seed were required to apply it to themselves. The faithful do that. "Bless Jehovah, O my soul,... who remits all your iniquities and heals all your diseases" (Ps. 103:1, 3). "Who shall separate us from the love of Christ?" (Rom. 8:35). "The life I now live in the flesh I live by faith in the Son of God, who loved me and gave Himself for me" (Gal. 2:20). "He chose us in Him" (Eph. 1:4). "Now we are sons of God" (1 John 3:2).[15]

XVI. Antecedent Acts of Faith: Knowledge (*Notitia*), Humiliation, Denial of Oneself, and Pious Struggle

The acts of faith are concerning its proper object, whether antecedent, accompanying, formal, or consequent. The antecedent acts are knowledge (*notitia*) of Christ and His benefits. This is the image of the embryo from which faith is born, and not only explicit by reason of the foundation but also implicit by reason of the whole Word of God. Moreover, it is necessary in regard to that (τὸ ὅτι) because "this is eternal life, that they may know You the only true God" (John 17:3), and "the faith of the elect" is "knowledge of the truth according to piety" (Titus 1:1; John 3:33). *Theoretical assent* (*assensus theoreticus*) is that through which the faithful person confesses the truth known about Christ so that, convicted about it through the Holy Spirit, he willingly perceives as true and divine what God reveals in His Word about Himself, His grace, longsuffering, virtues, and Jesus Christ. For the "one who receives His testimony seals that God is true" (John 3:33). It is as it were to suck the breasts of the divine promise, which is no less accepted by God than it is pleasing to the mother when the infant sucks her breasts. *Humiliation* before God is that whereby the sinner "is pricked" (κατανύγεται) (Acts 2:37). *Denial of oneself* is necessary because man first ought to despair of himself before he trusts in Christ, and *pious struggle* because the one called in the Word and Spirit to faith does not snore as if asleep. Rather, embraced in Christ, he is eager to act.[16]

XVII. The Accompanying Acts of Faith: Practical Assent, Flight to Christ, and Contrition

The *accompanying* acts of faith are *practical assent* (*assensus practicus*) or *trusting* (*fiducialis*) assent whereby the one who believes the gospel concerning Christ

15. *Medulla*, XXXIX–XLII.
16. *Medulla*, XLII–XLVI.

judges not only that it is true but also that it is good and good for him, most worthy of all love and devotion, and that the promises of grace are also most certain to him. The former is full persuasion (πληροφορία) concerning the grace of God pertaining to him (Rom. 4:21; Col. 2:2), the "shouting of the king" (Num. 23:21; Jer. 49:2), whereby Christ the king is followed with joyful shout. Holy *flight* is that whereby "as the deer pants for the river beds of water, so the soul of the one who believes pants for God and thirsts for the living God" (Ps. 42:1–2). Finally, saving contrition of spirit is not from fear of punishment but from love of Christ.[17]

XVIII. The Formal Act of Faith

The *formal* act of faith is *trusting apprehension of Christ*, reception of Him, and *union* with the same. Indeed, this is to believe in Christ (האמין) (πιστεύειν εἰς Χριστὸν)—namely, proving Him. It is to commit to obtain salvation in Christ, to throw oneself on Him as the arm of the Savior in that manner in which nurslings commit themselves to nurses and are sustained by hanging from their breasts, "to receive" (λαμβάνειν) Christ (John 1:12), "to accept" (ὑπολαμβάνειν) Him, to take up His life as Head and treasure (Col. 2:6), "to lean on" Him (Isa. 10:20; 50:10), "to throw oneself upon the beloved" (Song 8:5), "to recline upon Him and to lean on" Him (Ps. 7:6; Isa. 48:2), "to apprehend the refuge of salvation" (Isa. 17:5), "to put on Christ" (Gal. 3:27), and "to be united to Him" (Ps. 86:11). That cannot happen without trust (*fiducia*) in Christ, who is apprehended. Nevertheless, trust, which is in faith in regard to its formal act, ought to be distinguished from trust in its accompanying act or *practical assent* and consequent assent or *acquiescence* in Christ.[18]

XIX. The Consequent Acts of Faith: Life-Giving, Purifying, Quieting, Strengthening, and Fruit-Bearing

The *consequent* acts of faith are also diverse. The pure grace of justifying faith is *life-giving* because "the righteous live by faith" (Hab. 2:4), apprehending Him who is "life" (John 14:6) and in whom is "life" (John 1:4). Hence it revives (ἀναζωπυρεῖται) all our gifts and duties (2 Tim. 1:6). It is *purifying* because, as the sky is purified by light, so "hearts are purified by faith" (Acts 15:9). It is *quieting* because "the justified by faith have peace with God, access of faith received for grace, in which they stand and boast" (Rom. 5:1–2). It is *strengthening* because "we can do all things in Christ who strengthens us" (Phil. 4:13), and "faith" is "our victory" (1 John 5:4–5). Finally, it is *fruit-bearing* because faith, as

17. *Medulla*, XLVI.
18. *Medulla*, XLVII–XLVIII.

a pregnant mother, is immediately impregnated with good works and is "efficacious through charity" (Gal. 5:6).[19]

XX. The Trust (*Fiducia*) of Faith

Faith is not free from trust in regard to antecedent *practical assent*, *apprehension* of Christ, and *quieting* act or *acquiescence*, which it follows. The very names of faith in Christ (πίστεως εἰς Χριστὸν), (בטחה), (האמונה), to which fear (פחד) is opposed (Isa. 12:2), include persuasion (πεποίθησις), full persuasion (πληροφορία), confidence (παρρησία), and even paraphrases of faith. One such is "the substance of those things which are hoped for, demonstration of those things which are not seen" (Heb. 11:1), because things so hoped for stand present in the soul of the one who believes and the *not seen* as seen. To that degree things hoped for are demonstrated certain and firm to the one who believes. Moreover, that trust may also be described through "substance" (ὑπόστασιν) (Heb. 3:6, 14) and "boasting in substance" (καύχημα ὑποστάσεως) (2 Cor. 9:4). In addition to that, faith and trust have the same opposites, such as "doubt" (Matt. 14:31), "to have taste of high things" (Luke 12:29), "fear and timidity" (Isa. 12:2; Luke 8:50), "diffidence" (Rom. 4:20). Finally, the effects that the Scriptures attribute to faith cannot be free from trust.[20]

XXI. Love Is Not the Form of Faith

Neither is true faith destitute of love, nor is love the form of faith but the fruit that emanates from the same. Indeed, although love, a certain witness of faith, is also in a testimony, its form is nevertheless not that love which is carried in all the attributes and works of God and to neighbor, but rather the effect emanating from it as its cause. For "love is not imitated by faith" (1 Tim. 1:5), and "faith works through love" (Gal. 5:6) because through it, as its work and fruit, "it demonstrates" that it is true (James 2:18). Apart from love faith is dead, an empty corpse, and nothing (James 2:20, 26).[21]

19. *Medulla*, XLIX.
20. *Medulla*, L–LIV.
21. *Medulla*, LIIIff.

LOCUS XXII

On the Grace of Justification

I. The Nexus of Calling and Justification

The grace of justification is most closely joined with the grace of calling. "Those whom God called He also justified" (Rom. 8:30). For God "calls into communion of His Son" and His righteousness (1 Cor. 1:9).[1]

II. The Words "to Justify": הצדיק, etc.

The words "*to be justified*" owe its origin not to Latin but to the church, to express to the devout the emphasis of the words "הצדיק" and "δικαιοῦν." Moreover, the force of the original words, above all, is not to make righteous but is taken in a forensic and intransitive sense. Δίκαιον νομίζειν means *to repute*, *to declare*, and to that degree *to absolve* as *righteous* in *judgment*. For opposed to that are "to condemn" (הריע), not to make wicked (Deut. 25:1; Prov. 17:15), "to pronounce perverse" (עשק), not to make perverse (Job 9:20), and "to accuse" (ἐγκαλεῖν) (Rom. 8:33).[2]

III. Justification of the Sinner Is Defined

Justification is either of the sinner or of the righteous. *The former* is *the act of God the Judge whereby He freely, on account of Christ, remits the sins of man the sinner who believes in Him and adjudicates the right of eternal life*. The apostle declared this nature of justification in whole, saying, "We are justified freely by His grace through the redemption that is in Christ Jesus, whom God set forth as propitiation through faith in His blood, for the demonstration of His righteousness, on account of the remission of sins made before, in the tolerance of God, for the display of His righteousness in the present time, that He is just and the One who justifies him who by faith is in Jesus Christ" (Rom. 3:24–26).[3]

---

1. *Medulla*, I, II.
2. *Medulla*, III.
3. *Medulla*, IV.

IV. Its Principal Cause

It is therefore "God who justifies" (Rom. 8:33). In economy it is God the *Father* as *Judge* who "reconciles the world to Himself in Christ, not imputing sins to them" (2 Cor. 5:19). It is the *Son* who is Sponsor and "Advocate" (Rom. 8:34). It is the Holy Spirit who is *Door-keeper*, the certification of absolution who pronounces the sentence of God in the hearts of the elect.[4]

V. The Internal Cause of Justification

The *internal* cause moving God to justify man is the grace of God or gracious favor. For we are justified "freely" (חנם) (Isa. 55:1–2), "freely by His grace" (δωρεὰν τῇ αὐτοῦ χάριτι) (Rom. 3:24). For the gratuitous favor of God is the fountain of all benefits, and justification singularly comes forth from the love of God. For that righteousness, on account of which we are pronounced righteous in the judgment of God, admitted and defined from the eternal love of God alone toward men, is given in time, and what is given in the judgment of God is accepted.[5]

VI. The External Cause of the Same

The cause outside God, moving the same to justify, is work (δικαίωμα) or perfect righteousness that the law of God demands from Him who deserves to be justified. For because God prescribes the cause of the right of claiming life "to do" (τὸ עשות) that which the law commands (Lev. 18:5) and threatens death to the one who does not do it, He cannot so omit that cause in judgment whereby He justifies the sinner as just, holy, and truthful, that He can justify anyone without it. Otherwise, the "judgment" of God would not be "according to truth" (Rom. 2:2), and "He would absolve by absolving" without righteous requirement (δικαίωμα) (Ex. 34:7).[6]

VII. This Is the Righteousness of Christ and Redemption

This cause in the judgment of God is not inherent in the righteousness of man the sinner, infected indeed with sin, imperfect, and not even possessing any true legal righteousness. Instead, it is the righteousness and redemption (ἀπολύτρωσις) of Christ. "We are justified freely by His grace through the redemption that is in Christ Jesus" (Rom. 3:24). For He is "our righteousness" (צדקנו) (Jer. 23:6), "was made righteousness by God" for us (1 Cor. 1:30), and is

4. *Medulla*, V–VIII.
5. *Medulla*, VIII.
6. *Medulla*, IX.

"the righteous" who "suffered for the unrighteous" (1 Peter 3:18). This righteousness is especially necessary and above all efficacious.[7]

VIII. And It Is Imputed to the Sinner

But although the righteousness of Christ is the single cause of justification, in a certain manner it nevertheless ought to be ours, and it cannot prevail except in the judgment of God. But although the righteousness of Christ is foreign in *quality*, indeed inherent in Christ, it is nevertheless ours in *law* and *judgment*. For sin is not imputed to us, but the righteousness of Christ is imputed; that is, it is attributed, given, and adjudicated to us, which is the cause of life. "Blessed are those whose sins are forgiven, whose sins are covered. Blessed is the man to whom God does not impute sin" (Ps. 32:1–2; Rom. 4:7, 8). For hence the apostle gathers that "God imputes righteousness without works" (Rom. 4:6), as verse 5 had said that "faith," Christ received by faith, "is reckoned (λογίζεσθαι) for righteousness." The same is in the antithesis of the first and second Adam, where he substitutes for the word "imputation" "justifying work" (τοῦ δικαιώματος) or "cause of righteousness," His "gracious giving" (χάρισμα) (Rom. 5:15), "giving in grace" (δωρεὰν ἐν χάριτι), and "gift" (δώρημα) (Rom. 5:16). Both the righteousness (δικαίωμα) of the second Adam, Christ, and the fall (παράπτωμα) of the first Adam on those whom both represented, could not be except by imputation.[8]

IX. Faith Is Not Imputed as a Work

And faith is not imputed by justifying as a work—that is, the Christian religion and its exercise—because "the wicked is justified" (Rom. 4:5), not the faithful. For "all have sinned and fallen short of the glory of God" (Rom. 3:23), and the "grace of God," without works, indeed is given "freely, through the redemption in Christ Jesus" (Rom. 3:24). Otherwise faith would abolish the law because God would admit another righteous requirement (δικαίωμα), another righteousness than required by the law. But faith "establishes the law" (Rom. 3:31). Moreover, Christ would have died in vain, and faith could no longer be opposed to works.[9]

X. The Legal Righteousness of Christ Imputed: It Was Made Perfect in His Sufferings

That righteousness of Christ, which is imputed by justifying, is not the essential righteousness of God, because otherwise man would be deified. Rather, it is the legal righteousness of Christ, that obedience which He demonstrated by

7. *Medulla*, X–XVI.
8. *Medulla*, XVI–XX.
9. *Medulla*, XX, XXI.

ordering His whole life to the norm of the law and by suffering and which was also active in death itself, having died out of love. For not sufferings alone or righteousness, which they call passive, are imputed by justifying. "By the obedience of one (indefinitely) many are established righteous" (Rom. 5:19). The finishing touch of His obedience was His sufferings, having died out of love. For He was *obeying* God the Father not only in death, but "until death" (μέχρι θανάτου) (Phil. 2:8). In addition, Christ was Sponsor with the Father of His fulfilling the law, which man was obligated to fulfill according to the command, "Do this and you shall live." If this fulfillment of the law is not imputed to man, neither did Christ fulfill the promise, nor can man "live," because neither he nor another for him and in his place "did" or fulfilled the law perfectly.[10]

XI. The Parts of Justification: Remission of Sins

The parts of justification are remission of sins and adjudication of life. *Remission of sins* is the *judicial act of God whereby He pardons for the sinner* who believes *the guilt and penalty of sin on account of Christ*. David speaks about this: "Blessed are those whose sins have been remitted" (Ps. 32:1–2). Moreover, sins are remitted, not expelled, as the acts of which have already crossed over. But since guilt is abolished, the penalty is also pardoned. Indeed, sins were taken away in the cross differently than they are in justification and sanctification. In the *cross* Christ took them away by expiating, in *justification* He took them away by not imputing and not condemning, and in *sanctification* He takes them away by weakening and abolishing innate vice little by little. Moreover, eternal guilt and punishment having been remitted, temporal punishment is not retained by God because, the cause having been taken away, sin, the effect, all punishment, is taken away. For "there is no condemnation for those who are in Christ Jesus" (Rom. 8:1). Christ "has perfected all who are sanctified in one offering" (Heb. 10:14).[11]

XII. Human Satisfactions, Indulgences

The same reason also cuts the throat of human *satisfactions*, both one's own and foreign. For they are insulting to the redemption and righteousness of Christ, which is the sole cause of remission of sins and life and is of infinite value. For "we are justified freely by the grace" of God "through the redemption in Christ Jesus" who alone is "Propitiator in His blood" (Rom. 3:24–25). This redemption and satisfaction of Christ is not applied through any human satisfaction, being incompatible (ἀσύστατον) with it, but through faith alone in Christ. Since there are no satisfactions of this kind, there can be no place for *indulgences* by men performing the grace of imposed satisfactions. This also leans on false

10. *Medulla*, XXII–XXV.
11. *Medulla*, XXV–XXIX.

hypotheses, which are by no means among the last *treasures* of foreign human satisfactions or rather worthless things and "the key of the shaft of the abyss" (Rev. 9:2). For even saints cannot make satisfaction for themselves or for others. Moreover, no satisfactions of Christ not yet applied in the plan of God are given, and to that point they are superfluous.[12]

XIII. The Adjudication of Life

The second part of justification is the *adjudication of life*. For man absolved from his sins does not have the right to obtain life unless the same righteousness of Christ attributes that whereby He made satisfaction in whole to the law that promises heavenly life. Therefore, the word of righteousness (צדקה) most often signifies the right to the good thing. "This inheritance of the servants of the Lord and their righteousness is from Me" (Isa. 54:17). That righteousness is man's which is from the Son of God and heir of all things.[13]

XIV. The Condition of Imputing Righteousness Is Faith Alone, Which Justifies as Instrument

The righteousness of Christ is not imputed to the sinner without condition. This is neither the same righteousness that the law demands nor one's own satisfactions nor sacrifice nor love or good works, but faith in Christ. "We conclude that man is justified by faith without the works of the law" (Rom. 3:28). Moreover, it justifies not as preparation, disposition, part of righteousness accepted for the whole, or a work, but as an instrument or hand by which one grasps and applies Christ and His righteousness as refuge of one's salvation and from the "fullness" of the same "grace for grace" (John 1:16). For faith without Christ is an eye without light, an ear without sound. Therefore, everywhere Scripture attributes justification, life, and communion with Christ to faith. For "the righteousness of God is revealed from faith to faith" and to that extent by faith alone as the ultimate end (*archetele*) (Rom. 1:17). "We are justified by faith without works of the law" (Rom. 3:28). "The just shall live by faith" (Hab. 2:4; Rom. 1:17). Faith does not do this *properly* but *by metonymy*, by virtue of the *object* apprehended, so that of those words, *faith justifies*, the proper sense is *Christ and His righteousness apprehended by faith justifies*. Next, works, as causes, are removed from justification, life, and communion with Christ. For "man is justified by faith without works of the law" (Rom. 3:28) and "not except by faith" (ἐὰν μὴ διὰ πίστεως) (Gal. 2:16). "To the one who works the reward is imputed by debt. But to him who does not works but believes in Him who justifies the wicked, his faith is imputed to him for righteousness" (Rom. 4:4–5). Therefore, works of

12. *Medulla*, XXIX–XXXIV.
13. *Medulla*, XXXIV.

any kind are excluded, even those done from grace, because works do not cease to be. Even the works of Abraham done from grace are removed (Rom. 4:1, etc.). Finally, justification consists in the remission of sins, which can accept nothing besides faith.[14]

XV. Justification Is One in Species in All and One in Number in All

Justification is *one in species* in all because God justifies all who believe freely by grace, through the redemption of Christ. Moreover, it is *one in number in all* because at the same time the bringing of perfect remission of sins to the believer is never revoked. For it is "a gift of righteousness" (Rom. 5:17), and "the gifts of God" proper to the elect are "without repentance" (Rom. 11:29). "I wipe away your transgressions like a dense cloud and your sins like a cloud" (Isa. 44:22).[15]

XVI. Active and Passive Justification

The act of justification is undivided and perfect in itself. Yet by method it has a divided sense, is imperfect and unequal. For justification is twofold: active and passive. The *former* is the sentence of God the Judge absolving, perfect and equal to all. The *latter* is the sense of the same once received by faith. In respect to all the justified of the Old Testament and New Testament it was and is divided, imperfect, and unequal, yet so that it never perishes in general.[16]

XVII. Justification of the Righteous

There was the justification of the *sinner*. The justification of the *righteous* or *justified* is the *declaration of righteousness once received by faith whereby, justified by faith, demonstrating the same righteousness of faith or its sincerity through works as fruit, truly faithful in conscience before God men, the person is declared justified through faith*. The former is of the *sinner*, a priori, the cause by faith alone. The latter is of the *righteous*, a posteriori, the effect completed by works alone. Saint Paul says about this, "If Abraham was justified by works, he had boasting, but not before God" (Rom. 4:2). Saint James also says, "Abraham our father was justified by works, offering his son.... Therefore, you see that man is justified by works and not only by faith" (James 2:21–24). The twofold judgment of God, the twofold accusation of Satan, and the twofold tribunal of God demand both the justification of the sinner and the righteous.[17]

---

14. *Medulla*, XXXV–XL.
15. *Medulla*, XL.
16. *Medulla*, XLI.
17. *Medulla*, XLII, XLIII.

XVIII. The Effects of Justification, Adoption: Its Cause

There are various effects of justification by faith, yet very important ones are adoption and freedom. *Adoption* is the *gracious sentence of God whereby He adopts those justified and reconciled to God by faith through and on account of Christ above, and as sons and heirs, coheirs with Christ.* For "to those who received" Christ by faith "He gave the power to become sons of God" (John 1:12). "You have received the Spirit of adoption" (Rom. 8:15). "God sent out His Son, in order that we might receive adoption" (Gal. 4:4–5). "He predestined us to sonship" (Eph. 1:5). Indeed, its *decree* is assigned to God the Father, its *acquisition* to God the Son, "vindicating us in freedom" (John 8:36), and its *sealing* to the Holy Spirit, effective with His inner testimony and breath, in order that we may approach the Father with confidence in Christ and call Him Father (אבא).[18]

XIX. And Difference

Adoption is taken broadly, narrowly, and most narrowly. *Broadly* taken it is the state of sons but with "no difference from the servants" (Gal. 4:1). *Narrowly* it is taken merely of sons who "did not receive the spirit of servitude again for fear" (Rom. 8:15). *Most narrowly* it is taken of the glorified sons. The apostle writes about this: "We ourselves who have the firstfruits of the Spirit also groan within ourselves, awaiting adoption, the redemption of our body" (Rom. 8:23). Indeed, sonship is perfected in the liberation of the body from death.[19]

XX. Essential Freedom: Accidental or Christian

Freedom is a fruit of justification and a companion of adoption, and it is either essential or accidental. *Essential freedom* is immunity from the curse of the law and servitude to sin. "The law of the Spirit of life, which is in Christ Jesus, has set me free from the law of sin and death" (Rom. 8:2). *Accidental freedom*, which is also called *Christian*, is proper to the faithful of the New Testament. It is a greater degree and perfection of freedom—namely, immunity and exemption from the carnal precept and the authority of the law and of men as guardians of the law. "If the truth has set you free, truly (ὄντως) you will be free perfectly" (τελείως) (John 8:36). There are rules of this latter liberty, lest it degenerate into lust or license, which makes *servants of corruption*, in order that faith and love may direct the same in the use of things indifferent. For "whatever is not from faith is sin" (Rom. 14:23), and "knowledge puffs up but love edifies" (1 Cor. 8:1). Finally, let it not become a pretext for mastery. For "all things are lawful to me. But I will not be reduced to the power of any" (1 Cor. 10:23).[20]

---

18. *Medulla*, XLV, XLVI.
19. *Medulla*, XLVI–XLIX.
20. *Medulla*, XLIXff.

LOCUS XXIII

On the Grace of Sanctification

I. The Nexus of Sanctification with the Remaining Benefits

The grace of sanctification immediately follows the grace of justification. It is understood under *calling* as its continuous progression, under *justification* as its fruit, and under *glorification* as the beginning of the same.[1]

II. Its Definition

Sanctification is the *grace* or *the gracious favor of God whereby He, on account of Christ the Redeemer, through the Holy Spirit, restores the corrupted nature of the man justified by faith according to the Word of God more and more to His image so that in turn he daily dies to sin and lives to righteousness for salvation in Christ.* Indeed, it is the preservation of the first regeneration and a certain continual progression.[2]

III. And Necessity

There is the greatest necessity of sanctification. For "without it no one will see the Lord" (Heb. 12:14). "The one who has been born from God does not sin" (1 John 3:9). Indeed, all things seriously demand it, including the eternal election of God; the grace and redemption of Christ; the Spirit of Christ; calling, conversion, and regeneration of man; justification; adoption; faith in Christ; the kingdom of Christ; the hope of glory to be revealed in us; consolation of conscience; sincerity of faith; freedom of Christians; the beginnings of eternal life; the promises of God; the way to heaven; heavenly glory; and the course and struggle imposed on us in that way.[3]

---

1. *Medulla*, I.
2. *Medulla*, II, III.
3. *Medulla*, IV.

IV. It Consists in Restoration to the Image of God

The essence of sanctification is not in change of actions alone but in continual restoration of man to the image of God. "That we may be restored in the spirit of our mind and put on the new man who was created according to God in righteousness and the holiness of truth" (Eph. 4:23–24). This restoration is continual conversion from darkness to light, from the power of Satan to God. Hence, in it evil is removed through *mortification of the old man*, vicious qualities being put away more and more, and good is restored through *vivification of the new man*, good qualities being infused, preserved, and increased.[4]

V. The Parts of Sanctification: Repentance

The parts of sanctification are repentance and new obedience. Repentance *broadly* signifies the whole conversion of man and also embraces faith itself (Matt. 3:2; 9:13; Acts 2:38). *Narrowly* it signifies contrition and conversion placed opposite to faith (Mark 1:15; Luke 24:47). *Most strictly* it signifies restoration alone, distinguished from sorrow according to God (2 Cor. 7:10). In this passage repentance is taken *narrowly*, defined as *sorrow from the knowledge of sins together with trust in remission of the same, producing change of heart from evil to good.*[5]

VI. Its Parts: Acknowledgment of Sins, Confession of Them Done to God, to Men, but Not into the Ears of a Priest

The parts of repentance are acknowledgment of sins, confession of the same, sorrow and sadness, imploring of remission, and plan of changing life. *Acknowledgment of sins* is that whereby they are acknowledged from the law. "I have known my transgressions, and my sin is always before me" (Ps. 51:3). *Confession* of the same is twofold: one is made to God, another to men. It is made *to God* either *publicly* to the whole church (Dan. 9:5–7) or *to individuals*, of which sort was David, the publican, and those baptized by John. Both of the former are necessary, inevitable, and joined with shame in the face. Sins in a certain condition must be confessed *to men*, such as of the *church* offended by sin, and to "one another," some having offended others with sin (James 5:16). They also may be confessed *to pastors*, to whom the faithful lay bare the wounds of conscience, but freely and of consultation rather than confession. But it is foreign, which happens in the ears of the priest, of every sin and their circumstances, to procure absolution from the priest. This is not instituted in the Word of God, and it assigns to the priest what belongs to God alone and torture of the soul. The snare of desperation fosters license to sin, and it is the fetter of the papal kingdom.[6]

---

4. *Medulla*, V–X.
5. *Medulla*, XI.
6. *Medulla*, XI–XVI.

VII. Sorrow and Sadness, Imploring of Remission, Plan of Changing Life

Sorrow and *sadness* is that whereby man on account of sin acknowledged and confessed is sad "according to God" (2 Cor. 7:10), so that sin displeases him in the same manner in which it displeases God. In the former there is saving "compunction" (κατάνυξις) (Acts 2:37). *Imploring of remission* is that whereby the contrite person humbly asks pardon from God. "Be gracious to me, O God, according to Your goodness" (Ps. 51:1). "O God, be propitious to me a sinner" (Luke 18:13). Finally, there is a *plan of changing life*. For "in Christ one is a new creation" (Gal. 6:15).[7]

VIII. New Obedience: Good Works

New obedience is exercised through good works. Moreover, there are *good works, voluntary actions of the sanctified, which come from a pure heart, love of God, true faith in Christ, according to the law of God, for His glory, one's own salvation, and the usefulness of neighbor.* For in order that a work be good, concursus of all causes is required. This includes *its beginning*, which is the disposition of the will or the "treasure of a good heart" (Matt. 12:35), "a good tree" (Matt. 7:17), a "pure heart" (1 Tim. 1:5); *conformity with the law of God* because those things "must be done" that "God commands" (Deut. 12:32); and also *rectitude of circumstances* because goods are necessary to be conducted well. Moreover, *love of God* is introduced because "love is the fulfillment of the law" (Rom. 13:10) and the root of good works (1 Cor. 13:4). *Faith* is also introduced because "whatever is not from faith is sin" (Rom. 14:23), and "love from faith is not feigned" (1 Tim. 1:5). The *end* is *intention* of right, which the person who wills orders to the glory of God and salvation of neighbor, according to His Word. "If your eye is simple, the whole body will be lucid" (Matt. 6:22). But the good works noted in the latter are distinguished from the works of the unregenerate, Gentiles, and hypocrites. Moreover, the works exacted even of the regenerate for the rigor of the same bring forth their imperfection in this life, so that none can be found without adhering vice.[8]

IX. The Necessity of Those

Good works of adults and of those who can produce them are in a sense as necessary as sanctification itself. For although they do not justify, they are nevertheless fruits of justifying faith. They do not indeed serve the interests of meriting salvation, but taking possession of it. They are a consequence of the

7. *Medulla*, XVI–XXI.
8. *Medulla*, XXII–XXX.

adjoined antecedent, faith. "Let your light so shine before men, that they may see your good works, and glorify your Father, who is in heaven" (Matt. 5:16).[9]

X. They Do Not Effect or Merit Salvation

Yet good works neither effect nor merit eternal life. For "eternal life" is "a gift of God" (Rom. 6:23), opposed "to debt" (ὀφειλήματι) (Rom. 4:4). Moreover, it depends on Christ alone and faith in Him (John 17:3; Acts 4:12), and it is given as "an inheritance" (Matt. 25:34; Rom. 8:17; Eph. 1:18). For all boasting must be excluded from salvation. "Where is boasting? It is excluded through the law of faith" (Rom. 3:27). But the one who merits can boast. Yet it is "not from works, lest anyone boast" (Eph. 2:9). Finally, works merit neither from condignity, nor from pact, nor from congruency. They do not merit *from condignity*, because not even "our sufferings," still less actions, "are worthy of the glory of God to be revealed in us" (Rom. 8:18), and we are debtors of doing those things for God by right of creation and redemption. God has no *profit* when "we render our ways perfect" (Job 22:2–3), and "we are the workmanship of God, created in Christ Jesus for good works" (Eph. 2:10). They do not merit *from pact*, because God nowhere promised life to one meriting it, and legal sin cannot be entered from pact. They do not merit *from congruity*, because God promised the reward of merit not apart from perfect obedience, as from merit.[10]

XI. The Species of Good Works: The Christian Life, Denial of Oneself, Bearing of the Cross, the Function of One's Own Calling

The special species of good works are the Christian life and prayer. *The Christian life* is *that whereby the sanctified who imitate Christ throughout it furnish new obedience by denying themselves, bearing the cross, and working those things that are of their own calling*. Indeed, first in the Christian life is *denial of oneself*, which is a laying aside and emptying of oneself or of that for which one ought to be ashamed and renounce. "If anyone wishes to come after Me, let him deny himself." Above all, "impiety and worldly lusts" ought to be denied (Titus 2:12). *The bearing of the cross* follows it. "And let him take up his cross" (Matt. 16:24). "If we died together, we also live. If we endure we will also reign together" (2 Tim. 2:11–12). Indeed, this was the condition of Christ the Head and ought to be the same for His members. For since our cause suffered, in order that we may be conformed to Him and give requital to Him, we ought "in turn to fulfill what is lacking of the afflictions of Christ in the flesh for His body" (Col. 1:24). *The function of one's own calling* follows this. Saint Paul says about this, "We implore you to devote

---

9. *Medulla*, XXX.
10. *Medulla*, XXXI–XXXVII.

yourselves to rest, to do your own things, and to do work with your hands" (1 Thess. 4:10, 11).[11]

XII. Prayer

Prayer is *that whereby the pious request necessary goods from God in the name of Christ by faith, avert evil, and give thanks to God for received benefits*. Indeed, one must pray "as it is necessary" (καθὸ δεῖ) (Rom. 8:26) to "God" alone (Deut. 6:13) in the name of Christ (John 14:13–14). For it is not permitted to approach the Father without the Son the Priest (Heb. 7:25), and God is glorified in Christ alone. We must pray "from faith" (James 1:6), certain in Christ that whatever we ask in His name we shall receive (John 14:13). We must not pray for few goods but for all, *necessary ones* above all, because we need all things for salvation, but some more than others.[12]

XIII. Its Species

The species of prayer are petition (δέησις) of help amid evils; prayer (προσουχὴ) for goods; intercession (ἔντουξις), whereby we avert the evils of others; and thanksgiving (εὐχαριστία) for benefits received by others and us (1 Tim. 2:1). *Thanksgiving*, which is an invitation for a new benefit, ordinarily goes first. It is followed by *prayer* for goods. "First are the kingdom and righteousness of God, to which others are added" (Matt. 6:33), the former absolutely, the latter with condition. To this is added *petition* of help amid evils, which are either *faults*, simply to be averted, or *punishments*, which, being eternal and spiritual, must also simply be averted together with a temporal condition. *Intercession*, which demands love of neighbor, closes. "Be vigilant in prayer for all the saints" (Eph. 6:18).[13]

XIV. The Species Subdivided: Mental, Vocal, Song, the Remaining Species

Prayer of any sort is either mental or vocal. The *former* does not go outside the mind of the one praying. The *latter* goes outside the mind. "We return the calves of our lips" (Hos. 14:2). "Through the tongue we bless our God and Father" (James 3:9). *Song* is added to this. "Be full of the Spirit, speaking to one another with Psalms (also through musical instruments, which ψάλλονται are mentioned), hymns (songs of whatever sort), and spiritual songs (constant in singing), singing the Psalms in your heart to the Lord" (Eph. 5:19; Col. 3:16). Some prayer is *sudden*, while some is *premeditated* and composed, and those

---

11. *Medulla*, XXXVII–XLI.
12. *Medulla*, XLII–XLVI.
13. *Medulla*, XLVI–L.

either conceived or prescribed. Some are *private*, solitary or domestic, others are *public*, ordinary or extraordinary.[14]

XV. The Lord's Prayer: Its Parts, the Action of Addressing God the Father
Many formulas of prayers occur in the Old and New Testament. But the *Lord's Prayer* first seized the hand for all as a *formula* for praying according to the precept of Christ: "When you pray, say, 'Our Father,'" (Luke 11:2). It must be used as *exemplar* for other formulas according to the precept of the same Christ: "Thus (Οὕτως) you pray, 'Our Father,'" (Matt. 6:9). Its parts are the action of addressing God the Father, the body of the prayer, and the closing. The *action of addressing* is in these words: "Our Father, who is in heaven." There the action of addressing "Father" is the state of sons toward God. Invoking "our" is the innate character of faith that applies the promise and love toward our neighbor. Finally, the action of addressing Him who is "in heaven," the place of glory, the native land, home, which Christ occupied for us, testifies to our free access to God and the ardor of our prayers.[15]

XVI. The Body of the Same: Petition 1, Petition 2, Petition 3
The body of the prayer is summed up in six petitions, as in two tables: the first concerns the glory of God and the second the salvation of neighbor. The first three petitions, as the first table of the prayer, look at the *glory of God*. The *first* petition is in the words, "Hallowed be Your name." There the "name" of God signifies God Himself and His virtues. Its *hallowing*, which is used most broadly, as absolutely holy, includes separation from all profane use and glorification. The *second* petition is in the words, "Your kingdom come"—that is, preserve and govern all creatures, as King, above all the church, which is the kingdom of heaven; as its King, rule in this life by Your Word and Spirit, protect against all enemies, and fulfill the next life of heavenly glory. The *third* petition is "Your will be done, as it is in heaven, so also on earth"—that is, let Your will both *decreeing*, as of our King, be fulfilled on earth through us, as serving the interests of Your counsel, and *prescribing*, through our cheerful prompt obedience, as it is fulfilled in heaven, our native land, where Christ, the angels, the perfected ones of the Spirit, righteousness, peace, and holiness dwell and reign.[16]

XVII. Petition 4, Petition 5, Petition 6
The remaining three petitions, as the second table of the prayer, concern *our* salvation and that of our *neighbor*. The *fourth* petition is comprehended in these

14. *Medulla*, L–LIV.
15. *Medulla*, LIV, LV.
16. *Medulla*, LVI–LIX.

words: "Give us today our daily bread." "Food and clothing" are necessary for our life (1 Tim. 6:8), nature, calling, future necessities, peace, good rule, parents, leaders of the republic and the church, and so on. We acknowledge that all of these depend on Your blessing to bestow to us "today" because tomorrow is of its own care. The *fifth* petition sounds thus: "Remit us our debts, as we also remit our debtors." Pardon the sins that we confess, provide a happier sense of having been pardoned, strengthen and enlarge our faith in Christ, seal for Your grace love toward neighbor, inspire pardoning of his offenses, and restrain remaining wrath toward him. The *sixth* petition is conceived in these words: "And lead us not into temptation, but deliver us from evil." We do not avert temptation in general but those that belong to us: turn away the impending danger of temptations from the flesh, Satan, the world, and the Antichrist, lest you reveal the shame that is in us, and if anywhere temptation prevails, deliver us from it, lest we remain under its power and be conquered by the gates of hell. Finally, crush Satan and his scales, above all the Antichrist, under our feet in a short time.[17]

XVIII. The Closing

The *closing* contains doxology (δοξολογίαν) and pledge of the one praying. The *former* is in these words: "For Yours is the kingdom, the power, and the glory forever." For God, because He has the *kingdom*, has the will of dispensing His treasures. Since He is *powerful*, "He can do, from superabundance, above all of those things that we ask or think" (Eph. 3:20). Since He has *glory*, it is of interest to Him that the faithful heed the heralds of His glory. *Pledge* and trust is declared in the exclamation of the particle "Amen," which is the image of a seal and has the sense of desiring and affirming the thing as exceedingly fixed with God.[18]

XIX. Characteristics of Extraordinary Prayers: Fasting—Its Exercise, Bodily and Spiritual

The characteristics of extraordinary prayers are fasting and feasting. Fasting is religious abstinence from food, drink, and other temporal comforts instituted by God. The purpose is to pray more assiduously, meditate with more fixation, avoid more suitable things, and humble ourselves more lowly before God. Its exercise is twofold: bodily and spiritual. The *former* is abstinence from eating, drink, and other comforts of life. The *latter* is humiliation before God, rending of the heart, solemn confession of sins, singular contrition, and attestation of faith.[19]

---

17. *Medulla*, LIX–LXII.
18. *Medulla*, LXII–LXV.
19. *Medulla*, LXV, LXVI.

XX. Fasting: Legal, Evangelical

Fasting is either legal or evangelical. *Legal fasting* prevailed under the law and expired in regard to all that was shadowy in it. *Evangelical fasting* prevails under the gospel when "the spouse is taken away" (Matt. 9:15) and consists in the abstinence from food, drink, and all luxuries and comforts of life, so much as human fragility permits. It does not consist in abstinence from enjoyment of foods, which is not true fasting but the "doctrine of demons" (1 Tim. 4:1–3). "Do not let anyone condemn you on account of food or drink. If you have died with Christ, why, as living in the world, do you endure commands," which are of this sort: "Do not touch, do not taste (flesh), do not handle" (Col. 2:16ff.). Nor are there stated and defined times of fasting, because one must fast when "the spouse is taken away" (Matt. 9:15) who is not taken away at stated times.[20]

XXI. Feasting

Feasting is public thanksgiving for a singular benefit gathered out of the ordinary and is a spiritual attestation of happiness. The feasts in the Old Testament were declared publicly. In the New Testament a perpetual spiritual feast must be held "in the unleavened bread of truth and sincerity" (1 Cor. 5:8). About another feast the church has freedom whether it wants to regard certain times festively for commemorating the benefits of God, provided that the faithful are not burdened and that superstition, expectation of worship, and necessity cease.[21]

XXII. Pledge: Its Species, Conditions, Material

Pledge is also referred to prayer. It is a *religious, spontaneous, and solemn promise lawfully made to God, with a dedicated spirit and firm plan of heart, of promising about a thing or act for the honor of the same and good of neighbor or oneself.* It is either general or special. *A general pledge* is that whereby we pledge and devote ourselves and all our things to God, as happens in baptism and the Supper. *A special pledge* is that in which we singularly pledge something to God. Its *conditions* are that He be called purposely, with mature judgment, and prudently, and the calling must not trust oneself or have one's own strength. The *material* is neither evil nor indifferent, but what makes for the honor of God, our salvation, and our neighbor's salvation has been commanded in the law of God at least in general, and we are persuaded pleases God. For that reason pledges ought to be "spontaneous" (נדיבות) (Deut. 23:23), not because they are made about an indebted thing but by natural reason of a new obligation that comes up.[22]

20. *Medulla*, LXVI–LXXII.
21. *Medulla*, LXXII.
22. *Medulla*, LXXIII–LXXIX.

XXIII. Sanctification Is Imperfect: And It Continues to Grow from Day to Day

The sanctification of this life is imperfect because the sanctified consists of two principles: "the Spirit and the flesh," which are "struggling against" one another as contraries (Gal. 5:17). But yet in the conflict of the two the former continues to grow and strives for perfection. "We do not lose heart. But even if our outer man is corrupted from day to day, our inner man is renewed from day to day" (2 Cor. 4:16). "We complete holiness in fear" (2 Cor. 7:1).[23]

XXIV. Spiritual Struggle: Its Cause, Adversaries, Armor, the Manner of Struggling

A *spiritual conflict* consists in the conflict between the Spirit and the flesh. *It is that struggle whereby the faithful so wage war with the Spirit of Christ as leader against the flesh or sin remaining after regeneration and its champions, Satan and the world, with true faith in Christ. Desiring good according to the inner man, they nevertheless repeatedly succumb according to the outer man. Nevertheless, with the Spirit of God as victor they complete holiness with true faith and are saved in the day of the Lord.* In this struggle God is our principal *Struggler*, *Jehovah* our *courage*, *Jehovah, Rock, Refuge, Liberator* (Ps. 18:2). Less principal is the regenerate man, "faithful unto death" (Rev. 2:10). The *adversaries* are God our friend and those hostile to Him, His professed enemies, flesh, blood, and principalities. The *armor* is spiritual, full, arms sustaining and enduring attack (Eph. 6:11–19), opposed to terrible armor of the enemy, equipped with power and cunning or uncommon methods (μεθοδείαις). Finally, the *manner* of struggling is with *God* through obedience, trust, prayers, and humility. It is with the professed *enemy*, whose every attack the struggler not only blockades, lest Satan the serpent escape from the Siren, but also strenuously wages war, gathering his step, and finally prevails by conquering, confounding, and putting to flight.[24]

---

23. *Medulla*, LXXIX.
24. *Medulla*, LXXXff.

LOCUS XXIV

On the Constancy of the Covenant of Grace

I. Parts of the Constancy of the Covenant of Grace: Perseverance of the Saints

Now the last *grace of the constancy of the covenant of grace* consists in the perseverance of the saints and certitude of salvation. The *perseverance of the saints* is the *grace* or *gift of God whereby He gives the elect justified by faith and sanctified unconquerable constancy as they persist to struggle against sin and the troubles of this age or even to rise from falls through repentance in grace once given until the day of their redemption*. Therefore, it does not pertain to *any whatsoever* but only to the elect, nor *anything whatever* but those who struggle with sin and the troubles of this age, succumbing at some time but rising again and surmounting a difficulty on account of the inserted seed of regeneration. Finally, it is so a *gift* of God that the *moral* image of the disposition is not in man, acquired in repeated acts of believing, but is supernatural, spiritual, and *theological*, produced by the strength of the Holy Spirit in persevering. "I will give fear in their heart, that they may not withdraw from Me" (Jer. 32:40). "I am persuaded that He who began a good work in you will complete it until the day of Jesus Christ" (Phil. 1:6).[1]

II. The Foundations of Perseverance Are the Economic Operations of the Persons of the Trinity: Election of the Father

The foundations of the perseverance of the saints are the economic operations of the persons: the election of the Father, the redemption of the Son saving the elect in the covenant of grace undertaken as Mediator, and the sealing of the Holy Spirit. Its first basis is the election *of God the Father* because "it is not possible that the elect be led astray" (Matt. 24:24), "election follows on" (Rom. 11:7), and the foreknown and predestined "are glorified" (Rom. 8:30).[2]

1. *Medulla*, I–V.
2. *Medulla*, V.

III. The Redemption of the Son, the Promise of the Covenant of Grace in Christ

The second basis of perseverance is the economic operation of the Son of God *redeeming* the elect in the covenant of grace undertaken as Mediator. For the covenant of grace, whose mediator is Christ, has the promise of persevering grace. "I Jehovah have called you with righteousness and have seized your hand, and I will keep you and give you as a covenant people as a light to the Gentiles, that their blind eyes may be sharpened, to take out the chain from the bolt" (Isa. 42:6–7). "This is the covenant that I will cut. I will give My law in their midst, and I will write it on their heart. They will know Me from least to greatest" (Jer. 31:33–34). "I will give fear in their heart, that they may not withdraw from Me" (Jer. 32:40). For that covenant is "eternal" (עולם) (Isa. 55:3), "firm for him" (Ps. 89:28). It consists in perpetuity flowing into the covenanted, because the indwelling of the "Holy Spirit in" their "hearts" is also promised to them (Ezek. 36:27) as is God's "doing" (τὸ עשה)—that is, to perfect and "complete the work" (Phil. 2:13) and protect them against enemies, lest the "sheep" of Christ "could be snatched" from His "hands" (John 10:27–30).[3]

IV. Confirmation of the Same

The confirmation of that promise in a comparative manner, consisting in deeds and signs, confirms perseverance. For *it is compared* especially with stable things, such as "marriage" (Hos. 2:19–20; Eph. 5:32), "testament" (Gal. 3:15; Heb. 9:17), the immovable *statutes* of eternal providence, the movement of "the sun and the moon" (Jer. 31:35–36), the decree about not allowing the "flood" (Isa. 54:9). Such have been made, which men apply for the strengthening of the promises, above all covenantal. These are public acts, books, tables, oath, witnesses, sacrifices, the blood of the testament, memorials, and so on. Feast *signs* are sacraments, a pledge.[4]

V. The Cause of the Covenant of Grace Is Impulsive and Final

In addition, the cause of the covenant of grace is *impulsive*—the love of God toward the covenanted, who is supreme (John 3:16; Rom. 5:8–11; 1 John 4:10) and "eternal" (Isa. 54:8). It is also *final*, the manifestation of the glory of grace, not imperfect but most full, not only being offered but also being conferred because the end and means cohere in an indivisible nexus.[5]

3. *Medulla*, VI.
4. *Medulla*, VI–XI.
5. *Medulla*, XI.

VI. The Foundation of the Covenant of Grace, Christ, Proves Perseverance, Not Only in Undertaking but Also in the Execution of the Office of Mediator

The chief *foundation* of the covenant of grace, Christ—Servant, Sponsor, and Mediator—brings perseverance to pass not only in undertaking the office of Mediator but also in execution of the same. In *undertaking* it He promised and furnished vicarious obedience to God the Father, as faithful *Servant, Sponsor*, and *Mediator*, to gather a peculiar people for Himself. In turn God awarded an inheritance and private possession, of which He would be the heir, Head, and Lord, as we have seen in its own place. But as Christ neither gave up as Surety nor could He give up, so God the Father could not rob Him of the promised reward. Moreover, it is not for nothing that Christ is Head of the church and confers to the same the Spirit and the gifts of His Spirit, righteousness and life. In *execution* of the same office He redeemed and saved His people and conquered their enemies. To that extent, being Redeemer and Savior at the same time as Victor and the Triumphant, He has arranged the perseverance of the saints in safety.[6]

VII. The Sealing of the Holy Spirit

The last basis of perseverance is the *sealing* of the Holy Spirit. For He has been promised to "remain" with us "forever" as the "Spirit of truth" in the giving of whom is found a true and certain promise (John 14:16–17). In the same "believers are sealed" as in "the Spirit of promise" who is the "pledge of our inheritance and acquisition of redemption," so that we are redeemed as "bought with a price." That is to say, we are fully set free "for the praise of His glory" (Eph. 1:13–14).[7]

VIII. The Same Applies the Graces of God and Preserves to the End

The same Holy Spirit is also the Spirit "of power," who works powerfully (2 Tim. 1:7). He works in the faithful by applying the graces of God and by preserving them until the end. For Scripture declares that constancy of the benefits of grace conferred by the Holy Spirit not only *generally* when it calls those "steadfast graces for David" (Isa. 55:3), "gifts of God without repentance" (Rom. 11:29), but also *singly* when it teaches that the benefits of grace, gathered apiece, last many years. In general, above all is *union with Christ* (Eph. 3:17), with various likenesses, foreshadowed in *natural things*, of the vine and vine branch, bread and the head; in *economic things*, of spouses; in *forged things*, of the house, foundation, and clothing; and in *supernatural things*, of the persons of the Holy Trinity (John 17:22). There is *justification*, which is irrevocable, the cause of

6. *Medulla*, XII–XV.
7. *Medulla*, XV.

which is "the righteousness of the ages" (Dan. 9:24), "eternal redemption" (Heb. 9:12). There is *adoption* through Christ that only belongs to certain persons, to such who "will inherit salvation" (Heb. 1:14). There is *sanctification*, which, as a certain spiritual resurrection, is compared with the bodily resurrection of Christ (Rom. 6:8–9) and comes in the name of *regeneration*. Such is sealed in *the sacraments* of circumcision and baptism. Finally, the effect of sanctification, *holiness*, consists in new life and singular virtues, chiefly that triad of virtues: faith, hope, and love. "These three remain (μένουσι): faith, hope, and love" until perfection arrives in heaven (1 Cor. 13:13). "You have stood in the faith" (2 Cor. 1:24). "The one who believes Him who sent Me has eternal life" (John 5:24). "Hope" is the "safe and firm anchor" of the soul, "penetrating into the inner curtain," heaven, where it clings to the Rock of eternity (Heb. 6:19, 20). "Love never perishes" (1 Cor. 13:8) but "remains" (1 Cor. 13:13).[8]

IX. The Certitude of Salvation

The *certitude of salvation* is the undivided companion of the perseverance of the saints. This is that persuasion of the faithful elect whereby they, relying on faith in the divine testimony of the Holy Spirit and the sense and experience of grace working in them in regard to the foundation and disposition of trust, for the measure of faith and the Spirit can certainly trust that they are in a state of grace in the present. They can also certainly trust that they will persevere until the end in the same, although not without struggle and temptation, and to that extent be infallibly saved.[9]

X. Its Foundations

The foundations of that certitude include *the same perseverance of the saints*, the supports of which disclose themselves among believers in certain signs, so that they cannot doubt the *promise of the covenant of grace*. It commands "not to fear" but to hold God for His "reward and protection" (Gen. 15:1), also interceding with an oath (Heb. 6:17). Another foundation is the *mutual pledging between God and the faithful*, God pledging His Spirit, the sense of which is most affected in the heart, and making Himself known as witness (Rom. 8:16), while the faithful pledge themselves to God, their salvation, as a "deposit until the day of the advent" of Christ (2 Tim. 1:12). Another foundation is the *divine promise* not only *general*, whereby salvation is promised to all believers and to that extent individuals because the individuals stand under the universal (Mark 16:16), but also special and distinctly (1 Cor. 1:6–7; 2 Cor. 1:21; James 1:6, 8) the *innate character* of saving *faith*, which is certain of its assent and trust. The *nature of*

---

8. *Medulla*, XVI–XXIV.
9. *Medulla*, XXIV, XXV.

hope is also a foundation of perseverance because it is "living" (1 Peter 1:3) and does "not make ashamed" (Rom. 5:2–6). Moreover, there is *the character of love*, which cannot exist without the sense and certitude not only of the one who loves, but also of the mutual love of God who is loved when "the love of God is poured forth into our hearts through the Holy Spirit" (Rom. 5:5). Other foundations include *union and communion with God*, which believers cannot let lie hidden, and the *necessity of confirming election and calling* (2 Peter 1:10), which, if it always wavers, unstable, cannot be commanded. There is also the *efficacy of prayers* because we are preserved by God to claim remission of sins and eternal life (Matt. 6:10, 12) and, claiming, can trust that He is heard clearly (1 John 5:14–15). *The sealing of the sacraments* is also a foundation of perseverance because those, as signs and seals of grace, effect certitude in the thing promised. Finally, there are the *examples* of Abraham (Rom. 4:18, 21), David (Ps. 23:4, 6), Paul (Rom. 8:38), and all the faithful who say, "We know that we have crossed over from death to life because we love the brothers" (1 John 3:14).[10]

XI. It Also Belongs to Persevering Grace

These signals strengthen the certitude not only of *present* grace but also of *persevering* grace. "If sons, also heirs" (Rom. 8:17). Moreover, on account of the immutability of the testament, the inheritance cannot be overturned. For God Himself "sustains the lot" of Christ and of us (Ps. 16:6). Moreover, the Holy Spirit, as *pledge* and *firstfruits*, also promises and testifies concerning the future inheritance.[11]

XII. The Imperfection of Certitude

Nevertheless, the certitude of grace in this life does not achieve the highest degree so that it always excludes all fear of the opposite. For the certitude of experimental proofs is repeatedly impaired in no small degree by the remnants of the flesh and temptations of Satan. Even the faith of heroes struggles on earth but surmounts the difficulty in heaven. The same faith, that spiritual hand, repeatedly suffers punishments inflicted in the lower world. Nevertheless, all certitude does not so perish, because rays of hope shine through the midst of the anguish (Ps. 42:10–11), and "the grace of God" ought "to be sufficient" (2 Cor. 12:9). Moreover, satisfaction is promised to those who hunger and thirst for righteousness, consolation to those who mourn, and rest to those who labor (Matt. 5:4–5; 11:28).[12]

---

10. *Medulla*, XXVI–XXIX.
11. *Medulla*, XXIX.
12. *Medulla*, XXX.

LOCUS XXV

On External Worship, above All on the Sacraments of the New Testament

I. The External Worship of the Gospel

The covenant of grace under the gospel has peculiar worship and external rites. Although this worship is bodily, the same is nevertheless spiritual because the Spirit of promise works it and has His seat especially in the mind and will of man and to that extent in his *spirit*. For "bodily exercise" without spiritual exercise "is useful for little" (1 Tim. 4:8). The same worship is also "rational" (λογικὸς) (Rom. 12:1).[1]

II. The Exercise of the Worship of the New Testament

The exercises with singular reason pertaining to external worship of the New Testament are the preaching of the Word, prayers, hymns, alms, and the use of sacraments, about which we have devoted a large section. Preaching has this in peculiar: it is generally evangelical, not domineering as for slaves but pleasant as for the free, and a certain encouragement (παράκλησις) rather than domineering legislation (2 Cor. 5:20).[2]

III. The Sacraments of the New Testament: There Are Two—Baptism and the Supper

We have written above about the sacraments in general and in the species of the Old Testament. The sacraments of the New Testament are more perfect because they no longer reduce to servitude but render believers more certain about communion with Christ and perfection through Him. There are two: Baptism and the Supper. For just so many and not more have the requisites of true sacraments and are put forth by Saint Paul as corresponding to (ἀντίστοιχα) the sacraments

1. *Medulla*, I, II.
2. *Medulla*, II–VII.

of the Old Testament (1 Cor. 10:1–5). "In one Spirit we all have been baptized into one body, and you all have been drunk into one Spirit" (1 Cor. 12:13).[3]

IV. The Definition of Baptism: Its Institution

Baptism is the sacrament of regeneration whereby, through the sprinkling and washing of water in each and every one of God's covenanted people, internal washing from sins is declared and sealed through the blood and Spirit of Christ. The Hebrews handed down the opportunity of *baptism of proselytes* before Christ for its *institution*. Its use appeared to have been put forward much, as Christ instituted the sacrament for Gentile proselytes.[4]

V. The Baptism of John, of the Disciples of Christ; Ministers of Baptism

John, called *the Baptist*, first baptized in the New Testament, about which we have spoken above. The disciples of Christ followed him who, with the authority of their Teacher Christ, not only before the resurrection (John 4:2) but also after it were sent to preach and baptize (Matt. 28:19). They administered this sacrament. The baptism of both differed in the substance of the thing, the sealing of regenerating and justifying grace. To that extent the same differed in the particular manner of revealing and gathering the gifts that before the glorification of Christ could be offered only commonly to the faithful, not only to some. Both also, as ministers called by God to preach, baptized. "Go teach the nations, baptizing them" (Matt. 28:19). Therefore, unless legitimately called, they could neither preach nor baptize.[5]

VI. Its Element: Water

The element of baptism is clear *water*, especially fitting to signify regeneration through the obedience of Christ and the sanctification of the Spirit. For water has the force of suffocating and mortifying the buried and at the same time of washing the filth of the body, which square with the death of Christ and the operation of the Holy Spirit from the beginning.[6]

VII. The Baptismal Rite

This water of baptism, sanctified by the Word, is applied through the *rite* of the same, which is "purification" (καθαρισμὸς) (John 3:25–26). It is carried out either through *dipping* or *immersion* of the whole body into water in the custom of the Jews, washing "the whole flesh" (Lev. 15:16), or through *sprinkling* or

3. *Medulla*, VII, VIII.
4. *Medulla*, IX.
5. *Medulla*, X–XIII.
6. *Medulla*, XIII–XVI.

dipping of part of the body. Sprinkling (ῥαντισμὸς) of this sort is also used in the law. The word "βαπτισμοῦ" signifies both: *immersion* properly and narrowly and *sprinkling* with a general and metaphorical notion (Heb. 9:10; Luke 11:38; Joel 2:28). Moreover, both have mystery.[7]

VIII. The Mystery of Baptism

The thing signified or the *mystery* of baptism in general is the gospel of Christ, specifically regeneration through Christ and the Holy Spirit. For in baptism is the "washing of regeneration" (λουτρὸν παλιγγενεσίας) (Titus 3:5) or vivification and resurrection from the death of sin (John 5:25). Since regeneration is completed through the merit of Christ and the sanctification of the Spirit, water has likeness to both. For it nourishes bodily life, revives, allays thirst, is bought with no price, is common to all, is sufficient for all, and purifies the impure body, all of which the blood of Christ and the Holy Spirit furnish. Moreover, each rite of immersion and sprinkling is not an obscure hieroglyph of the death, burial, and resurrection of Christ and of ours (Rom. 6:3–8; Col. 2:11–12). Baptism is not the cause of all these benefits, but the seal. For "it saves," not as "a putting off of the filth of the flesh" or by virtue of the sacrament by which it is such, but as an "appeal of good conscience to God." That is to say, it is a seal of trust toward God in which we are rendered more certain about salvation and remission of sins (1 Peter 3:21).[8]

IX. Infant Baptism

The subject of baptism is the faithful people of God, without any distinction of nation, sex, or age. Indeed, infants of the covenanted must be baptized as equally as the infants of the covenanted were once circumcised because the promise made to Abraham and his seed, Christ having been revealed, was not diminished but enlarged through the mouth of Peter: "The promise is yours and your children's" (Acts 2:39). In this argument Saint Peter commanded each one (ἕκαστον) to be baptized (Acts 2:38). Indeed, the Israelites, who once were "near," and the faithful from the Gentiles, who once were "far off" (Acts 2:39), are held with no distinction under the New Testament (Gal. 3:28). For the children of the faithful Gentile, notwithstanding infidelity of the other parent, are "holy" (1 Cor. 7:14). Therefore, since baptism as equally as circumcision seals that covenant for those who believe, into which their children have been received as holy, in the same right baptism is administered to these as circumcision once was to those. For Christ commanded "to make disciples and to baptize the nations," with no distinction of age (Matt. 28:19). Therefore, those who are born in the lap of the

---

7. *Medulla*, XVI, XVII.
8. *Medulla*, XVIII–XXII.

church are fit at the age of infant to begin the institution and must be baptized as equally as their parents. Therefore, the apostles baptized whole "households" (1 Cor. 1:16).[9]

X. The Necessity of Baptism

The necessity of baptism is not *absolute* and *of the center*, but *limited* and *of the precept*. For it is not a law first established for the grace of Christ, but confirms and seals what has already been obtained by the merit of Christ and applied by faith as a seal. This sealing is so great a pledge of the love of God and a support for faith. Nevertheless, when it does not occur without the proper fault of man, "the grace of God is sufficient" (2 Cor. 12:9). He who denies the seal does not therefore deny grace, because He can save by His Word alone, just as He can confer benefit by command alone as King. That God wills to save those not baptized without their own fault is similar to the examples of those saved who were uncircumcised (2 Sam. 12:18–23). The nature of baptism, which hangs on a positive precept, is never regarded as among the means of obtaining salvation. The innate character of all ceremonies, none of which are absolutely necessary; the condition of infants not baptized (ἀβαπτίζων); the righteousness of God, who punishes no innocent person; and finally the effect of baptism, which is not properly salvation but a degree of greater consolation and happiness, do not allow for doubt.[10]

XI. The Lord's Supper

The Lord's Supper is *the other sacrament of the New Testament whereby, through the distribution of the broken bread and the wine poured out and perception among the faithful, communion of the body of Christ is declared and sealed for them in the broken cross, the blood having been poured out for them for redemption of sins and eternal salvation*.[11]

XII. Its External Ministry in Regard to Persons

The parts of the Holy Supper are its external ministry and mystery. In the *external ministry* the persons, symbols, and rites about the same must be considered. The *person administering* in the first Supper was Christ, and next were apostles and pastors. But those communing in the first Supper were Christ Himself and His apostles, not even Judas excepted (Luke 22:21), and after it were the faithful and Christian adults who examined themselves (1 Cor. 11:28).[12]

---

9. *Medulla*, XXII–XXVI.
10. *Medulla*, XXVI–XXXI.
11. *Medulla*, XXXI.
12. *Medulla*, XXXII.

XIII. The Symbols

The symbols of the feast were bread and wine. Indeed, the reason of each feast that Christ had prepared to institute was requiring the mystery of spiritual feeding. "Wine gladdens the heart of man and makes the face to shine before oil, and bread supports the heart of man" (Ps. 104:15).[13]

XIV. Bread and the Rite about the Same

The *bread* employed in the first Supper was unleavened on account of the circumstance of the time. Outside of the circumstance of the time, unleavened, or perhaps fermented, does not refer to the substance of the thing, provided that the bread is not covered with scum or an image of coin makers. There were *rites* about the same bread that Christ "took up" (Matt. 26:26) and, having been taken up, "blessed," and by blessing, sanctified the same for its use, "giving thanks" (Luke 22:19); the bread having been blessed, "He broke it," and having been broken, "He gave it to His disciples" or distributed it and said, "Take and eat" (Matt. 26:26). This is diametrically opposed to private Masses and the preservation of the bread.[14]

XV. Wine and the Rites concerning It

The other symbol of the feast is *wine*. That was the "fruit of the vine" (γενήμα ἀμπέλου) (Matt. 26:29; Luke 22:18), for the custom and place of the nation, diluted perhaps with water, without necessity outside custom and place. The rites employed concerning that are nearly the same as those concerning the bread. For Christ "took the cup," "blessed" it or "gave thanks," uncertain which form of words was used or more sublime, He simply "gave" it and for the custom of those feasting with the eloquent command, "Drink from it all" (Matt. 26:27). Therefore, this necessity of eating the bread is the same necessity of drinking the wine because Christ, in the same way (ὡσαύτως) that "He took and gave" the bread, took and gave "the cup." He commanded that "all" (πάντας) drink from it and also that they "do this" (Luke 22:19, 20). This was said to the apostles, not as apostles but "disciples" (μαθηταῖς) (Matt. 26:27)—that is, to the faithful, representing any sort of faithful. For in those words gathered from the evangelists and Saint Paul about the bread and the wine, there is no distinction, not even the least, in regard to the command of eating and drinking. That is to say, Christ wisely instituted the diverse symbols to enjoy communion with Him with their equal necessity because He wished thereby to foreshadow the perfect and complete redemption of our body and soul. For the bread represents His body

13. *Medulla*, XXXIII.
14. *Medulla*, XXXIV–XXXVIII.

and the wine His blood—that is, the soul, once foreshadowed by the prohibition from eating the blood of beasts.[15]

XVI. The Mystery of the Supper: The Sealing of the Spiritual Feast

The *mystery* of the Supper, a bodily feast, is the sealing of the spiritual feast. Scripture speaks about this everywhere. "Taste and see that Jehovah is good" (Ps. 34:8). "They will eat and will admire all the riches of the earth" (Ps. 22:29). "You prepare a table before me. You have anointed my head with oil. My cup overflows" (Ps. 23:5). "I have come into my garden, my sister, my spouse. Eat my honeycomb with my honey. Eat, friends, drink and be drunk" (Song 5:1). "O those thirsting, come to the waters. Come, buy wine and milk without money and without price. Eat good, and there will be delight in your rich soul" (Isa. 55:1–2). "Many will come from the east and the west, and they will recline at the table with Abraham, Isaac, and Jacob in the kingdom of heaven" (Matt. 8:11).[16]

XVII. Its Food: The Body and Blood of Christ

The food of this feast is the *body* and *blood* of Christ. "This is My body. This (cup) is the blood of the New Testament" (Matt. 26:26). "The cup, which we bless, is it not communion of the blood of Christ? The bread, which we break, is it not communion of the body of Christ" (1 Cor. 10:16)? Therefore, the bread signs and seals to the believer the body, the wine the blood of Christ, and communion with Him, the right for making each, as seal, pledge, and "commemoration" (ἀνάμνησις) of it, commemorates the image of the pledge, the certitude of entire possession. Hence, the food and drink of the Eucharistic feast is twofold: one *symbolic, bodily,* and *visible*, bread and wine; and another *spiritual* and *invisible*, the body and blood of Christ, or communion with the body and blood of Christ or with the whole Christ in regard to foundation and fruit, first (πρώτως) killed and second (δευτέρως) made alive and reigning in heaven. As members of His body, we are thereby sharers of His death, merit, righteousness, and life, and regenerated, are made alive in this life, kept, fed for eternal life, and delight in Him only. This communion alone, necessary and uniquely saving, is in agreement with the spiritual feast and contains the kernel of the whole gospel.[17]

XVIII. The Gathering of the Symbols and Rites with the Spiritual Feast of the Body and Blood of the Lord

The symbols and rites excellently represent this mystery of the eucharistic feast. For Christ instituted the *bread* and the *wine* at the same time that He sealed full

15. *Medulla*, XXXVIII–XLII.
16. *Medulla*, XLII.
17. *Medulla*, XLIII.

redemption and complete nourishing of body and soul. Communion of the *blood* symbolizes communion of the violent death, and communion of the *body* His communion as broken and at the same time revived to life in the symbol of the bread broken and the wine poured out. The bread "received" of Christ the Sponsor carries the conspicuous image of those received by God. The "blessing" and consecration of the bread and the wine symbolizes the anointed and consecrated of Christ by the Holy Spirit. The "breaking" of the bread and the "pouring out" of the wine symbolizes the death of the body and soul and spiritual nourishing. The "distribution" to eat and drink symbolizes Christ given to all the faithful and applied for spiritual food. Finally, the *eating* of the bread and the *drinking* of the wine symbolize the same being converted into the drink and blood of spiritual life, indeed of the one living in us.[18]

XIX. The End of the Supper Is Remembrance and Announcement of the Death of Christ

Therefore, the special end and use of the Lord's Supper is "remembrance" of Christ, of all His words and deeds (Luke 22:19; 1 Cor. 11:24–25), and "announcement of His death until He comes" (1 Cor. 11:26). It is not weakly taken but powerfully, not only *theoretical* but also *practical*, whereby he who *remembers* the death of Christ and *announces* it recalls all the benefits acquired by the death of Christ as pleasant in his mind, applies them to himself in faith through the symbols confirmed, and has communion with the death and life of Christ. For he *remembers* Christ and *announces* His death, not as of a foreigner but of one who belongs to Him, whereby he feeds in the spiritual feast and at the same time is united and connected with Christ the Head as He is with His body. "We many are one bread, one body" (1 Cor. 10:17). In addition, there is the subordinate end: confirmation of our faith about remission of sins through the death of Christ, public profession of Him, an increase of love and happiness, peace of conscience, and hope of eternal life in the Holy Spirit.[19]

XX. The Presence of the Body and the Blood of the Lord in the Eucharist

The presence of the body and blood of Christ in the Eucharist is neither bodily nor imaginary but true and real. It is not *bodily*, because even the faithful before Christ ate the "same spiritual food" among them and with us, and they "drank the same spiritual drink," drinking from the "rock to follow," which is "Christ" (1 Cor. 10:3–5). Nevertheless, the former was not bodily communion. The gospel sets forth the body and blood of Christ as its special object, although not bodily present. Indeed, it is the same object of the Eucharist and the gospel.

18. *Medulla*, XLIV.
19. *Medulla*, XLV.

In addition, "we remember" Christ and "announce His death until He comes" (1 Cor. 11:25–26). The same remembrance establishes the body of the Lord delivered, although already glorious, and His blood poured out, although previously emptied, as very present. It is not *imaginary*, but *true* and *real*, because faith makes it so that "those things which are hoped for stand" in the soul of the one who hopes and "those things that do not appear are demonstrated" (Heb. 11:1). Finally, contact of bodies or commingling of the same is not required for communion.[20]

XXI. The Symbolic and Spiritual Manner of Presence

Indeed, the manner of presence is twofold: symbolic or relative, and spiritual. The *symbolic* whereby, according to Christ's institution, the bread and the wine, the breaking and eating of the former, and the pouring out and drinking of the latter are ordained to signify, seal, and display the promised goods. This manner consists in the relation hanging on symbols and rites. But the power is great of the related things, above all divine things. The *spiritual* is that whereby the Holy Spirit offers the foundation and the fruit, the body and blood of the Lord together with all His benefits, through the external symbols and word of the gospel, gives to the faithful and calls them His own so that, stronger in faith each day they may be more and more united. These two manners of the presence and communion of the body and blood of Christ suffice for salvation because there are only two *parts* of the Lord's Supper: the symbols and the things signified. There are only two *instruments* of taking up both: the mouth of the body and of the soul. There are only two kinds of those who administer and who commune: *ministers* extend the symbols and the *Holy Spirit* dispenses the former internally and writes them on the heart, and people commune *worthily* or *unworthily*. Finally, there are two adequate *ends*: primarily, remembrance and announcement of the death of Christ, and secondarily, confirmation of faith.[21]

---

20. *Medulla*, XLVI.
21. *Medulla*, XLVIIff.

LOCUS XXVI

On the Church

I. The Notion of the Church

The subject of the covenant of grace is the *church*. In this word is the notion of calling (κλήσεως). For they are said "to be added to the church whom the Lord called" (προσκαλέσται) (Acts 2:39, 47). Therefore, the church is, by the force of the word, the *assembly* of those *who are called*.[1]

II. Distinction: The Definition Properly Called

Since calling is either special and internal or general and external, the twofold notion of the true church emerges. For it is taken either *properly* and *narrowly* or *improperly* and *broadly*. *The former* is *the assembly or gathering of elect men who, effectually called through the Word of the gospel, believe in Christ and prove this faith not only in profession but also in newness of life*. The angel himself more briefly defines the church, indicating those who make war with the "Lamb," as "of those ruling with the Lord and the King of kings, called, elect, and faithful" (κλητοὺς, ἐκλεκτοὺς καὶ πιστοὺς) (Rev. 17:14). For the church is not simply the assembly of the elect but of the elect, called, and faithful.[2]

III. Its Gathering Is through the Command and Word of God

The calling of God, whereby the assembly of the elect is called, is the powerful command and order of the same so that those who have been called are brought in. Nevertheless, ordinarily the bringing in of the former is not without calling, which is set forth according to the command of God through men, heralds of the Word. "How shall they believe, if they do not hear? How shall they hear without one preaching?" (Rom. 10:14).[3]

---

1. *Medulla*, I, II.
2. *Medulla*, III.
3. *Medulla*, IV, V.

IV. The Form of the Church Is Faith

Internally, faith in Christ and virtues flowing from the same as its form constitute the church. For calling makes the church, union and communion shows it, and faith, the end of calling, constitutes it—namely, it imparts to the church its existence (τὸ εἶναι). For it is found in all equally called as their form, and to that degree is the form of all the gathered. Hence, all the promises made to the church pertain to each and every one of the faithful by force of the relation of faith in Christ, and Christ belongs to the church and the church to Christ. "My beloved is Mine, and I am his" (Song 2:16). "Remain in Me, as I in you" (John 15:4).[4]

V. The Church Is the Communion of Saints

The church is the *communion of saints* because it is the union, society, and assembly of all the faithful, whether gathered in the same place or dispersed, who have a certain communion with one another. But Christ is the common (κοινὴ) thing, the Head of the church, and the goods that flow into the body from Him as Head. Hence, this is twofold, with *Christ the Head* and His *body* or members of the body among themselves. In *the Head*, Christ imparts to the church all things for life and salvation, and the church in turn imparts gifts in receiving them: love, worship, and thanksgiving. In *the body* the *saints* who live commune with either the living through mutual and equal affection, gifts of the Spirit and body, or the dead, through praises and imitation of them. "Hearing of your faith in the Lord Jesus and your love toward all the saints, I do not cease" (Eph. 1:15–16).[5]

VI. It Is Invisible

The church is properly called *invisible* because "we believe" it, and those things that we believe are "of those that are not seen" (Heb. 11:1). For election, calling, faith, and internal union and communion flee our senses. "All glorious is the daughter of the king internally" (Ps. 45:14). "God knows who are His" (2 Tim. 2:19). "A white stone, and no one knows the new name inscribed on it, except the one who receives it" (Rev. 2:17).[6]

VII. One, Holy, Yet Not Free from All Error and Vice

The church is also one, holy, and catholic. It is *one* with spiritual reason, numerical unity, and to that extent singular. "My dove is one, My whole, singular to My mother" (Song 6:9). "One body, one Spirit" (Eph. 4:4–5). "We many are one body in Christ" (Rom. 12:5). "There will be one flock" (John 10:16). It is *holy* not

4. *Medulla*, VI.
5. *Medulla*, VII.
6. *Medulla*, VIII.

only by *imputation* but also *inchoately* through the restoration of the regenerating Spirit (Titus 3:5) and by *separation* because it is a peculiar (περιούσιος) people (Titus 2:14). But it is not so holy that it is free from all error in intellect and vice in will and to that extent sinless (ἀναμάρτητος) in the world. For the reason of faithful individuals is the same of the whole church. But faithful individuals can err in this life, not indeed in the foundation but besides it, and fall, not willingly but through the weakness of the flesh. Therefore, Saint Paul wished to see the Thessalonians "to restore their defects of the faith" (τὰ ὑστερήματα τῆς πίστεως) (1 Thess. 3:10). "We all stumble in many ways" (James 3:2).[7]

VIII. Catholic

It is also *catholic*, *universal*, and one but with a certain extension, not according to *act* but according to *power*. It is that either *absolutely*, since all members have the same saving faith in particulars in time and in unison, which the faithful have professed and will profess in every place, or *oppositely* to the chair of Moses, because of assemblies of heretics and worldly commands. The absoluteness is seen either *universally* by reason of the whole multitude of believers in every time and place or *particularly*, now in it that reigns in *heaven* and now in it that makes war on *earth* as the assembly collected as particulars or wanders about outside them.[8]

IX. The Church Improperly and Broadly Called

The members of the true church, properly called, also burn with mutual desire for communion and external gathering, as often as it can prevail. "I am a companion of all who fear God" (Ps. 119:63). "If we walk in the light, we have communion among one another" (1 John 1:7). For the very opposition (ἀντιπρίστασις) of the world joins the faithful in the world. Hence, the other notion of the church *broadly* and *improperly* called rises, according to which the *church* is *the assembly or gathering of those who profess Christ their Lord and are associated with the communion of the divine Word preached and the sacraments*. In this sense they are said "to have daily increased" in the church (Acts 16:5), and Christ commanded "to tell it to the church" (Matt. 18:17). Yet any assembly so associated is not the church, but only that which has the faithful mixed. On account of this the commingled assembly comes in the name of the church improperly, according to association, opinion, and love owed. But the church is not thus twofold because *properly called* is distinguished from *improperly called* not in the manner of existing in the world but in the manner of considering.[9]

---

7. *Medulla*, IX, X.
8. *Medulla*, XI, XII.
9. *Medulla*, XIII, XIV.

X. The Marks of the External Church

The external church and improperly called is infallibly discerned in certain marks and ought to be discerned on account of the necessity of gathering with some particular church. These marks imported from the same form, which is the confession of faith, are three: *truth of doctrine* or confession of *faith* conformed to the Word of God, *worship* of the external Word in proclamation and consisting in the administration of the sacraments, and *rectitude* and *order*, or the direction of the *church*. Indeed, in these marks the nature of the external church is declared, and the true church is discerned from the false, and to that extent the essentials of the church and the properties are inseparable from it. The *essentials* are inseparable from the church because they are aimed at from the form itself of the external church. Its *properties* are inseparable from it because those individuals of the one and only true external church, certainly flowing from its essence, flow, if not in regard to act, at least in regard to preparation of spirit. They are *inseparable* because they begin and end with the established rite in the established church.[10]

XI. The External Church Is Visible

The external church is visible, fallible, and failing easily. It is *visible* since what the faithful do in the name of Christ by preaching and professing the Word of God, conforming their teaching and lifestyle to it, can be judged by others and known among themselves. By doing these things it ought to be regarded the true church of Christ to which they can and ought to gather themselves to be saved. "Tell the church. If he does not listen to the church, let him be to you as a heathen and publican" (Matt. 18:17). "They were enduring in the teaching of the apostles, in communion, the breaking of bread, and prayers" (Acts 2:42). "If you remain in My Word, truly you will be My disciples" (John 8:31). "In this all will know that you are My disciples, if you have love toward one another" (John 13:35). But the church is not visible to all, but only to those who learn, acknowledge, and love the teaching of Christ. Moreover, it is not visible "with pomp" (μετὰ παρατηρήσεως), which sort belongs to the worldly city (Luke 17:20). It is visible with the broad distinction of interior purity, the state of the exterior sometimes flourishing more and sometimes being more obscure. For however visible, its splendor does not bring forth a common place and operation in the kingdom of Christ more than of Satan and the Antichrist, which is more noticeable.[11]

10. *Medulla*, XV–XVIII.
11. *Medulla*, XVIII.

XII. Fallible

Next, the external church is also *fallible*, much more than properly called. For in it are housed not only the elect but also hypocrites, secret infidels, and atheists. From such people the greatest error and corruption can pollute and be brought into the external communion, with those prevailing and dominating yet without danger to the elect. "The kingdom of heaven is similar to man sowing good seed in his field. But when the men were asleep, his enemy came, and sowed tares among the wheat, and departed" (Matt. 13:24–25). Hence, the former prophecies must be brought forth about *apostasy* through the Antichrist, *the son of perdition* in the church. Indeed, "the image of God, from the law in the temple of God, will sit down" and will "dominate" (1 Tim. 4:2; 2 Thess. 2:3–4; 1 John 2:7).[12]

XIII. It Is Falling Easily

Finally, it is also *falling easily*, not as a whole, so that at any time several faithful may fall in the name of the gathered of Christ, sometimes very obscurely and sometimes very clearly. But since any particular church, none excepted, can err even in the foundation, so it can fall. The fall is either from *truth* and *life* so that it ceases to be and perishes deep within in regard to pastors and sheep, or at least from *flower* and *vigor*, so that it is obscured, diminished, and corrupted so that nearly nothing appears although it exists and lives. The experience of all times teaches this in respect to any church, even the external universal church. But if anywhere a particular church lacks any of these virtues and the universal is obscured, the elect do not perish. Instead, before death they are called forth to the Lord, migrate to another, are preserved from corruptions at least in regard to the foundations of saving teaching, go into hiding, or set themselves in opposition to the corruptors, stirred up by the divine voice. Moreover, they either conquer by enduring martyrdom or establish a separate assembly with God's help.[13]

---

12. *Medulla*, XIX–XXIII.
13. *Medulla*, XXVIff.

LOCUS XXVII

On the Government of the Church

I. The Church Cannot Lack Government

The church of Christ cannot lack government and polity, because it is a certain religious society, which cannot be preserved without distinction between those commanding and those being subject.[1]

II. That Principal Government Belongs to the One Head of the Church, Christ

The external government of the church is either principal or ministerial. The *principal external government* belongs to Christ. "All power in heaven and on earth has been given to Me" (Matt. 28:18). Scripture also makes Him the one Head of the church. "He gave Him (not another) Head over all things to the church" (Eph. 1:22–23). "He (Αὐτὸς) is the Head of His body, the church" (Col. 1:18–20). Therefore, He alone properly and with emphasis is the Head of the church in regard to *dignity* over members of the church, angels, and "all sharers" (μετόχους) (Heb. 1:4, 9), "firstborn among brothers" (Rom. 8:29). He is also Head of the church in regard to *communion of nature*, from which He has the right and duty to love and save the church. Moreover, He is Head in regard to *union* with the church, as His body to which He is most closely united, so that the latter exists, lives, and remains in the former. He is also Head in regard to the *dependence* of the church on Him as the root from which the goods and gifts of the Holy Spirit pour forth into it (Isa. 11:10; Rev. 5:5). Through various ministries and gifts "He suitably arranges the body" for Himself (1 Cor. 12:27; Eph. 4:12, 16; Col. 2:19). Finally, He is Head in regard to *dominion*, which applies to Him as our King and Lord. All this has analogy with a natural head.[2]

1. *Medulla*, I.
2. *Medulla*, II.

III. The Ministerial Government: Ecclesiastical

The *ministerial* government of the church is that *whereby God governs the church gathered from the world by the ministry of men*. It is either ecclesiastical or civil. *Ecclesiastical* government is that whereby God *governs the church through ecclesiastical persons, ministers of God and Christ, according to His Word and the rules of the church that agree with the same Word*. That also comes in the name of ecclesiastical *polity*, which sort God defined in the Old Testament and Christ in the New Testament with certain laws and established with the order of common governance. Indeed, He administered the former not as proper to men but in the divine authority of Christ, joined to *gifts* that Christ distributed as ordinary and extraordinary through His Spirit (1 Cor. 12:8, etc.) and *ministries* that are also ordinary and extraordinary and which flow from the gifts (Eph. 4:11). To be sure, extraordinary ministries demanded extraordinary gifts, and ordinary ministries demanded ordinary gifts.[3]

IV. The Necessity of Ministry

There are ordinary ministries. For "faith is from hearing, and hearing is from the message and the sent" (Rom. 10:15, 17). In the ministry of the apostles and others, all (πάντες) the saints until the end of the world ought "to grow into perfect men according to the measure of the stature of the fullness of Christ" (Eph. 4:13). For the same reason Paul commanded Timothy to establish in Crete "elders town by town" (Titus 1:5) and prescribed laws for elders, bishops, and teachers, according to which they would feed the church (Acts 20:28; 1 Tim. 3:1, etc.; Titus 1:6, etc.). Finally, Christ gave to Peter the power of the keys for the whole church (Matt. 16:18–19; 18:18; 28:19–20; John 20:23).[4]

V. Ministers of the Old Testament and New Testament

Ordinary ministers of the Old Testament were *patriarchs*, *elders*, *the firstborn*, and surrogates in their place, *Levites*. Those of the New Testament are "pastors," teaching and governing, and "teachers" (Eph. 4:11). The office of *pastors* is to "attend to themselves and to the whole flock" because they have been "established" for that "by the Holy Spirit." They are required "to feed the church bought with His (Christ's) own blood." Since "wolves" are imminent, it is necessary for pastors "to be vigilant" against them, "by day and night exhorting everyone with tears" (Acts 20:29, 31).[5]

---

3. *Medulla*, III, IV.
4. *Medulla*, V, VI.
5. *Medulla*, VII.

VI. The Calling of Ministers: Its Author, Christ the Head; Extraordinary or Ordinary

Calling is necessary to attend to this ministry. "No one takes the honor upon himself but who is called by God, as Aaron" (Heb. 5:4). "How will they preach unless they have been sent" (Rom. 10:15). Its author is Christ the Head who "gives" some as "pastors" and "teachers" (Eph. 4:11), imparting the gifts necessary, the stamped of which He provides as stamps in the church. That calling is either extraordinary or ordinary. The *extraordinary calling* is carried out by the special breath and inspiration of the Holy Spirit alone. The *ordinary calling* is carried out not only "by aptitude" (ἱκανότητι) to attend to the office (2 Cor. 3:5–6) but also by *will* and love toward God and neighbor "to desire" that office as "good work," precious, praiseworthy, and beautiful (1 Tim. 3:1). They also have the right of calling by certain orders in the church.[6]

VII. Their Testing and Ordination

Those to be called ought to be tested. "Let them first be tested and then minister" (1 Tim. 3:10). "Lay hands on no one (not closely tested) quickly, and do not share with the sins of others" (1 Tim. 5:22). This testing consists in the examination of *aptitude* or *faculty*, and *will* and *fidelity*. "What you have from me" through "many witnesses, commend to faithful men who are suitable (ἱκανοὶ) to teach others" (2 Tim. 2:2). Those only who have been thus tested ought to be ordained with the sign "of the laying on of hands" (1 Tim. 4:14) or without it, by consideration alone. For Christ ordained without the laying on of hands, with breath alone (John 20:22), and was able to be king although not crowned king.[7]

VIII. The Order of Elders and the Office

Elders not teaching but *governing* are distinguished from pastors or teaching elders. The institution of those is divine because Christ commanded that one or two more prudent be summoned for the refutation of the brother sinning, and the church for those who have not listened—that is, "more" (πλείονας) should be approached (2 Cor. 2:6; Matt. 18:16, etc.). "Having gifts…whether ministry by ministering or teaching by teaching," and "the one who leads (ὁ προϊστάμενος) leading with devotion" (Rom. 12:6–8). Elsewhere "those administering" (κυβερνήσεις) are mentioned as distinct from those teaching (1 Cor. 12:28). Paul above all makes this point clearly: "Those who lead, elders, are worthy of double honor, especially those who labor in word and teaching" (1 Tim. 5:17). Their *office* agrees with the office of pastors, except that they neither teach nor dispense the sacraments. They rule the church concerning

6. *Medulla*, VIII–XI.
7. *Medulla*, XI–XV.

another common counsel, and "presiding over" (περιοδευταὶ) (Ezek. 39:14), they surround and watch over all and exercise refutation.[8]

IX. The Order of Teachers: Their Office

Next is the order of *teachers*. For Christ "gave" some "teachers," who do nothing except teach (Eph. 4:11). "Those having prophecy according to the conformity of faith, or teaching by teaching" (Rom. 12:7). Their *office* is *to teach*, to speak frequently, not to order, and to teach not new revelation but to demonstrate to the conscience the revelation of Christ and the apostles. For it is not permitted "to teach another" (ἑτεροδιδασκαλεῖν) foreign doctrine (1 Tim. 6:3) or "to sell the Word" (καπηλεύειν) of God, to mix foreign doctrine as salesmen are accustomed to do (2 Cor. 2:17). It is the special piety of the teacher to shun with devotion to the *truth* opinions rejected in the Word of God, and with devotion to *love* not to fight boldly about all things.[9]

X. The Order of Deacons and the Office

The order of deacons, who are the sacred guards of bodily things of treasure and economy, have been called by God to this office through the church (Acts 6:1–2). Their office consists in the holy collection of treasure and in the just dispensation of the same. Above all, "simplicity" (ἁπλότης) is required in them, opposition to fraud, and devotion to those in want, not to their own commodities (Rom. 12:8). The apostle describes in detail many requirements for them (1 Tim. 3:8–13).[10]

XI. Power in the Minister of the Church Consists in the Power of the Keys

The government of the church through these ministers consists not only in office but also in power. This power, above all of pastors, is placed in the power of the keys. It is not *lordly* and principal, which belongs to Christ alone, but *economical*, the sort that belongs to stewards and servants. "I will give to you (Peter, and in this paradigmatically the church and its ministers) the keys of the kingdom of heaven. And whatever you bind on earth will be bound in heaven. Whatever you loose on earth will be loosed in heaven" (Matt. 16:19). There "to bind," with Christ as interpreter (John 20:23), is "to retain sins," and "to loose" is to "remit" the same. Therefore, in general the *power of the keys* is the power from special calling to preach the gospel to Jews and Gentiles, and to that end teaching, admonishing, refuting, consoling, and binding.[11]

---

8. *Medulla*, XV, XVI.
9. *Medulla*, XVII, XVIII.
10. *Medulla*, XIX–XX.
11. *Medulla*, XXI.

XII. The Form of Ecclesiastical Government

Therefore, the form of ecclesiastical government is properly ministerial, not monarchical, aristocratic, or democratic, because the lordly power belongs to Christ alone. But it is *economic* because the ministers govern the church as the house of the living God as "stewards and dispensers of the mysteries of God" (1 Cor. 4:1). Moreover, that power is not of the sword but of the keys. Finally, in general matters the government is immutable and uniform, whereas in particulars it is mutable and varied.[12]

XIII. It Concerns Persons and Things

The government of the church concerns persons and things. All *persons* are citizens of the church, variously distinct among themselves. "About those who are within, you judge. But about those who are outside, God judges" (1 Cor. 5:12–13). The *things* are the teaching of the Word of God, ceremonies, sacraments, discipline, and the goods of the church.[13]

XIV. As Concerning the Doctrine of the Word of God, and Its Institution, Not Only Public but Also Private

"The teaching of the Word of God in the manifestation of the truth for conscience" (2 Cor. 4:2) is "through the words taught by the Holy Spirit" (1 Cor. 2:13). Indeed, preaching of the written Word of God alone falls on the pastor. "This gospel of the kingdom will be preached in the whole habitable world as a testimony to the Gentiles, and then will be the end" (Matt. 24:14). The architectonic end of that herald is to set forth God's will from His Word for the edification of the church, and not only of all as a whole but also of any and every individual. "You know how we were with you as a father with his children, admonishing, consoling, and appealing that you may walk worthy of God who calls you into His kingdom and glory" (1 Thess. 2:11–12). Hence, it ought not to be a public institution but also private for individuals. For one sheep that has been lost demands more struggling care than all the rest (Luke 15:4). For it is required of the good pastor "to seek the lost sheep, to lead back the one who has veered away, to bind the broken one, to strengthen the weak one, to rout the fat and powerful one, and to feed with judgment" (Ezek. 34:15–16).[14]

XV. And Also Catechetical

Since God not only declares Himself in His covenant as ours but also as the God of our seed (Gen. 17:7; Acts 2:39) and Christ even commanded "children

12. *Medulla*, XXII, XXIII.
13. *Medulla*, XXV.
14. *Medulla*, XXVI–XXVIII.

to come" to Him (Mark 10:14), those also ought to be imbued in the knowledge of God "from childhood" (2 Tim. 3:15). This institution comes in the name of catechesis (χατηχήσεως), which is either domestic or public. The domestic is carried out by the parents and the latter by the ministers of the church and school. Indeed, through this as certain *songs of steps* the youth are promoted from milk to solid food and more sublime mysteries.[15]

XVI. Concerning Ceremonies: Sacraments above All, and Laws of Good Order

The government of the church concerns *ceremonies* because man, in what he is weak, cannot commonly be taught in the teaching of the Word of God and built up in faith in Christ and His kingdom without external stays. The former are of two kinds: *instituted by the divine will*, to which *sacraments* pertain above all, discussed above, or of *good order*, which define the order and decorum of external worship. The exercise of these consists not in a certain part of divine worship, which has been defined in the Word of God, but in ecclesiastical order, prudence, and specification of the church. Therefore, whatever sort of ceremonies are chosen, these are neither necessary, outside the case of scandal, nor mystical.[16]

XVII. Concerning the Discipline of the Church: The Necessity of Which Is Asserted

The next matter of government concerns *discipline*, which is *the application of the will of God declared in His Word and sealed through the sacraments, something personal to be guarded against or warded off through censures for scandals of doctrine and life*. For that reason Christ gave the power of the keys to the church and its ministers so that they might not only preach the will of God but also apply it to persons by binding and loosing. He also prescribed the same degree of rebuke and separation from those unwilling to repent (Matt. 18:15, etc.). But it is of interest to the glory of God and salvation of the church that the chains of this discipline not be broken. For through it the name of God is hallowed, human corruption is impeded, regeneration is promoted, the kingdom of Christ grows, and thus the church judges itself, lest it have to be necessary to be judged by God. Communion with foreign sins is thereby avoided and the church, purged from scandals, retains its splendor.[17]

15. *Medulla*, XXVIII.
16. *Medulla*, XXIX.
17. *Medulla*, XXX–XXXVIII.

XVIII. Concerning the Temporal Goods of the Church

There remains the government of the church concerning *temporal goods*, which the church can painfully lack on account of various things that must be paid for ministers, the poor, the sick, and building charges. After His ascension into heaven, Christ, the apostles, and the first Christians had more struggling care for these (John 13:29; Acts 4:34). Their *use* ought to be pious, lest the *spots live in the love feasts* with the faithful and they "feed themselves without fear" (Jude 12). Their *administration* ought to be religious, "lest man rob what is God's," which those who do are "cursed" (Mal. 3:9).[18]

XIX. Gathering of Many Churches in Synods, Sanhedrin, and Councils

Many churches can also gather in Sanhedrin, synods, and councils, and rule each other by themselves in a certain manner. For the brotherhood and communion of the saints extends itself into the whole world. Moreover, those who are in different places are equally members of one another and are held to please each other, help, and communicate to one another, yet in a way that no church be reduced into servitude (ἐξουσιάζεῦται) by another, which could deprive it from freedom. "How good is it for brothers to sit as one" (Ps. 133:1). "Where two or three have been gathered in My name, I will be in their midst" (Matt. 18:20). Therefore, Saint Paul, lest he should run in vain, sent by the Antiochenes to Jerusalem, conferred with the apostles and the church in that very place (Acts 15:2; Gal. 2:1–2), and he also sent his Jerusalem decree to Antioch to others. At Miletus, Paul summoned the Ephesian elders (Acts 20:17–28). Moreover he had wandering companions, "the apostles of the churches" sent by the churches (2 Cor. 8:19, 23). This is the origin of synods and councils.[19]

XX. The Civil Government of the Church

The former was the ecclesiastical government of the church. *Civil* is that whereby *the faithful magistrate, armed with the sword by divine will, if faithful, takes care of the church together with the republic and promotes and protects the pure worship of God as guardian of both tables.*[20]

XXI. The Origin of the Magistrate

The origin of the magistrate is divine. "There is no power except from God. Moreover, the powers that have been set in order have been set in order by God" (Rom. 13:1). "For" God "teaches the nations" and keeps them in discipline (Ps. 94:10). "He girds and accompanies kings" (Job 12:18). "Through Me kings

---

18. *Medulla*, XXXVIII, XXXIX.
19. *Medulla*, XL–XLIII.
20. *Medulla*, XLIII.

reign. Through Me princes exercise command" (Prov. 8:15–16). Indeed, since all men are sinners by nature and children of wrath, it is from God that people who are not mad, stupid, or simple but very talented, wise, and apt must carry the helm of the republic. Indeed, some people are born not savage, but gentle, compliant, and humble. The origin of all power also demonstrates that. For all "have been born from one blood" (Acts 17:26), are also brothers, dwell together, and love one another, but not without order of those commanding and those obeying, from the gift of God.[21]

XXII. The Legislative and Judicial Power of the Magistrate

The power of the magistrate consists in legislation and in the constitution of judgments. "In Me princes decree righteousness"; namely, they make law according to which the subjects are ruled (Prov. 8:15). To be sure, there is "one Lawgiver, powerful to save and destroy" (James 4:12)—namely, supreme, alone exerting power with authority for conscience and religion. He established men, nevertheless, as "lawgivers" (מחקקי) (Gen. 49:10), imparting power to them whereby they rule society with extensive laws. Moreover, since the power of laws is ineffectual without judgments, the *judicial* power of the magistrate also coincides. "Establish judges and officers for you in all your gates" (Deut. 16:18). Christ also confirmed this power in the New Testament. "Be a friend to your adversary quickly, lest the adversary hand you over to the judge" (Matt. 5:25). "He is a minister of God for you for good. But if you do evil, fear. For he does not bear the sword in vain. For he is a minister of God, an avenger for wrath" (Rom. 13:4). Therefore, he can and ought to exercise not only civil judgments but also capital ones. Certainly the method of unity rather than of private individual ought to be held.[22]

XXIII. The Care of the Church Falls on the Magistrate

But very important care of the church falls on the magistrate. For not only is he held to subject himself to the kingdom of Christ but also to watch over it diligently by promoting it. "Kings, lead prudently. Judges of the earth be instructed. Serve Jehovah in fear. Kiss the Son" (Ps. 2:10–12). "Open, Oh gates, your heads, that the king of glory may enter" (Ps. 24:9). "Kings will come to the splendor of your rising" (Isa. 60:3). "You shall suck the breast of kings" (Isa. 60:16). "Kings shall be your bearers and princes your nourishing women" (Isa. 49:23). "The shields of the earth are God's" (Ps. 47:9). "The kings of the earth will bring their glory" into the new city (Rev. 21:24). For the magistrate is a guardian of the church and of divine law, "praising the one who does good, God's minister

---

21. *Medulla*, XLIV, XLV.
22. *Medulla*, XLVI, XLVII.

for good," established "for the praise of good work" (Rom. 13:3–4). But his best work is piety.[23]

XXIV. His Power concerning Religion

The power and care of the magistrate concerning religion must be held upwardly (κατ᾽ ἄρσιν). For he does not have formal ecclesiastical power concerning religion, because this power is entirely spiritual in the symbol of the keys and is gathered for the church alone. He must be far less dominating because this power belongs to Christ alone downwardly (κατ᾽ θέσιν). He can and indeed must do all that serves the interests of Christ and His kingdom through the power conceded to him by God, including enlarging it. For he is "God's minister" for all his subjects and the church in his empire in civil matters and in a certain manner in external order, "for good" (εἰς ἀγαθον) (Rom. 13:4). He ought to consecrate his "shields to God" (Ps. 47:9). Therefore, this ministry (διακονία) and responsibility (κηδεμονία) is in regard to Christ. Hence, as ministers of the church and all the faithful members of the church are kept to serve the interests of the same according to calling and gifts received from God, so the pious and faithful magistrate ought to so serve the interests of Christ and His kingdom, which is the church, that he neglects none of those things that pertain to his agreeable care of the church.[24]

---

23. *Medulla*, XLVIII.
24. *Medulla*, XLIXff.

LOCUS XXVIII

On Glorification

I. Glorification; Separation of the Soul

The finishing touch of the benefits flowing from the covenant is in glorification. This is either separation of the soul or of the whole man. *Separation of the soul* is the glorification *whereby the elect, having died in faith, immediately are transferred from death, according to the soul separated from the body, into heaven, are fully sanctified, and will live without this body until the consummation of the age.*[1]

II. The Death of the Faithful

The separation of the soul from body happens in death. For through it our "earthly home, a tabernacle, is destroyed" (2 Cor. 5:1). But the death of the faithful differs entirely from the death of the unfaithful in heaven and, far more than the latter, it "is precious in the eyes of the Lord" (Ps. 116:15). It is not "loss of soul" (Matt. 16:26) but "gain" (Phil. 1:21), not "retaliation" (ἀντιμισθία) for sin (Rom. 1:27) but "abolition of the body of sin" (Rom. 6:6), "departure to the Lord" (2 Cor. 5:8), having "crossed over from death to life" (John 5:24), "loosing" (ἀνάλυσις) from the body and migration to "Christ" (Phil. 1:23; 2 Tim. 4:6), "exit (ἄφιξις) and arrival" at the goal (Acts 20:29).[2]

III. The Burial of the Dead Body

After the death of one's body, the status of the soul is different. For the body as "dust returns to the earth" (Eccl. 12:7) into which it is sown, so that the corrupt in it may grow strong and be returned fitted for glory (1 Cor. 15:42). Hence, it also ought to be honorably led away to and buried in a fitting place, to mature corruption and testify to faith in the resurrection. "You are earth, and you shall return to the earth" (Gen. 3:19). Those words include a mandate for an

1. *Medulla*, I, II.
2. *Medulla*, III–IV.

honorable burial. "What you sow is not made alive unless dead" was a mandate to the earth and a corrupt, rotten tomb in it (1 Cor. 15:36).[3]

IV. Separation of the Soul: Migration to Heaven

The state of the soul after death is different. Indeed, the former "returns to God who gave it" (Eccl. 12:7). For separated from the body it is immediately fully sanctified and set free from all sin. "He who has died has been justified from sin" (Rom. 6:7) since he gains the full fruit of justification from sin. "If Christ is in you, certainly the body is dead on account of sin," ended and put off, "but the Spirit is life on account of righteousness." It is made alive through liveliness of new life on account of the righteousness given in Christ (Rom. 8:10). For in death "sanctification in the fear of God is made perfect" (2 Cor. 7:1). And so the soul fully sanctified and purged from sin is transferred into heaven, the place of blessedness. "Our earthly home, a tabernacle, having been destroyed, we have a building from God, a house not made by hand, eternal in heaven" (2 Cor. 5:1). "Today you will be with Me in paradise" (Luke 23:43). "I wish to be loosed and to be with Christ" (Phil. 1:23).[4]

V. The State of the Soul Is Glorious: It Neither Sleeps nor Is Idle (ἀέργος)

The state of the soul received into heaven is entirely glorious. "Immediately the lightness of our affliction is passing away," and "the eternal weight of glory is at work in us" (2 Cor. 4:17). For because God is also the God of men after death (Matt. 22:32), "He has prepared a better city for them, a heavenly one" (Heb. 11:16). For "it is much better (πολλῷ μᾶλλον κρεῖσσον) to be with Christ than to live in the flesh" (Phil. 1:23). Indeed, neither do souls in heaven sleep, because sleep is of the body and very long sleep is death rather than life, nor are they idle (ἀέργοι) but "are living" (Matt. 22:32; John 5:24; Rom. 8:10). But "to live" is to work (ἐνεργεῖν), to live in another life, and to see God. This life belongs to another life. Here the visions that John makes, in which the saints, "shouting with a great voice" (Rev. 6:9–10) and "adoring" (Rev. 19:1, 4) are introduced.[5]

VI. Its Knowledge and Power

The glorious souls do not or cannot know all things. For what they know on earth separately about anything is not carried within the spirit of man. "Abraham did not know us, and Israel did not acknowledge us" (Isa. 63:16). "If the sons increase (the dead grandsons), he does not notice" (Job 14:21). "The dead do not know anything of those things that are on earth" (Eccl. 9:5). Above all they

---

3. *Medulla*, VI–IX.
4. *Medulla*, IX–XIV.
5. *Medulla*, XV.

do not know the secrets of hearts, because only "God is the searcher of hearts" (Ps. 7:9; 1 Kings 8:39; Rom. 8:27). For they will easily lose the knowledge of inferior things, to which will be opposed far more sublime and glorious things to be contemplated. But the *power* of the same of any kind will always be finite and subject to the will of God.[6]

VII. Glorification of the Whole Man

Glorification *of the whole man* is that *whereby the elect who have died in faith are rendered as sharers of glory and perfect blessedness, according to soul and body, at the consummation of the age*. For "we await the redemption of the body" (Rom. 8:23). "We have been sealed by the Holy Spirit for redemption" by reason of the full efficacy of ransom (τοῦ λύτρου) (Eph. 4:30).[7]

VIII. Degrees of Glorification: The Advent of Christ to Carry Them Out

The degrees of that glorification are raising of the dead, final judgment, and eternal life. For their Deliverer will return from heaven. "The seventh from Adam, Enoch, prophesied, 'Behold, the Lord comes with His myriad of saints, that He may make judgment,'" (Jude 14). "That Jesus, who was received by you into heaven, will return, as you saw Him depart to heaven" (Acts 1:11). "For He will come in the clouds with angels to judge the living and the dead" (Matt. 24:30; 25:31; 2 Thess. 1:7–8; 2 Tim. 4:1) "with much power and glory" (Luke 21:27) in contrast to His first advent.[8]

IX. Its Time Is Uncertain; Signs of It Approaching

The time of the advent of the Lord is uncertain. "About the day and hour on which the Lord will come no one knows, not even the angels of heaven or the Son, except the Father" (Mark 13:32). "The hour will come in which you are not thinking" (Matt. 24:50), "as a thief in the night" (2 Peter 3:10). But yet certain *signs* will precede it, from which its approaching can be predicted. "When these things begin to happen, raise your heads. For your redemption is near" (Luke 21:28). These are "signs of the times"—that is, what is done in distinct times to signify another imminent time and God's work over talebearers (Matt. 16:3). They even come in the name "of trumpets." As their blast once broke down the walls of Jericho, so they will break down the kingdom of Satan, and the kingdom of Christ will rise (Rev. 8:2, etc.). Christ Himself established those signs predicting the imminent advent of Christ as the proclamation of the gospel in the whole world and His kingdom more consummate. "The gospel of the

6. *Medulla*, XVI–XXII.
7. *Medulla*, XXII.
8. *Medulla*, XXIII.

kingdom will be preached in the whole habitable world as a testimony to all nations, and then the end will come" (Matt. 24:14). "The seventh angel sounded the trumpet, and great voices were made in heaven, saying, 'The kingdoms of this world have been made our Lord's and His Christ, and He will reign forever'" (Rev. 11:15–18).[9]

X. The Raising of the Dead

The first work of the arriving Christ will be the raising of the dead whereby He *by His omnipotent Word will revive the elect who have died in faith to life, their bodies restored from the earth and again joined to their souls and conformed to the glorious body of Christ.* The testimonies of Scripture above all demonstrate this. Many testimonies exist in the Old Testament and New Testament, and the latter are better. "I am the God of Abraham, Isaac, and Jacob" (Ex. 3:6, 16). From these words Christ Himself proved the resurrection of the dead through evident consequence because "God is not the God of the dead but of the living" (Matt. 22:32; Luke 20:38). "You return man to the least, and you say, 'Return sons of men'" (Ps. 90:3). "I will see Your face in Your righteousness. I shall be satisfied, when I awake, with Your likeness" (Ps. 17:15). Christ more clearly put it: "The hour will come in which all who are in graves will hear His voice, and all who did good will come forth to the resurrection of life but those who did evil will come forth to the resurrection of judgment" (John 5:28, 29). But Saint Paul demonstrates the principal truth in many arguments (1 Cor. 15:1–34) and exposes that whole mystery (1 Thess. 4:14–18). Moreover, there is no lack not only of *examples* of those raised but also of *types*: Enoch, Isaac, Baculus, Aaron, Elijah, the people of Israel rising again from the death of afflictions (Isa. 26:3–4, etc.; Ezek. 37:12–14). There are also many reasons for their resurrection.[10]

XI. The Body Rises Again the Same in Number

The body rises again the same in number in which it died. For we believe the resurrection *of this flesh*, as it rightly has the Aquiline (*Aquilejense*) symbol. "The kinsman Redeemer at last will stand over the dust.... From my flesh I will see God, whom I will see, and my eyes will behold, and not another" for me (Job 19:25–27). "It is necessary that "*this* corruptible (τὸ φθαρτὸν τοῦτο) put on incorruption, and *this* mortal put on immortality" (1 Cor. 15:53–54). "The life of Christ ought to be manifest in our body, our mortal flesh" (2 Cor. 4:10). For our flesh that is glorified is not unbecoming, as it is an image in the singular counsel of the Trinity (Gen. 1:26–27) in whom man believes, was the temple of the Holy Spirit, and is a sharer of the sacraments. Moreover, since Christ, our Head, rose

9. *Medulla*, XXIV–XXX.
10. *Medulla*, XXX–XXXV.

again in the same body that He received from Mary—namely, in which Thomas could seize the traces of the nails (John 20:27)—our lowly body also ought to become conformed to the body of Christ (Phil. 3:21) and must rise again the same in number. The righteousness of God above all demands this, as does the word itself of resurrection, which is a new creation. Finally, it is fitting to restore what He made. For how much more is it to have made than to have restored?[11]

XII. The Resurrection Will Be Universal

The resurrection will be universal, not only of the just but also of the unjust. "Those who did good will come forth to the resurrection of life, and those who did evil will come forth to the resurrection of judgment" (John 5:29). "I have hope in God, as also they await the future resurrection of the dead, the just and the unjust" (Acts 24:15). For those not rising again cannot be judged. But it is necessary that "before the tribunal of Christ all things (πάντας) be made manifest, in order that everyone may be paid back for what He did through the body, whether good or evil" (2 Cor. 5:10).[12]

XIII. The Changing of Those Surviving

The changing of those surviving will be analogous to the resurrection of the dead at the advent of the Lord. For Paul taught us as mystery that "we will not all sleep, but we all will be changed" (ἀλλαγησόμεθα) (1 Cor. 15:51). "We say this to you in the Word of the Lord (only Him revealing), that while we are living, those who are surviving will be at the advent of the Lord. We will not outrun those who sleep,… because the dead in Christ will rise first,… then we who are living, who will be left, will be gathered together with them in the clouds in the way to the Lord" (1 Thess. 4:15–17). The manner of that changing is secret, except that through it mortality and corruption are put off. To that extent there is a certain analogy to death, and from the same will be the resurrection.[13]

XIV. The Final Judgment

The final judgment will be that most solemn *act whereby Christ, judge of the universe, will gather the elect raised through His angels from the whole world and will separate them from the reprobate, a public and solemn sentence of eternal life, the inheritance soon to be taken possession of, and will transfer the reprobate to eternal death, immediately to be taken possession of.* That is everywhere predicted in the Scriptures. For "the seventh from Adam prophesied about it" (Jude 14). "Will the judge of the whole earth not make judgment?" (Gen. 18:25). "He will judge

11. *Medulla*, XXXV, XXXVI.
12. *Medulla*, XXXVII–XXXVIII.
13. *Medulla*, XXXIX.

the world in righteousness, He will judge the peoples in rectitude" (Ps. 9:8, 9). "The Lord will judge the just and the wicked" (Eccl. 3:17). "God commanded us to testify what He (Jesus of Nazareth) has been established by God as Judge of the living and the dead" (Acts 10:42). "It is necessary that we all be manifested before the tribunal of Christ, that everyone may report according to those things which he did through his body, whether good or evil" (2 Cor. 5:10). Christ describes the progress of that whole judgment (Matt. 25:31, etc.). Most serious reasons from the righteousness of God, His truth and immutability, the nexus of resurrection and judgment, the universal expectation of the pious, the aim of particular judgments, and so on, confirm its truth.[14]

XV. God Will Be the Judge, Singularly Christ

The judge will be the Triune God, with common authority and power. The Son of God with a singular visible exercise will judge with authority. For "all power and all judgment from the Father has been given" to the Son (John 5:22, 27), and the power of judging is part of His office as King. "The Father judges no one" (John 5:22) apart from the Son to whom He gave judgment "because He is the Son of Man" (John 5:27). If He were not the God-man (θεάνθρωπος), He could not judge singularly.[15]

XVI. Preparation and Administration of Judgment

The method of judgment consists in preparation and administration. *Preparation* will happen in that manner which Christ the "judge will sit over the throne of majesty" (Matt. 19:28). Before His tribunal "all will be manifested" (2 Cor. 5:10), "every knee will bow itself to Him" (Rom. 14:11), and the gathered will stand divided into two parts, some at His right and others at His left, for a sign for good and evil (Matt. 25:33). The *administration* will have knowledge of the cause, delivery of the sentence, and execution. The *knowledge of the cause* consists in revelation by divine power of all things done that anyone throughout their whole life knew, said, and did. For God "will bring to light the secrets of darkness and will make manifest the plans of the heart, and then there will be praise to each one from God" (1 Cor. 4:5). The *delivery of the sentence* will have the tenor that the "pious will enter into eternal joy" and the impious "into eternal fire" (Matt. 25:34, 41, 46). The *execution* of the sentence will follow this, and it will close judgment. "The cursed will depart into eternal fire, but the just into eternal life" (Matt. 25:46).[16]

---

14. *Medulla*, XL, XLI.
15. *Medulla*, XLII, XLIII.
16. *Medulla*, XLIV, XLV.

XVII. The End of the World

The end of the world and the consummation of the age follow the last judgment. This was everywhere predicted. "You have established the earth, and the heavens are the work of Your hands. Those will perish, but You will remain. All those, as clothing, will grow old, as a garment You will change them, and they will be changed" (Ps. 102:25–26). In the New Testament many things are said for the same matter (Matt. 5:18; 24:14, 35; 2 Peter 3:7). To this extent "the restoration of all things" (Acts 3:21), the "regeneration" of the world (Matt. 19:20), and the "new heavens and new earth" (2 Peter 3:13, etc.) happen.[17]

XVIII. The Burning of the World

God, not nature, will put an end to the world. "As a garment You will change them, and they will be changed" (Ps. 102:27; Heb. 1:11). "The Lord will judge in fire" (Isa. 66:16). "The heavens will pass with a crash" (ῥοιζηδὸν) (2 Peter 3:10). The effect of this burning will not be the annihilation of the world but the restoration of it. For the working of fire is not to annihilate but to melt and purge. For that reason Saint Paul taught that the "creation will be set free from the bondage of corruption into the liberty of the glory of the sons of God" (Rom. 8:19–23). For God did not so surrender the creation to futility on account of the sin of man that it would be perpetually subject to him, but that in its own time it would be set free from it together with the sons of God. And the "anxious expectation" (ἀποκαραδοκία), which sort in verse 19 is also assigned to the sons of God, can be none other than of changing into a better state. "All these things, as clothing, will grow old. The image of the garment, You will change them, and they will be changed, and as an outer garment, You will carry them away, and they will be changed" (Ps. 102:26–27).[18]

XIX. The Hell of the Condemned

One state of man in the future age is of the damned, another, far away, of the saved. For the condemned will be expelled into hell, to the eternal punishment of fire. "The wicked will return to hell (לשאלה)" (Ps. 31:17). "The image of sheep place themselves into hell and death is fed them. Their rock departs into the clouds of hell" (Ps. 49:14). "Their worm will not die, and their fire will not be quenched" (Isa. 66:24; Mark 9:43–44). Most clearly Christ said, "Depart from Me into eternal fire" (Matt. 25:41).[19]

17. *Medulla*, XLVI, XLVII.
18. *Medulla*, XLVIII–LI.
19. *Medulla*, LII.

XX. The Punishments of Hell: Their Eternity, and Degrees

The punishments of hell will be either *privative* and *of damnation* or *positive* and *of sense*. *The former*, which are going away from the face of God, all grace, the mercy of God, peace and joy of the Holy Spirit, the hope of liberation, the fellowship of Christ and the saints, and the vision of God will be deprived of glory. *The latter*, by far more terrible, are either exterior or interior. *Exterior* will be bodily punishments, above all the "inextinguishable fire" (Isa. 66:24; Mark 9:43), which will be metaphorically related to the soul but could be properly related to the body. *Interior* punishments are compared with "pains of those in labor" (Luke 16:23), "in chains and bonds" (Ps. 11:6; Matt. 13:30), "plagues and scourges" (Prov. 19:29; Luke 12:48), *effectively* through "weeping and gnashing of teeth" (Matt. 8:12; 13:42) on account of the sense of one's own evils and envy or sense of foreign good. "The worm, which does not die" (Isa. 66:24; Mark 9:44)—that is, continual anguish of conscience and other things of this sort are described. In addition is the *eternity* of the punishments, most atrocious of all. For "who will dwell with eternal burnings?" (Isa. 33:14). "Their worm does not die, and the fire is not extinguished" (Mark 9:44). Nevertheless, there will be *degrees* of punishments. "It will be more tolerable for the land of Sodom and Gomorrah on the day of judgment than for that city that did not listen to you" (Matt. 10:15).[20]

XXI. Eternal Life

Meditation of eternal life puts the finishing touch on the instruction, which is the *consummate blessedness of the elect, called, justified, and raised into heaven, whereby they, seeing God face to face, enjoy a full sense of His favor and even perfect communion of His image forever.* This is also everywhere promised in doing the law and in believing the gospel. "God gave us eternal life. And this life is in His Son" (1 John 5:11). All the elect, raised according to body and soul, the faculties and parts of each, will be sharers.[21]

XXII. The Goods of Eternal Life: God Is the Highest Good; The Work of Man concerning It

Of what sort the eternal life will be is clear not only from lack of all evils, but also from the position of goods. The basis of their goods is the highest good, which is not in any creature but is God alone. "Many will say, 'Who will make us to see good?' Raise over us the light of Your face, Jehovah" (Ps. 4:6). "Blessed is the people whose God is Jehovah, whom He has chosen for His inheritance" (Ps. 33:12). "Say to my soul, 'I am Your salvation'" (Ps. 33:12). He also gives

20. *Medulla*, LIII–LVIII.
21. *Medulla*, LVIII–LXII.

Himself to all the saints to possess and enjoy. "I will be your God and that of your seed after you" (Gen. 17:7). "I am the God of Abraham, Isaac, and Jacob" (Ex. 3:6, 16). That cannot happen without the working of man concerning God as highest good. This working concerning God, the highest good, is the best, most holy, uncorrupted working of man, and its knowledge, love, and enjoyment, through which he clings incessantly (ἀδιαλείπτως) to Him as highest good, is most closely united. Its beginning is this present life, and the consummation will be another.[22]

XXIII. It Comes in the Name of Vision

The perfection of the knowledge and love comes in the names of the *vision of God*, His *face*, and *knowledge*. "From my flesh I will see God" (Job 19:26). "I will see Your face in righteousness. I will be satisfied, when I awake, with Your face" (Ps. 17:15). "Blessed are the pure in heart because they will see God" (Matt. 5:8). "Now we see in a mirror, in obscurity, then face to face" (1 Cor. 13:12). "We shall see Him as He is" (1 John 3:2). Of what sort that vision will be we will see when we will see. It is certain that it will not be of essence, because God is "wonderful" (פלא) (Isa. 9:6). Moreover, it will be no dry contemplation, because "we will know, just as we are known" (1 Cor. 13:12). But God *knows* and *is known* through love. Therefore, the vision of God, His virtues, works, intellect and will, is through the most pure love of God because no one can be blessed who does not love God and enjoy His love. This vision will be joined with the full sense of the favor of God because it will not simply be a vision of the face of God, which also can be indignant, but the "light of the face of God" (Ps. 36:9). "Let Jehovah make His face to shine over You, and pity you" (Ps. 31:16). There is "life in the light of the face of the King" (Prov. 16:15).[23]

XXIV. The Happiness of Eternal Life

The vision of God and sense of His favor will have as companion incomparable happiness. "The satisfaction of happiness is with Your face, and of delights which are at your right hand forever" (Ps. 16:11). "I draw near to God, the happiness of my joy" (Ps. 43:4). "The righteous will be happy, will exult before God and will be cheerful in happiness" (Ps. 68:3). That joy will be in God—namely who "will be all in all" (1 Cor. 15:28)—and all the faculties and senses of the whole man will fulfill itself and all its charms (θελκτηρίοις). "What eye has not seen nor ear has heard and has not ascended into the heart of man, which God prepared for those who love Him (which sort were in the time of Christ, when heaven was

22. *Medulla*, LXII–LXVI.
23. *Medulla*, LXVI, LXVII.

opened and God was manifest in the flesh)" God will most fully "reveal" there a cause for ineffable joy (1 Cor. 2:9–10).[24]

XXV. The Perfection of the Image of God

From the beatific vision of God the perfect renewal of His image will follow. For because "we shall see Him as He is," we will be like the same (1 John 3:2). "With unveiled face beholding the glory of the Lord, we will be transformed to the same image from glory to glory, as by the Spirit of the Lord" (2 Cor. 3:18).[25]

XXVI. Which Shines Not Only in the Soul

The perfection of the divine image shines in the soul and the body. For all faculties *of the soul*, intellect, will, and power, will be similar to God. Perfect wisdom and knowledge of the mysteries of God will illuminate the *intellect*. "When He comes, Who is perfect, then what is from part will pass away" (1 Cor. 13:10). We will recognize the mysteries to which our stupor in this life did not penetrate. Also the saints will know each other much more, as Adam never knew Eve before sight (Gen. 2:23). Health, holiness, rectitude, freedom, and most exact harmony of reason and affections will perfect *will*. For the will shall inseparably cling to the perfectly known highest good and shall be fastened together through love. And in what he adheres to his good more freely, this will be more free. No longer will the affections and wills of God and men be discordant. For there will be no will there except what God does, and what the one God wills all shall will, and what one and all will, God shall will.[26]

XXVII. But Also in the Glorious Body

The *bodies* of the blessed will also be perfected in glory. "Jesus Christ will transform our lowly body, that it may become conformed to His glorious body" (Phil. 3:21). For "we expect adoption, redemption of our body" (Rom. 8:23). While the substance of the body remains and the corruptible qualities have passed away, glorious qualities worthy of glory will follow. "What is sown in corruption is stirred up in incorruption (because there will be nothing there contrary, corrupting, destroying), what is sown in worthlessness is stirred up in glory (majesty, lovability, splendor), what is sown in weakness is stirred up in power (above all *active*, because the spirit will instantly be moved without being encumbered and *slender*, without superfluous thickness), what is sowed as an animal body is raised

24. *Medulla*, LXVIII.
25. *Medulla*, LXIX.
26. *Medulla*, LXX.

spiritual (by the Spirit immediately inhabiting to make alive, move, and rule)" (1 Cor. 15:35–39).[27]

XXVIII. The Accidents of Blessedness

The habitation of the whole man, society, multitude of goods, universality, continuity, and eternity will increase blessedness. For *they will dwell* in heaven, the house of the Father, Paradise, which "the glory of God makes bright" and whose "lamp" will be "the Lamb" (Rev. 21:23). They will have *companions*: Christ, the angels, all the saints, patriarchs, prophets, apostles, martyrs, and Reformers. From this society mutual love (ἔρως καὶ) and ineffable joy will come forth. *Goods—many*, unexhausted in the highest good; *universal*, because that inheritance will not diminish the abundance of possessors and coheirs; and *continual*, because they will not fall into any vicissitude of evils. For the crown of these will be blessed *eternity* because they can no longer die whose blessedness will be perfect and in whom "God will be all in all" (1 Cor. 15:28).[28]

XXIX. Inequality of Glory in Regard to Degree

While the blessedness in regard to its essence will be equal for all, it will be different in degrees, not from the merit of works but from the esteem of God, who will crown His gifts for His pleasure. "Those who are wise will shine the likeness of the splendor of the firmament, and justifying many, as stars forever" (Dan. 12:3). "There is one glory for the sun, another for the moon, and another for the stars. For star differs from star in glory. So it will be in the resurrection of the dead" (1 Cor. 15:41–42). For God "returns to each one according to his works" (Rom. 2:6). And the "distinction of gifts" of this life (Rom. 12:6; 1 Cor. 12:4–5) carries the distinction of rewards of another after it.[29]

XXX. Epilogue

Indeed, to Him who can keep us free from hindrance and cause us to stand before His glory guiltless in exultation, to the only wise God our Savior be glory, magnitude, authority, and power, both now and forever. Amen.[30]

THE END

---

27. *Medulla*, LXXI.
28. *Medulla*, LXXII.
29. *Medulla*, LXXIII, LXXIV.
30. *Medulla*, LXXV.

Scripture Index

OLD TESTAMENT

Genesis

1:1 30, 41–43
1:1–2 41
1:2 34, 42–43
1:3 30, 41
1:6–8 43
1:9 44
1:11–12 42, 44
1:14 44
1:16 44
1:20–21 45
1:24–25 45
1:26 30, 45–47
1:26–27 204
1:28 47, 103
1:29 63
1:31 46, 55
2:1 55
2:3 99
2:7 45
2:8–9 44
2:9 62, 64
2:16 65
2:17 46, 64
2:19 45
2:23 46, 210
2:24 47, 102
3:1 45, 55
3:7–8 68
3:15 30, 59, 69, 80, 83, 118
3:19 201
3:20 46, 69, 84
3:22 65
3:22–23 68
4:1 84
4:4 86
4:5 87
4:8 87
4:25 84
4:26 85
5:24 84, 87
5:29 84, 87
6:2 80, 85
6:5 67, 69, 72
6:9 84
8:21 69
9:4 86
9:6–7 101
9:9–10 84
9:9–17 86
9:26 27, 85
9:28 85
12:1–3 84
12:2 84
12:7 84
13:16 84
14:18 23, 84
14:20 27
15:1 84, 174
15:5–6 84
15:6 80
15:13 84
17:1 22
17:1–2 84
17:6 84
17:7 150, 195, 209
17:7–8 30
17:8 84
17:9–15 87
18:18 84
18:19 85

Genesis (*continued*)
18:25 26, 205
19:24 30
20:7 85
22:16 98
22:17–18 84
37:28 87
49:8–10 84
49:10 116, 137, 198
50:20 52

Exodus
2:2 89
3:2 32
3:4 32
3:6 81, 84, 204, 209
3:7 32
3:14 23, 30
3:14–15 22
3:16 204, 209
4:22 80
7:3 52
9:16 53
12:13 92
15:13 90
15:26 89
16:31 92
17:1–6 92
17:7 34
18:12 85
19:3–6 89
19:8 91
20:1–18 89
20:2 90
20:2–3 96
20:4–5 97
20:5 90
20:7 90, 97
20:8–11 99
20:10 90
20:12 90, 100
20:13 101
20:15 103
20:16 105
20:16–17 96
20:17 106
20:21 90
21:14 101
21:23 101
22:2 102
22:25 104
23:20 32
23:20–21 30
24:8 91
31:15 99
33:19 37
33:20 91
33:23 91
34:6 26
34:7 154
34:27 16

Leviticus
15:16 178
16:2 34
17:10 86
17:14 114
18:5 154
18:6 102
19:3 100
19:11 105
19:18 96
21:9 114
23:7 99
26:1 115

Numbers
10:9 102
10:31 102
11:16 113
12:6–8 91
15:30 71
15:38–39 109
16:30 41
20:2–11 92
21:8–9 93
23:21 151
24:21 112
27:21 91
30:5–6 101
35:22 101

Deuteronomy
4:7 91
4:15 101
4:32–36 29
5:26 24
5:29 91
6:4 23, 30
6:4–5 95
6:5 63
6:13 57, 98, 165
10:16 87
10:17 27
10:20 98
12:32 163
16:18 198
16:21–22 115
17:14ff 113
18:11 58
18:18–19 131
21:23 124
23:2 118
23:19–20 104
23:23 168
24:1 102
25:1 153
27:26 63, 72
29:29 25
30:1 137
30:6 137
30:11–12 127
31:25–26 15
32:4 26
33:3 56

Joshua
1:6 102
3:10 24
24:27 15

Judges
13:18 22

1 Samuel
2:2 26
8:11–19 113
10:25 15
10:26 51
16:7 25
17:36 24
26:19 90

2 Samuel
12:11 53
12:18–23 180
16:10–11 53
22:32 30
23:3 34
24:1 53

1 Kings
8:27 24
8:39 25, 203
18:39 29

1 Chronicles
19:8–9 113

2 Chronicles
16:9 24
34:14 89

Nehemiah
8:8 17

Job
7:1 xi, 51
9:20 153
10:4 24
11:7–9 23
12:16–17 52
12:18 197
14:4 69
14:5–6 51
14:21 202
15:15 42
19:25 76, 84
19:25–27 204
19:26 209
22:2–3 164
22:14 42
26:7 44
33:4 33

Job (*continued*)
33:23 76
33:23–24 84
37:18 43
38:7 55

Psalms
1:2 18
2:6 130, 136
2:7 31
2:8 33, 76, 136
2:10–12 198
2:12 33
4:6 208
5:4 52
6:1 73
7:6 151
7:9 203
8:4 118
8:5 119, 126
9:8 26
9:8–9 206
11:6 208
16:6 175
16:10 125, 127
16:11 209
17:15 204, 209
18:2 24, 169
19:7–8 16
19:8 17, 71
22:2 124
22:2–3 126
22:14 124
22:29 182
23:4 175
23:5 182
23:6 175
24:2 44
24:9 198
25:8 26
29:3 27
31:16 209
31:17 207
32:1–2 98, 155–56
32:2 80
32:5 80
33:6 34
33:12 208
33:13–14 49
34:8 182
36:6 50
36:9 24, 209
40:7–8 76
41:9 124
42:1–2 151
42:10–11 175
43:4 209
45:2 33
45:6 137
45:7 120
45:14 186
47:5 127
47:9 198–99
49:14 207
51:1 163
51:3 162
51:5 69
51:10 147
65:3 134
68:3 209
68:11 142
68:19 127
69:2–3 126
81:12 52
86:10 30
86:11 151
89:28 172
90:2 23
90:3 204
90:4 23
94:10 197
99:7–8 34
102:25–27 207
102:27 24, 42
103:1 150
103:3 150
103:20 56
103:21 55
104:4 55
104:5 44
104:15 181
104:28 50

104:30	34, 50
106:20	96
110:1	128
110:2	136–37
110:3	146
110:4	133
115:3	25
116:15	201
119:63	187
119:96	16
119:105	17
133:1	197
139:7–8	34
144:1	102
145:3–4	23
145:17	26
147:5	24
148:2	55
148:4	43

Proverbs

2:17	102
3:12	26
6:17	105
8:1	32
8:15–16	198
8:23	129
11:12	105
14:30	100
16:4	36, 39
16:15	209
16:33	51, 98
17:15	153
19:29	208
20:27	10
21:1	51
25:9–10	105
30:4	32
30:9	104

Ecclesiastes

3:11	50
3:17	206
7:29	46–47
9:5	202
12:7	45, 201–2

Song of Solomon

2:16	186
5:1	182
6:9	186
6:10	14
8:5	151

Isaiah

2:3	136
4:2	110
5:16	26
6:8	34
6:9	146
7:8–9	137
7:14	118
7:16	137
8:18	138
8:19–20	18
9:6	136–37, 209
10:20	151
11:3	32
11:10	191
12:2	152
14:26	35
17:5	151
26:3–4	204
28:11	15
29:22	143
31:9	93
33:14	208
34:11	43
38:14	76
40:3–6	142
40:18	23
40:22	42
41:4	22
41:9	39
41:23	25
42:6–7	172
42:8	27
44:22	158
45:21	129
46:10–11	36
47:6	90
48:2	151
49:1–3	123

Isaiah (*continued*)
49:4 76
49:7 137
49:23 198
50:1–2 32
50:10 151
52:6 131
52:7 142
53:9 125
53:10 76, 127, 134, 136
53:11 124
53:12 134
54:5 33
54:8–9 172
54:9 87
54:9–10 86
54:17 157
55:1–2 154, 182
55:3 172–73
59:21 15
60:3 198
60:16 198
60:21 36
61:1 130–31
61:3 36
62:8 128
63:9 30, 89
63:16 202
63:17 52–53
64:8–9 77
65:17–18 41
66:1 23, 43
66:16 207
66:24 207–8

Jeremiah
4:2 98
4:10 53
10:10 24
10:13 44
13:23 72
17:13 39
23:5–6 32
23:6 154
29:6 101
30:21 76
31:22 41
31:31 93
31:31–35 140
31:33 16, 136, 146
31:33–36 172
32:27 27
32:40 171–72
49:2 151

Ezekiel
8:11 113
11:5 25
16:60–61 140
18:20 72
18:24 63
21:3 27
31:16 43
31:18 43
34:15–16 195
36:25 112, 148
36:26 51
36:27 172
37:12–14 204
39:14 194

Daniel
7:10 56
8:13 131
9:5–7 162
9:23ff 137
9:24 133–34, 137, 174
11:27 83
12:3 211
12:7 98

Hosea
1:6 39
2:3 39
2:19–20 172
2:21–22 50
6:7 62
7:3 105
9:3 90
12:5 22
13:9 53
14:2 165

Joel
2:28 179
2:32 142

Micah
5:2 32

Habakkuk
2:4 19, 151, 157

Haggai
2:7–9 137

Zechariah
6:12 75
9:9 136
9:12 33
12:1 47

Malachi
1:2–3 39
3:1 137, 142
3:6 24
3:9 197
4:4–5 15
4:5–6 142
4:6 93, 132, 143

NEW TESTAMENT
Matthew
1:18 118
1:21 38, 129–30
3:2 136, 143, 162
3:8 143
3:15 143
3:17 30, 149
4:10 57, 97
4:17 132, 136, 141
5:4–5 175
5:8 209
5:16 98, 164
5:18 15, 207
5:25 198
5:44 91
6:9 166
6:10 56–57, 175
6:12 175
6:22 163
6:30 51
6:33 165
7:17 163
7:18 72
7:29 132
8:11 182
8:12 208
9:13 162
9:15 168
10:15 208
10:19 144
10:28 38, 45
10:29–30 51
11:4–6 138
11:12–13 142
11:19 25
11:25 10, 38, 41
11:27 24
11:28 175
11:29 133
12:24–25 132
12:26 57
12:28 71
12:32 71
12:35 163
13:24–25 189
13:30 208
13:42 208
14:26 58
14:31 152
16:3 203
16:17 29
16:18–19 144, 192
16:19 194
16:24 164
16:26 201
17:5 149
18:10 56
18:15 196
18:16 193
18:17 187–88
18:18 192
18:20 197

Matthew (*continued*)
19:6 101
19:9 102
19:20 207
19:26 27
19:28 206
20:15 27
20:16 38
20:28 134
22:29 11
22:30 57
22:31–32 11
22:32 202, 204
22:36 95
22:37 63
23:19 130
24:14 195, 204, 207
24:24 39, 171
24:30 203
24:35 207
24:40 38
24:50 203
25:31 203, 206
25:33–34 206
25:34 164
25:41 72, 206–7
25:46 206
26:26 124, 181–82
26:27 181
26:28 134–35, 139
26:29 142, 181
26:38–39 126
26:39 118
27:45–46 125
27:51 125
28:1 126
28:18 191
28:19 14, 30, 34, 178–79
28:19–20 192
28:20 32

Mark
1:4 143
1:15 76, 132, 162
1:22 132
9:43–44 207–208
10:14 196
11:22 149
13:32 203
15:33 125
16:15 143
16:16 174
16:19 127

Luke
1:3 15
1:17 132
1:32–33 136
1:33 137
1:35 70, 118–19
1:42 118
1:68 135
2:21 129
2:40 120
2:52 120
3:14 102
3:18 123
3:23 123
4:6 58
4:8 97
4:32 132
8:30 57
9:27 142
8:50 152
9:58 123
10:1–2 144
10:16 144
10:20 39
11:2 166
11:38 179
12:12 144
12:29 152
12:48 208
15:4 195
15:7 57
15:10 57
16:23 208
17:20 188
17:20–21 136
18:13 163
20:38 204
21:27–28 203

22:7 124
22:18–20 181
22:19 183
22:21 180
22:29 37
22:44 124
22:69 128
23:43 64, 202
23:46 118
24:39 118
24:44 15
24:47 162
24:49 143
24:51 127

John
1:1 32
1:3 32, 42
1:4 151
1:4–5 91
1:10 32
1:12 77, 151, 159
1:13 118
1:14 117, 119
1:15 143
1:16 157
1:18 24, 130–31
1:29 92, 143
2:3–5 123
2:19 126
2:25 32
3:5 147
3:5–6 33, 69
3:6 72, 119
3:13 32, 131, 120
3:14–15 93
3:16 135, 172
3:25–26 178
3:33 150
3:34 120
3:36 149
4:2 178
4:13 92
4:24 23
5:17 49, 51
5:18–19 32
5:20 37
5:22 206
5:23 33
5:24 174, 201–2
5:25 179
5:26 32
5:27 206
5:28–29 204
5:29 205
5:32 31
5:34 14
5:39 16, 18
5:41 14
6:44 147
6:48 65, 110
6:48–50 92
6:50 65
6:68 32
8:31 188
8:36 159
8:44 56–57
8:50 33
8:58 32
10:11 135
10:16 186
10:17–18 76
10:18 126
10:27–30 172
10:28 130
10:30 32
12:27 126
12:31 59
12:40 52
12:48 18
13:18 39
13:29 197
13:35 188
14:2 43
14:6 151
14:13–14 165
14:16 31, 33
14:16–17 173
14:26 144
15:4 186
15:19 38
15:26 33–34

John (*continued*)
16:7 33
16:9 59
16:11 59
16:13 15, 105, 144
16:14–15 33
17:3 9, 150, 164
17:9 135
17:19 134
17:21 141
17:22 173
17:23 141
18:36–37 136
19:30 125, 143
19:34 92, 125
20:22 193
20:23 144, 192, 194
20:27 205
20:31 16
21:17 32

Acts
1:3 127
1:5 144
1:11 203
1:22 143
2:1–4 144
2:37 150, 163
2:38 162
2:38–39 179
2:39 185, 195
2:41 144
2:42 188
2:47 185
3:6 33
3:12 33
3:21 43, 207
4:12 164
4:27–28 52
4:34 197
5:3 34
6:1–2 194
8:19 144
10:38 130
10:40–42 143
10:42 206
10:43 77
10:45 149
13:12 131
13:48 38, 77
14:16 52
15:2 197
15:9 151
15:11 80
15:18 24
16:1 149
16:4 63
16:5 187
16:14 146
16:31 80
17:25 24
17:25–26 42
17:26 50, 62, 95, 101, 198
17:28 42, 46, 49–51
19:6 144
20:17–28 197
20:27 16
20:28 32, 120, 130, 192
20:29 192, 201
20:31 192
24:15 205
28:25–26 34

Romans
1:3 118
1:3–4 117
1:4 31–32
1:5 140
1:17 132, 157
1:19 11
1:19–20 9
1:24–25 103
1:25 29, 97
1:27 201
1:32 52, 68
2:2 154
2:4 146
2:6 211
2:15 11
2:18 19
3:23–24 155
3:24 154

3:24–25 134, 156
3:24–26 153
3:27 164
3:28 157
3:31 155
4:1–2 158
4:4 64, 164
4:4–5 157
4:5–8 155
4:11–12 148
4:13 150
4:16 150
4:17 41
4:18 175
4:20 152
4:21 151, 175
4:25 126
5:1–2 151
5:2–6 175
5:5 149
5:8 134
5:8–11 172
5:10 91
5:12 69–70
5:14 62
5:15–16 155
5:16 68, 135
5:17 158
5:18 135
5:19 156
6:3–8 179
6:6 201
6:7 135, 202
6:8–9 174
6:12 70
6:23 46, 72, 164
7:7–10 69
7:14 63
7:14ff 148
7:17 70
7:23 67
7:24 70
8:1 70, 156
8:2 159
8:3 59, 134
8:7 70
8:10 46, 202
8:11 34, 130
8:15 159
8:16 39, 174
8:17 164, 175
8:18 164
8:19–23 207
8:23 159, 203, 210
8:26 165
8:27 203
8:29 35, 37, 39
8:30 38, 153, 171
8:33 153
8:33–34 154
8:34 135
8:35 150
8:38 175
9:5 32
9:11 35, 37, 40
9:13 135
9:16 37
9:18 40
9:21–23 40
9:22 37
9:22–23 38
9:24 40
10:2 10
10:3–6 90
10:13–17 142
10:14 185
10:15 192–93
10:17 16, 192
11:7 39, 171
11:8 146
11:29 158, 173
11:33 23, 35
11:33–36 40
11:34 24, 35
11:36 51
12:1 177
12:2 19
12:6 211
12:6–8 193
12:5 186
12:7–8 194
13:1 197

Romans (*continued*)
13:4 198
13:3–4 199
13:9 95
13:10 163
14:5 19
14:11 206
14:17 63
14:23 159, 163
16:26 23
16:27 25

1 Corinthians
1:6 131
1:6–7 174
1:9 153
1:16 180
1:21 29
1:23 149
1:26–27 38
1:27 14
1:29 14
1:30 131, 134, 149, 154
2:8 120
2:9–10 210
2:10 19, 33
2:10–11 34
2:11 17, 23
2:12 14
2:13 12, 195
2:14 10
2:15 19
3:5–6 10
3:11 11
4:1 78, 195
4:5 206
4:15 148
4:21 144
5:3 144
5:5 144
5:8 168
5:12–13 195
6:11 34
6:12 18
6:18 71
6:19 34
7:14 179
7:15 102
7:23 18
7:26 102
7:28 102
7:34 102
7:38 101
8:1 159
8:6 30–32
8:8 63
9:1 143
9:15 100
10:1–5 92, 178
10:3–5 183
10:4 92
10:11 92, 140
10:15 19
10:16 182
10:17 183
10:23 159
11:10 57
11:24 110
11:24–26 183
11:25–26 184
11:26 110
11:28 180
11:32 73
12:4–5 211
12:6 49–50
12:8 192
12:11 19, 33
12:13 178
12:27 191
12:28 193
13:4 163
13:9 12
13:10 210
13:12 209
13:13 174
14:1 144
14:29 19
15:1–34 204
15:4 127
15:5–6 126
15:22 69
15:25 137

15:28 137, 209, 211
15:29 112
15:35–39 211
15:36 202
15:41–42 211
15:42 201
15:47 32
15:51 205
15:53–54 204

2 Corinthians

1:12–13 16
1:18 10
1:21 174
1:24 18, 174
2:6 193
2:17 9, 16, 194
3:5–6 193
3:6 146
3:15 90
3:17 34
3:18 90, 210
4:2 18, 195
4:3 17
4:6 10, 14
4:10 204
4:13 149
4:16 169
4:17 202
5:1 201–2
5:8 201
5:10 205–6
5:14 135
5:18–19 130
5:19 154
5:20 177
5:21 134
6:18 27
7:1 169, 202
7:10 162–63
8:19 197
8:23 197
9:4 152
9:13 77, 140
10:5 10
10:13 146
10:13–16 144
10:15 146
11:13 16
11:14 56
12:4 43
12:9 148, 175, 180
12:12 144
13:13 30, 34

Galatians

2:1–2 197
2:16 157
2:20 150
3:2 89
3:13 124, 134
3:15 172
3:16 84
3:19 89–90
3:24 90
3:27 151
3:28 179
4:1 159
4:4 76, 123
4:4–5 117, 159
4:6 33
4:19 148
5:6 87, 152
5:16 106
5:17 70, 148, 169
5:19 70
6:15 87, 163
6:16 18

Ephesians

1:2–8 37
1:4 35, 150
1:4–5 37–39
1:5 36, 159
1:6 37, 130
1:8 140
1:10 83, 140
1:11 25, 35, 37, 51
1:13 149
1:13–14 173
1:15–16 186
1:18 164

Ephesians (*continued*)
1:18–19 146
1:19 126
1:19–20 147
1:20 128
1:22–23 191
2:1 72, 147
2:2 58
2:3 69, 72
2:5–6 147
2:8 149
2:9–10 164
2:12 80, 89
2:15 63, 107
2:20 14, 16
3:17 173
3:20 167
4:4–5 186
4:8–9 127
4:11 144, 192–94
4:12 191
4:13 192
4:16 191
4:22–24 147
4:23–24 162
4:24 46–47
4:30 203
5:19 165
5:26 78
5:29 101
5:32 172
6:1 100
6:11 58
6:11–19 169
6:18 165

Philippians
1:6 171
1:11 104
1:19 33
1:21 201
1:23 201–2
2:6–11 123
2:7 119
2:8 124, 156
2:9–10 33, 126
2:13 172
2:15–16 14
2:17 73
3:3 87
3:16 18
3:21 205, 210
4:3 39
4:13 151

Colossians
1:15 110
1:15–16 42
1:16 32
1:18–20 191
1:21 80
1:23 80, 149
1:24 73, 164
2:2 29, 151
2:3 131
2:5 149
2:6 151
2:11 87
2:11–12 179
2:14 63, 107
2:16ff 168
2:17 90, 111
2:19 191
2:20 18
3:5 106
3:9 70
3:10 47
3:16 17, 165
3:22 100–101
4:6 105

1 Timothy
1:5 152, 163
1:15 130
1:17 23
1:19 149
2:1 165
2:5 76
2:5–6 139
2:6 83, 134, 142, 146
3:1 192–93
3:6 57

3:8–13 194
3:10 193
3:16 117, 126
4:1–3 168
4:2 189
4:8 177
4:14 193
4:15 12
5:17 193
5:21 56–57
5:22 193
6:3 12, 194
6:6 106
6:8 167
6:15 27

2 Timothy
1:6 151
1:7 173
1:12 174
2:2 193
2:11–12 164
2:19 38, 186
3:15 16, 18, 196
3:16 14
3:16–17 16
4:1 203
4:6 73, 201

1 Thessalonians
2:11–12 195
3:10 187
4:10–11 165
4:14–18 204
4:15–17 205
5:9 39
5:20 16
5:21 19

2 Thessalonians
1:6–9 72
1:7 56
1:7–8 203
2:3–4 189
2:11 52–53

Titus
1:1 12, 77, 149–50
1:1–2 10
1:5–6 192
2:10 98
2:11–12 140
2:12 164
2:13 32
2:14 187
3:4 26
3:5 179, 187

Hebrews
1:1 143
1:2 42, 131
1:3 32, 112
1:4 31, 191
1:6 33
1:9 191
1:11 207
1:14 55–57, 174
2:3 131, 143, 149
2:7 119
2:10 81, 126, 141
2:14 118
2:16 76, 119
3:1 34
3:5–6 127
3:6 152
3:14 152
4:12 18
4:13 24
5:4 193
5:7–8 123
5:13–14 xxii
6:1 xxii, 12, 70
6:6 71
6:16 98
6:17 174
6:19–20 174
7:2–3 87
7:3 32, 84
7:14 133
7:16 24, 107
7:16–17 133
7:19 142

Hebrews (*continued*)
7:21–22 133
7:22 76
7:25 135, 165
7:26 70, 76, 127
7:26–28 133
7:27 133
8:1 128
8:5 92
8:6 76, 139, 141, 149
9:8 34, 112
9:10 179
9:12 174
9:14 32, 133
9:15–16 76
9:17 172
9:19 91
9:24 135
9:26 133
10:1 92
10:3 112
10:5 118
10:5–10 109
10:14 156
10:22 148
11:1 149, 152, 184, 186
11:3 41
11:4 80, 84, 86
11:5 87
11:6 86
11:8–9 84
11:16 202
11:19 87
11:26 80
12:2 149
12:6 73
12:14 161
13:8 80, 117

James
1:2–4 73
1:6 165, 174
1:8 174
1:13 52
1:14–15 70
1:17 17, 24
2:5 38
2:18 152
2:20 152
2:21–24 158
2:26 148, 152
3:2 187
3:6 42
3:9 165
4:12 18, 198
5:16 162

1 Peter
1:3 147, 175
1:6–7 73
1:11 33
1:19 92
1:20 35
1:23 147–48
1:25 146
2:3 26
2:9 136
2:19 21
3:18 155
3:20–21 87
3:21 77, 179

2 Peter
1:3 141
1:4 106
1:10 39, 175
1:19–20 17
1:20–21 19
1:21 14
2:4 57
2:19 72
3:7 42, 207
3:8 23
3:10 43, 203, 207
3:12 42
3:13 207

1 John
1:7 130
2:1 135
2:23 29
3:2 150, 210

4:1 12
4:1–3 19
4:8 26
5:4–5 151
5:6 14
5:7 30–31, 34
5:8 148
5:11 208
5:14–15 175
5:20 32

1 John
1:1 32
1:5 67
1:7 112, 187
1:8 148
1:10 148
2:7 189
2:18 140
3:2 209
3:4 67
3:9 161
3:14 175
4:10 172

Jude
4 39
6 56–57
12 197
14 203, 205
14–15 85

Revelation
1:2 32
1:3 18
1:5 133
1:6 111
1:8 22, 27, 32
2:7 65
2:10 169
2:13 98
2:17 186
2:24 58
4:11 25
5:5 191
5:6 92
5:8 92
5:10 111
6:9–10 202
8:2 203
8:3 130
9:2 157
10:5–6 98
11:15–18 204
15:4 26
17:14 185
19:1 202
19:4 202
19:10 57, 91
19:13 32
20:10 59
21:23 211
21:24 198
22:20 15

Subject Index

Aaronic priesthood, 236
Abarbenel, Isaac, 180–81

Aaron, 85, 111, 133, 204
Abel, 84, 86, 87
abolition
  of ceremonies, 112
  of judicial laws, 116
  of legal economy, 93
Abraham, 80, 84, 85, 148, 175
accidental freedom, 159
active justification, 158
acts of faith, 151
actual sin, 70
Adam, 45, 61, 62, 68, 84
adjudication of life, 157
adoption, 159, 174
adultery, 102–3
affability, 105
Alsted, Johann Heinrich, xiii
Alting, Jacob, xxiv
Alting, Johann Henrich, xiii
Ames, William, xiii, xxiii
Amyraldian controversy, xx
Amyraut, Moses, xvii
Anabaptist theology, 12n10
angels, 36–37, 43, 55–59
animals, 45, 46, 47, 107–8, 110
announcement, 183
antecedent will, 38
Antichrist, 12, 19, 59, 167, 188, 189
Apocrypha, 15
apostasy, 132, 189
apostles, 143–44
Apostolic Creed, 125
apparitions, 127
aptitude, 193
Arminian Controversy, xviii
ascension, 127
Athanasian Creed, 125
atheism, 51
attributes, 32
authenticity, 14
authority, 14, 19, 30, 100
author of sin, 49, 53
Azazel, 111

Baculus, 204
baptism, 92, 144, 177–80
baptismal rite, 178–79
bare signs, 79
bearing of the cross, 164
Bellarmine, Robert, 12n10
betrayal, 124
Beza, Theodore, xiv
Blair, Ann, xxi
blasphemy, 71, 98
blessedness, 211
blessing, of man, 47
blood, 86
body, of man, 45–47, 201–2, 204, 210
bread, 181, 182–83
Bullinger, Heinrich, xiv
burial, 125, 201–2
Buxtorf, Johannes, 5

calling, 38, 145–52, 164
Calvin, John, xiv
Cameron, John, xvii
canon, 18
capital punishment, 114
catechesis, 195–96

catholic church, 187
cause, of faith, 149
certitude, 174–75
chastisement, 73
chastity, 102–3
children, 100–101
Christian freedom, 159
Christian life, 164
Christian republic, 116
church, 14, 18, 185–89, 191–99
circumcision, 87, 92, 129, 179
civil government, 197
civility, 101
clarity, of Scripture, 17
clothing, 112
Cocceius, Johannes, xiii, xvi
commission, 71
common calling, 145–46
communicable attributes, 24–27
communicatio idiomatum, 120
communion of saints, 186
concupiscence, 70
condignity, 164
confession, 162
congruity, 164
consequent will, 38
conversion, 147
councils, 197
counsel of peace, 75
counter-obligation, 77
covenant of grace, 75–81
  constancy of, 171–75
  vs. covenant of works, 81
  under the gospel, 139–44
  under the law of Moses, 89–93
  under the patriarchs, 83–87
covenant of works, 61–65, 81, 93
covetousness, 106
creation, 41–47
Crocius, Ludovicus, xii–xiii
cross, 124–25
crucifixion, 124–25

Daillé, Jean, xvii
Daneau, Lambert, xiv
David, 175
deacons, 194
death
  of Christ, 133–34, 183
  of the faithful, 201
  as penalty of sin, 68, 72
  threat of, 64
Decalogue, 95–106, 114, 116
de Chandieu, Antoine, xiv
decrees, of God, 35–40
decretal will, 25
defense, 137
de Labadie, Jean, 12n10
de la Faye, Antoine, xiv
denial of oneself, 150, 164
Descartes, René, xv
descent into hell, 125–26
devil, 58
Diodati, Giovanni, xiv
discernment, 19
disciples, 144, 178
discipline, 196
disposition, 149
divination, 98
divinity, 21
doctrine, 188, 194, 195
dominion, 191
doxology, 167
du Moulin, Pierre, xviii

earth, 43
ecclesiastical government, 195
ecclesiastical matters, 115
Eckhart, Meister, 12n10
economic laws, 115
economy, of divine persons, 31, 33, 34
Edict of Nantes, xix
efficacy, 146
efficient cause, 36
eighth commandment, 103–4
elders, 193
elect, 135, 146, 149
election, 38–39, 145, 171
Elihu, 84
Elijah, 204
eminent grace, 119
emotions, 25–26

end of the world, 207
enemies, 95
Enlightenment, xv
Enoch, 84, 85, 204
essential freedom, 159
eternity, 23, 64, 137, 145, 208–11, 211
Eucharist, 124
evangelical face, 90
evangelical faith, 148
evangelical fasting, 168
evangelical prophecy, 131
evangelists, 142, 144
Eve, 46–47, 68, 84
evil, 51, 52–53
evil angels, 57
exaltation, 126
examination, 193
example, of Christ, 132–33
execution, 142
existence, 41
ex nihilo, 41
expiation, 108, 111, 133–34
extension, 42
external cause, of justification, 154
external church, 188–89
external worship, 177–84

Fabricius, J. L., xii–xiii
faculty, 193
faith
  and the church, 186
  and covenant, 80, 90
  as duty, 76
  of the elect, 149
  example of, 148
  and justification, 157, 158
  law of, 140
  and reason, 11
  and sanctification, 163
fallible, church as, 189
false gods, 29
false witness, 105
fasting, 167–68
fate, 49
faults, 165
feasts, 111, 168, 172
fidelity, 100, 105, 193
fiducia, 151, 152
fifth commandment, 100
final judgment, 205–8
firstborn, 110
first commandment, 96
firstfruits, 110, 111
flood, 44
foreknowledge, 35
Formula Consensus Helvetica, xvii, xix
fornication, 103
fortune, 49
fourth commandment, 99–100
Franeker, xiii, xvi
freedom, 27, 46, 159
free will, 37, 46
fruits, 140

genre, xx–xxi
Gentiles, 163, 195
Gernler, Lucas, xviii
glorification, 201–11
glory, of God, 27, 96, 166
God
  as creator, 41–42
  decrees of, 35–40
  election of, 171
  existence of, 21
  as judge, 206
  name of, 22, 97–98
  as one, 30
  providence of, 49–53
  will of, 25
Gomarus, Franciscus, xiii
good, 26, 52–53
good angels, 56
good order, 196
good works, 163–64
gospel, 139–44
governance, 50
government, of the church, 191–99
grace, 26
gratitude, 100
guilt, 108

habitual graces, 119–20

happiness, 209–10
Heaven, 43, 64, 135, 202
Heinsius, Daniel, 5
hell, 125, 207–8
Helvidius, 118
Herod, 52
high priest, 109
highway robbery, 104
historical faith, 148
Hobbes, Thomas, xv
holiness, 26, 174
Holy Spirit, 184
  baptism of, 144
  blasphemy against, 71
  compelling of, 146
  pouring out of, 138
  sealing of, 159, 173
  as third person of the Godhead, 33–34
  witness of, 13–14
homicide, 101
honor, 100, 120
hope, 174–75
Hottinger, Johann Heinrich, xi, xvii
human nature, 118
humiliation, 150
hypocrites, 163

idolatry, 97
image of God, 46, 47, 101, 162, 210
images, 97
immensity, 23
immersion, 178
immortal, 45–46
immutability, 24
imperfection
  of certitude, 175
  of regeneration, 148
  of sanctification, 169
imputation, 69, 187
incarnation, 117
incest, 103
incommunicable attributes, 22–24
independence, 22
indulgences, 156–57
infant baptism, 179–80
inferiors, 100
infinity, 23
inheritance, 115
intellect, 24, 35, 55–56, 210
intercession, 135, 165
interest, 104
interior punishments, 208
internal cause, of justification, 154
internal governance, 137
interpretation, 17
invisible church, 186
irrationalism, 12n10
Isaac, 84, 85, 87, 204

Jacob, 84, 85
James, 127
Jerome, 118n4
Jesus Christ
  advent of, 203–11
  baptism of, 30
  body and blood of, 182, 183–84
  death of, 133–34, 183
  deity of, 31–32
  as head of the church, 191
  as judge, 206
  as mediator, 75, 89, 121, 130, 136, 139–40, 173
  office of, 129–38
  person of, 117–21
  righteousness of, 154–55, 157
  state of, 123–28
  suffering of, 155–56
  types of, 87
Jethro, 85
Jews, 29, 52
Job, 84
John the Baptist, 142–43, 178
Joseph, 87
Joshua, 113
Jubilee, 108, 111
Judas, 124
judges, 113
judgment, 18–19, 106, 154, 155, 205–8
judicial law, of Moses, 113–16
judicial power, 198
justice, 101–2
justification, 38, 153–59, 173–74

kingdom of Christ, 136
kingdom of Satan, 59
kings, 113
Klauber, Martin, xviii–xix
knowledge, 24, 57–58, 150, 202–3

labor, 99
Lamech, 84, 85
Lavater, Johann, 4
law, 62, 81, 89–93, 140, 155
legal face, 90
legal faith, 148
legal fasting, 168
legal justification, 64
legal prophecy, 131
legal purity, 109
legal righteousness, 63
legislative power, 198
Leiden, xiii, xvi
lending, 104
Levites, 109
lie, 105
light, 43
Lord's Day, 99
Lord's Prayer, 166–67
Lord's Supper, 177, 180–84
lot, 98
Louis XIV, xix
love, 26, 95–96, 152, 175
Luther, Martin, xiv

magic, 58, 97
magistrate, 113, 197–99
man, 45
manna, 92
man-stealing, 104
marriage, 46–47, 100, 102–3, 115
martyrdom, 73, 133
Mary, perpetual virginity of, 118n4
Mary Magdalene, 127
masterly power, 100–101
medulla, xxiii, 3, 7, 9n1
Melchizedek, 84, 87, 133
mercy, 26, 38, 104
merit, 130–31, 134, 164
Messiah, 137–38
ministers, 192–93
miracles, 32–33, 50–51, 79, 123, 132, 148
Molina, Luis de, 12n10
monastic vows, 140
Moses, 83, 113
Muller, Richard, xiv, xv
murder, 114
Muslims, 29
mutual communication of properties, 120
mystery
  of baptism, 179
  of Christ's two natures, 119
  of Lord's Supper, 182
  of offerings, 109
mystical theology, 11–12

name
  of God, 22, 97–98
  of Jesus, 129
Nathaniel, 127
natural law, 62–63, 68
natural theology, 9
Nazarites, 109, 111
neighbor, 95, 100, 101, 105, 166
new obedience, 163
New Testament
  books of, 15
  and covenant of grace, 139–40
  laws of, 116
  sacraments of, 92–93
  Trinity in, 30
  worship of, 177
ninth commandment, 105
Noah, 84, 85, 86, 87
notitia, 150

obedience, 62, 100, 163
object of faith, 149
Old Testament
  books of, 15
  sacraments of, 92–93
  Trinity in, 30
omission, 71
oral revelation, 13

order, 196
ordination, 193
original sin, 69, 72
ownership, 103

Paradise, 44, 64–65, 68
pardon, 71
parental power, 100–101
passive justification, 158
Passover, 92, 108, 124
pastors, 144
patriarchs, 83–87
Paul, 143, 175, 181, 197
peace, 115
peace offerings, 107–8, 110
Peace of Westphalia, xii
penalty, 72–73
Pentecost, 111
perfection, 210
permission, 52
perpetual laws, 116
perpetual magistrates, 113–14
perseverance, 63
perseverance of the saints, 171–75
persevering grace, 175
persons, 195
Peter, 127, 143
petition, 165–67
Pharisees, 71
piety, xxiii, 12n10, 140, 199
Pilate, Pontius, 52
pious struggle, 150
pledge, 168, 172
Polansdorf, Amandus Polanus von, xiv
political laws, 115
pope, 18
positive law, 63
poverty, 123
power
  of angels, 55–56, 58
  of God, 27
  of the keys, 194
  of the soul, 202–3
  of superiors, 100–101
practical assent, 150, 151
prayer, 165–67
predestination, 35, 36–37
preparation, 142
prescience, 51
prescriptive will, 25
preservation, 50
priests, 109, 111, 133
principle cause, of justification, 154
private ceremonies, 112
private power, 100
private revelation, 85
privation, 67
promise, 64, 76–77, 80, 90–91, 141, 172
prophecy, 85, 131, 138
prophets, 91, 108–9, 132, 144
Protestant orthodoxy, xiv, xv
providence, 49–53
public justice, 101–2
public revelation, 85
public rites, 107–8
punishment, 68, 72, 114, 165, 208
purifications, 109, 112

rainbow, 86
ratification, 142
rationalism, 12n10
reason, 10–11
Rechabites, 109, 111–12
reconciliation, 75, 130
redemption, 134, 154–55, 172, 203
Reformed orthodoxy, xv
regeneration, 37, 147–48, 174
religion, 10, 115, 199
remedies, 79
remembrance, 183
remission, 156, 163
Renaissance, xxi
repentance, 71, 76, 80, 90, 143, 158, 162
reprobation, 39–40
restoration, 162
resurrection, 126, 204–5
retaliation, 114
revealed theology, 9
revealed will, 25
revelation, 9, 10, 61, 85
rewards, 211
righteous, 158

righteousness, 26, 90, 153, 154–55
ritual law of Moses, 107–12
Rivet, André, xviii
robbery, 104
Roman Church, 17

Sabbath, 99–100
Sabellians, 31
sacraments
 and the church, 193, 196
 of covenant of grace, 78–80
 of covenant of works, 64
 of legal economy, 92
 of the New Testament, 177–84
 of the patriarchs, 86–87
 sealing of, 174, 175
sacred fire, 108, 110
sacrifices, 86, 107–8
sacrificial cakes, 107–8, 110
sadness, 163
salvation, 164, 174–75
sanctification, 119, 156, 161–69, 174
Sanhedrin, 113, 197
Satan, 58, 59
satisfaction, 134, 156
saving faith, 174
Scaliger, Joseph Justus, 5
scholastic theology, 11–12
scribes, 114
Scripture
 authors of, 13–14
 books of, 15
 clarity of, 17
 perfection of, 16
second commandment, 97
secret will, 25
self-sufficiency, 106
seventh commandment, 102–3
signs, 203
simplicity, of God, 23
sin
 acknowledgement of, 162
 author of, 49, 53
 of man, 67–73
 penalty of, 68, 72
 permission of, 51
 remission of, 156
 and reprobation, 40
Sinaitic covenant, 89–93
sitting at the right hand of God, 128
sixth commandment, 101
sorrow, 163
soul, 45, 201, 210
Spanheim, Friedrich, 5
special pledge, 168
specters, 58–59
Spinoza, Benedict de, xv, 29
spirits, 55
spiritual conflict, 169
spirituality, 23
spiritual significance, of rites, 109
sprinkling, 178–79
stoning, 114
Stucki, Johann Wilhelm, xiv
Suarez, Francisco, 12n10
subjection, 100
subordinates, 114
superiors, 100
symbols, 181, 184
Synod of Dort, xiii, xiv, xviii
synods, 197
systematic theology, xx–xxi

tabernacle, 108, 111
taciturnity, 105
Tauler, Johannes, 12n10
teachers, 144, 194
temple, 111
temporal goods, 197
temporary magistrates, 113
temptation, 167
tenth commandment, 106
testament, 77
testing, 73, 193
thanksgiving, 165
theft, 103–4
theology, 9
theoretical assent, 150
things, 195
third commandment, 97–98
Thirty Years' War, xii, xiii, xiv
Thomas, 127

threefold office of Christ, 131
time, 42
tithes, 110
translations, 17–18
Tree of Life, 64–65
Trinity, 29–34, 96, 130, 171
tritheists, 31
Tronchin, Louis, xix
Tronchin, Théodore, xiv
true church, 185, 187
trust, 150–51, 152
truth, 106, 126, 188, 194
Turretin, Francis, xvi, xvii, xviii, xix, 5
Turretin, Jean-Alphonse, xix
types, 87, 92, 109

union with Christ, 173
universal church, 187
universal resurrection, 205
University at Marburg, xii
University of Heidelberg, xii
unregenerate, 163
uprightness, 26
urbanity, 105

van Mastricht, Peter, xvi
Vermigli, Peter Martyr, xiv
victims, 107–8
violence, 101
virgin birth, 118
virtues, 26
visible church, 188
vision of God, 209
Voetius, Gijsbert, xvi
Vossius, Gerhardus, 5

Walaeus, Antonius, xiii
wantonness, 103
war, 115–16
Waser, Kaspar, xiv
washings, 109
water, 178
Wendelin, Marcus, xiii
Werenfelsius, Peter, 3, 4
Werenfelsius, Samuel, 3, 4
Westenius, Johann Rudolph, 3
whole burnt offering, 107, 110
will
  of angels, 55–56
  of God, 25, 35
  of man, 72
  of ministers, 193
  of the soul, 210
wine, 181, 182–83
wisdom, of God, 25
Wistius, Herman, xvi
Wollebius, Johannes, xiii, xiv, xxiv
Word, 16, 78, 85
works, 155, 157–58, 163–64
world, 42, 207
worship, 57, 99, 188

Xenophon, xxiii

Zurich, xi
Zwinger, Johann, 4, 5